Tolerance – A Concept in Crisis

I0131070

This book examines tolerance as a concept under crisis, exploring its origin and functions, and how it can be at risk of replacement by moral intolerance or retributive justice in turbulent societies.

Tolerance – A Concept in Crisis considers the contributions that can be made to understanding and elaborating tolerance, and its counterpart intolerance, by psychoanalysis and group analysis. The contributors, representing a range of countries, backgrounds, and specialisms, consider five key themes: conceptual and emotional challenges, tolerance and psychoanalysis, tolerance and group analysis, tolerance and the socio-political, and tolerance and intolerance in organizations and institutes. The project suggests that tolerance is an outcome of developmental processes (emotional, intrapsychic, intersubjective, and social) to agree and contain disagreement as part of mutual belonging. It also considers how it might be taken too far. The concept of tolerance is examined through its valid contributions to diversity and reduction of discrimination, promoting reflexive scepticism, critical pluralism, and durable forgiveness.

Tolerance – A Concept in Crisis will be of great interest to psychoanalysts and group analysts facing issues of conflict and its resolutions, as well as other professionals who are seeking new perspectives on tolerance.

Avi Berman, PhD, is a clinical psychologist, psychoanalyst, training analyst and a group analyst. He is a member of the Tel Aviv Institute of Contemporary Psychoanalysis and The Israeli Institute of Group Analysis. Avi is the initiator and co-founder of the Israeli Institute of Group Analysis and its first chairperson. He is the head of the group psychotherapy track in Tel Aviv University's psychotherapy program. He is a co-editor of *Sibling Relations and the Horizontal Axis in Theory and Practice* (Routledge).

Gila Ofer, PhD, is a clinical psychologist, training psychoanalyst and group analyst. She is the co-founder of the Tel Aviv Institute of Contemporary Psychoanalysis and past chairperson. Gila is the founding member of the Israeli Institute of Group Analysis, as well as a teacher and supervisor at both institutes and in the psychotherapy program in Tel Aviv University. She is the editor of *A Bridge Over Troubled Water: Conflicts and Reconciliation in Groups and Society* (Routledge).

The New International Library of Group Analysis (NILGA)
Series Editor: Earl Hopper

Drawing on the seminal ideas of British, European and American group analysts, psychoanalysts, social psychologists and social scientists, the books in this series focus on the study of small and large groups, organisations and other social systems, and on the study of the transpersonal and transgenerational sociality of human nature. NILGA books will be required reading for the members of professional organisations in the field of group analysis, psychoanalysis, and related social sciences. They will be indispensable for the "formation" of students of psychotherapy, whether they are mainly interested in clinical work with patients or in consultancy to teams and organisational clients within the private and public sectors.

Recent titles in the series include:

Group Analysis throughout the Life Cycle
Foulkes Revisited from a Group Attachment and Developmental Perspective
Arturo Ezquerro and Maria Cañete

The Tripartite Matrix in the Developing Theory and Expanding Practice of Group Analysis
The Social Unconscious in Persons, Groups and Societies: Volume 4
Edited by Earl Hopper

Intersectionality and Group Analysis
Explorations of Power, Privilege and Position in Group Therapy
Edited by Suryia Nayak and Alasdair Forrest

Group Analysis
A Modern Synthesis
Sigmund Karterud

Tolerance – A Concept in Crisis
Psychoanalytic, Group Analytic, and Socio-Cultural Perspectives
Edited by Avi Berman and Gila Ofer

"It is good to see a book on tolerance at this time when grey clouds threatening war are once again gathering over various parts of the globe. Tolerance and working with others have been the prime asset that has enabled the human race to succeed so emphatically. At the same time, nothing is perfect. We all have to tolerate imperfection and difference and indeed intolerance. Such prejudices unleash forces that undermine us with dismissiveness, ideology, and bigotry. Avi Berman and Gila Ofer have worked hard to gather authors with many important perspectives on the hidden unconscious turbulence which erupts in uncontrolled, ill-understood ways in our many different societies. It is essential that in the twenty-first century, we reflect on these potentially disastrous storms."

R. D. Hinshelwood, *Professor Emeritus, University of Essex, UK*

"Putting aside manic ideals of blissful harmony, Avi Berman and Gila Ofer turn their attention to the more human and more plausible attribute of tolerance. They have enlisted a number of distinguished contributors who compare and contrast tolerance with forgiveness, mutual recognition, and acceptance of difference. Together they elucidate such phenomena in a variety of contexts, ranging from groups, organizations, mobs, and, to wit, psychoanalytic associations. Given the radical demographic shifts, inter-ethnic conflicts, and other forms of sociopolitical schisms in our world of today, Berman and Ofer's book is of keen and urgent importance indeed."

Salman Akhtar, MD, *Professor of Psychiatry, Jefferson Medical College; Training & Supervising Analyst, Psychoanalytic Center of Philadelphia*

"A thought-provoking collection of papers that deepened my understanding of Tolerance – a psychological concept that is not easy to grasp in its nuance and sophistication and absorb into one's sensibility. An international group of scholarly clinicians approached tolerance from a number of therapeutic, geographic, moral, and political perspectives. Many contributions are deeply personal and reached me on that relational level."

Richard M. Billow, Ph.D., *Clinical Professor, Derner Postgraduate Programs; former director, Adelphi Postgraduate Group Program*

"Written by a diverse group of international experts, this book is an outstanding combination of different contemporary perspectives onto the concept of tolerance. It fills an important gap in theory and practice of development psychology, psychoanalysis, group analysis and politics (!) in these polarized times. The authors and editors succeeded in creating a fantastic blueprint, which the world really needs in view of the Kremlin's aggressive war against Ukraine, the competition between political systems and the fight of psychoanalytic institutes against their progredient insignificance. But blind tolerance, like epistemic mistrust, leads both individually and socio-politically to a dead end. In this respect, this book is also a wake-up call."

Ulrich Schultz-Venrath, Prof. Dr. med., *Professor of Psychosomatics and Psychotherapy (University of Witten/Herdecke), working in private practice as psychoanalyst (DPV/IPA) and training group analyst (D3G/EFPP/GASI)*

"In this Anthropocene era, there has never been a more important time for widespread understanding of mankind's own psychology. Central to our very survival is the issue of tolerance, over-tolerance, and the not tolerating of destructiveness in ourselves and others.

This is a wonderful collection of thought-provoking essays that range from developmental psychology to individual, dyadic, group, and societal psychology. All the essays are steeped in psychoanalytic studies and reflections.

The editors and authors are to be congratulated for producing this book. It deserves a very broad readership as part of the urgent need for the psychoanalytic field to play a greater part in bringing its understanding to a wider public in the interest of mankind's self-preservation."

Brian Martindale, *Honorary President of the European Federation of Psychoanalytic Psychotherapy*

"In a moment when expectations regarding democratic world diminished, stressing uncertainty, polarization and fear this book offers an essential and bona fide analysis of the concept of tolerance. Drawing on transdisciplinary research and exploring psychoanalytical, group analytical, sociocultural and organizational dimensions of the theme, the editors and authors from various countries permit an all-encompassing reflection on a fundamental topic to understand our current turbulent times."

Carla Penna, PhD, *psychoanalyst and group analyst in Rio de Janeiro. Member of the Group Analytic Society international. Former president of the Brazilian Association of Group Psychotherapy*

Tolerance – A Concept in Crisis

Psychoanalytic, Group Analytic, and Socio-Cultural Perspectives

Edited by Avi Berman and Gila Ofer

Routledge
Taylor & Francis Group

LONDON AND NEW YORK

Designed cover image: Normform / Getty Images

First published 2025
by Routledge
4 Park Square, Milton Park, Abingdon, Oxon OX14 4RN

and by Routledge
605 Third Avenue, New York, NY 10158

Routledge is an imprint of the Taylor & Francis Group, an informa business

British Library Cataloguing-in-Publication Data
A catalogue record for this book is available from the British Library

ISBN: 978-1-032-06010-1 (hbk)
ISBN: 978-1-032-06011-8 (pbk)
ISBN: 978-1-003-20025-3 (ebk)

DOI: 10.4324/9781003200253

Typeset in Times New Roman
by SPi Technologies India Pvt Ltd (Straive)

Contents

Contributors

Noga Ariel-Galor is an expressive arts therapist and a psychoanalytic psycho-therapist at a private practice in Tel-Aviv. She is a lecturer at the Multidisciplinary Program in humanities at Tel-Aviv university, the Art Therapy Program at Haifa University, and the Academic College for Society and the Arts. She is a board member of the Israeli chapter of the International Association for Relational Psychoanalysis and Psychotherapy (IARPP) and the Israeli Association for Psychoanalytic Psychotherapy.

Lewis Aron was the Director of the New York University Postdoctoral Program in Psychotherapy and Psychoanalysis. He had served as President of the Division of Psychoanalysis (39) of the American Psychological Association; founding President of the International Association for Relational Psychoanalysis and Psychotherapy (IARPP); founding President of the Division of Psychologist-Psychoanalysts of the New York State Psychological Association (NYSPA). He was the co-founder and co-chair of the Sándor Ferenczi Center at the New School for Social Research, an Honorary Member of the William Alanson White Psychoanalytic Society, and Adjunct Professor, School of Psychology, Interdisciplinary Center (IDC) Herzliya, Israel. Dr Aron had received the New York State Psychological Association (NYSPA) Distinguished Service Award and the Division of Psychoanalysis (39) Leadership Award. He held a Diplomate in Psychoanalysis from the American Board of Professional Psychology (ABPP) and was a Fellow of both the American Psychological Association and of the Academy of Psychoanalysis. Lewis Aron was one of the founders, and an Associate Editor of Psychoanalytic Dialogues and was the series editor (with Adrienne Harris) of the Relational Perspectives Book Series, Routledge. He was the Editor of the Psychoanalysis & Jewish Life Book Series, The Academic Studies Press. In 2012 he received the PEP Psychoanalytic Electronic Publishing ("PEP") Author Prize, presented to honor its most influential authors.

Avi Berman is a clinical psychologist, psychoanalyst, and a group analyst. He is a member in Tel- Aviv Institute of Contemporary Psychoanalysis. He is the initiator a co-founder of The Israeli Institute of Group Analysis and its first chairperson. He is a co-founder of "Be'Sod Siach" Organization for conflict resolution in Israel. He is the head of the Group Psychotherapy track in Tel-Aviv University (within the psychotherapy program of Sackler school of medicine). He is an active teacher and a supervisor in these institutes. His professional experience includes post traumatic therapy and supervision in "Amcha" (an association for treating holocaust survivors and their second generation's siblings. He is a co-author of *Victimhood, Vengefulness, and the Culture of Forgiveness* (together with Ivan Urlićand Miriam Berger).

Rina Dudai is a researcher of literature and a member of the Interdisciplinary Group at the Tel Aviv Institute for Contemporary Psychoanalysis. Her work focuses on patterns of poetic testimonies to extreme traumatic experiences, in the interface of literature, film and psychoanalysis. Her book *Tongue of Fire: Poetic Testimony to the Holocaust* was published in 2021.

Robert Grossmark teaches and supervises at the New York University Postdoctoral Program in Psychoanalysis, The National Institute for the Psychotherapies Program in Adult Psychoanalysis, National Training Program in Psychoanalysis, The Eastern Group Psychotherapy Society and other psychoanalytic institutes and clinical psychology doctoral programs. He has authored numerous papers on psychoanalytic process and group treatment and *The Unobtrusive Relational Analyst: Explorations in Psychoanalytic Companioning* which was nominated for the 2019 Gradiva Award for best book in psychoanalysis. He co-edited the books, *The One & The Many: Relational Approaches to Group Psychotherapy* and *Heterosexual Masculinities: Contemporary Perspectives from Psychoanalytic Gender Theory*, all published by Routledge.

Uri Hadar is professor of psychology in Tel Aviv University and the Ruppin Academic Center. His fields of research include psychoanalysis, nonverbal communication and the cerebral representation of natural language. His most recent book, *Psychoanalysis and Social Involvement* was published by Palgrave in 2013.

Earl Hopper is a psychoanalyst, group analyst and organizational consultant in private practice in London. He is a Fellow of the British Psychoanalytical Society, an honorary member of the Institute of Group Analysis, an honorary member of the Group Analytic Society International and a Distinguished Fellow of the American Group Psychotherapy Association. He is the editor of the New International Library of Group Analysis for Routledge.

Anat Hornung Ziff is a professor and senior international management consultant specializing in the theory and methodology of group relations. She has been a professor of conflict analysis and transformation at universities in the U.S., Europe, and Latin America, and co-founded non-profit organizations promoting leadership development and dialogue in Peru and Israel. Anat has her B.A. and M.A. from Ben-Gurion University where she is currently a PhD candidate.

Uri Levin is a clinical psychologist, group analyst and organizational consultant. He is a board member of the EFPP (European Federation of Psychoanalytic Psychotherapy). He teaches at the Tel Aviv University and supervises both in individual and group settings. He works mainly at his private practice in Tel Aviv with adults, couples and adolescents.

Martin Mahler is a clinical psychologist and psychotherapist in private practice. The IPA training and supervising analyst, the president of Czech Psychoanalytic Society in 2023–2025. The co-founder and past president of Rafael Institute, Prague. He initiated biannual Otto Fenichel's conferences on various multidisciplinary topics (antisemitism, fear of strangeness, psychic change) held in Prague, and Central European Seminars on psychoanalytic field theory (joint project of Czech, Italian, Austrian, Polish and Hungarian Psychoanalytic Societies).

Anne Morgan worked as a social worker in the UK before training as a Group Analyst at IGA London and a psychoanalytic psychotherapist at what was the Lincoln Institute. She moved to South Africa in 2000 and assisted in the establishment of the Working with Groups course at Ububele, the African Psychotherapy Centre in Johannesburg.

Leyla Navaro is an Individual, couple and group psychotherapist in private practice and Faculty and Supervisor at the Student Counseling Center in Bogaziçi University, Istanbul. She is the author and presenter of several issues on gender in the manifestation of powerful emotions such as envy, jealousy, competition, passion, desire, anger, use of power; currently working on family secrets, the 'untold known' and trans-generational transmissions.

Gila Ofer is a clinical psychologist, training psychoanalyst and group analyst. She has a BA in English and French literature, M.A and PhD in clinical psychology. Dr Ofer is a founding member and past president of The Tel-Aviv Institute of Contemporary Psychoanalysis and a founding member of The Israeli Institute of Group Analysis and serves on the faculty of both institutes. She also supervises and teaches at the Post-Graduate School for Psychoanalytic Psychotherapy, Tel-Aviv University. Dr Ofer has been the chair of the group analytic section and board member of the EFPP and coordinator of Eastern European countries EFPP. Currently she is the editor of the EFPP *Psychoanalytic Psychotherapy Review* and the book review editor of foreign language books in the *International Journal of Group Psychotherapy*. She writes on theoretical and clinical topics; has published her work in leading journals and presented her work and taught in Israel, Europe, East Asia and the US. Her edited book *A Bridge over Troubled Water: Conflicts and reconciliation in Group and Society* was published on 2017.

Monica Spiro is a clinical psychologist and group analyst working with individuals, couples, and groups in private practice in Cape Town, South Africa. She is the founder of the Centre for Group Analytic Studies in Cape Town, where she trains mental health professionals in group analysis.

Ella Stolper is a psychoanalytic psychotherapist and group analyst. She is a faculty member at the Group Facilitation Programs at Tel Aviv University (TAU), of the Israel Institute for Group Analysis (IIGA), of the Moscow Institute for Group Analysis (MIGA) and of the Kiev International School of Relational Psychoanalysis and Psychotherapy (KISRPP). Head and Founder of an Institute for Group Analysis in Russia. Conducts private practice (individual, group and pair) and supervised organizations.

Ivan Urlić is a neuropsychiatrist, psychoanalytic psychotherapist, and group analyst. As a professor of psychiatry and psychological medicine he teaches at the Medical School, and the Academy of Arts of the University of Split, Croatia, on several Universities in Croatia, Bosnia Herzegovina, and Italy, as well as internationally. He is a founder member of IGA Zagreb and IGA Bologna (Italy), where he is a training group analyst and supervisor. He has been chairperson of EGATIN, Board Member of GAS London, and board member of IAGP and of ISPS Int. He is co-founder and Deputy President of the ISPS Croatia, a board member of the IGA Zagreb where he is a training group analyst and supervisor, and a president of the Split branch of the Academy of psychiatric sciences of Croatia. He founded the Regional Center for Psychic trauma for Dalmatia (Croatia) for the treatment of war veterans and their family members.

He co-authored *Victimhood, Vengefulness and the Culture of Forgiveness* (with M. Berger and A. Berman) and is co-edited *Group Psychotherapy for Psychoses* (with Manuel Gonzalez de Chavez).

Chana Ullman is a clinical psychologist, a training psychoanalyst, and a faculty member at the Tel Aviv Institute of Contemporary Psychoanalysis. She is on the faculty and a supervisor at the relational track, the school of Psychotherapy, Sackler School of Medicine at Tel-Aviv University, and faculty at the doctoral program of Psychoanalysis at Tel Aviv University. Dr. Ullman is the past-president of the International Association of Relational Psychoanalysis and Psychotherapy. She is the author of the book *The Transformed Self: The Psychology of Religious Conversion* (Plenum Press,

1989) and of numerous publications regarding trauma and witnessing, polit-ical context, and the relational perspective on the psychoanalytic process. She lives and practices in Rehovot, Israel.

Liat Warhaftig Aran is a clinical psychologist, group analyst and a psychoana-lyst. She works in individual, couple, and group therapy in a private prac-tice. She is a staff member in the Israeli institute of group analysis, in the psychoanalytic psychotherapy program of Bar Ilan university and Barzilai medical center, and in Winnicott center. Liat is the co-founder and the aca-demic director of Kiev International school of relational psychoanalysis and psychotherapy.

Haim Weinberg is a licensed psychologist, group analyst and Certified Group Psychotherapist in private practice in Sacramento, California. He is the past President of the Israeli Association of Group Psychotherapy and of the Northern California Group Psychotherapy Society (NCGPS). Dr Weinberg is the list-owner of the group psychotherapy professional online discussion forum. He served as the Director of International Programs at the Professional School of Psychology in which he created and coordinates an online doctoral program in group psychotherapy. He co-edits a series of books about the social unconscious, wrote a book on Internet groups and co-authored a book on Fairy Tales and the social unconscious. His latest co-edited book is *Theory and Practice of Online Therapy*.

Shlomit Yadlin-Gadot is a practicing clinical psychologist and psychoanalyst, member of the Tel-Aviv Institute of Contemporary Psychoanalysis (TAICP). She is chair of the Psychotherapy Program, School of Medicine, Tel-Aviv University. She writes and lectures on the interface between philos-ophy, literature, and psychoanalysis. She is a director on the IARPP board of directors and co-chair of the international colloquium committee. Her book, *Truth Matters: Theory and Practice in Psychoanalysis*, was published by Brill in 2016. Her co-authored *Introduction to Lacanian Psychoanalysis* was published by Routledge in 2023. She lives and practices in Ramat-Hasharon, Israel.

Tamar Ziff is a freelance researcher focused on issues of justice and the rule of law, particularly in Latin America and Israel. She received her B.A. in Political and Social Thought from the University of Virginia.

Acknowledgment

Thanks are due to the contributors who devoted much time and effort to provide us with original and thoughtful papers. Thanks also to Galit Atlas who gave us permission to republish the paper by the late Lew Aron. We are grateful to our many patients from whom we have learned much about feelings, emotions, the human condition, and tolerance. Ms. Netta Shachaf patiently prepared this book's manuscript and Ms. Netta Keessom expertly edited some articles. Susannah Frearson and Jana Craddock provided excellent and supportive editorial assistance. To all these individuals, we offer our sincere thanks.

Foreword

Writing this Foreword a few weeks after Hamas perpetrated terrorist attacks on Israel, crossing territorial, personal, and moral boundaries, it is extremely difficult to find the intellectual and emotional space for expressing my appreciation of this much needed collection of papers on the topic of tolerance from the point of view of Group Analysis and Psychoanalysis of a contemporary kind. Most of the authors are Israelis, as are its two co-editors Dr Avi Berman and Dr Gila Ofer. Several of these colleagues are my personal friends. They understand that in human affairs there is no "absolute beginning". The Golden Rule of "Do unto others as you would have them do unto you" rarely takes precedence over what many of us have called the Leaden Rule of "Do unto others what they have done unto you". Moreover, unconscious identification is never based only on love and admiration; envy must also be taken into account.

Although "tolerance" is a concept in crisis, it is also highly dependent on its context. What is known in the philosophy of science as the "third, intermediate world" of social and cultural phenomena is a matter of meaning and narrative: a "speaker", an "audience", and perhaps a "chorus" are paramount. However, processes of tolerance are properties of the tripartite matrix of any social system: the foundation matrices of our contextual societies, the dynamic matrices of our organisations and groupings of various kinds, and of the interpersonal matrices of the participants in them (Hopper, 2024a). Thus, the problem of tolerance cannot be addressed in terms of any particular action but only in terms of our relationships to this particular action and to the perpetrators of it.

Always systemic, tolerance can be defined in terms of intolerance, which is not its binary opposite as much as it is an indication of an alternative paradigm. In this dialectical context, processes of tolerance and intolerance depend on the importance of processes of conformity to core values and moral norms. The more that the cohesion of a social system depends on the integration of its various patterns of relations rather than on the solidarity of its various patterns of beliefs, values and norms, the less likely it is that cohesion depends on conformity to these particular patterns of normation. Thus, conformity and non-conformity are likely to be defined in terms of a large range of deviation (Hopper, 2023).

These arrangements are rarely stable, of course. Under conditions of social trauma, whether of a stress, cumulative, or catastrophic nature, complex social systems are likely to regress, and, therefore, to become more "simple" in their structures and dynamics. Societies and organisations become more like groups. Their cohesion becomes more a matter of solidarity and similitude. Conformity and non-conformity are defined more rigorously. In fact, it is impossible to understand tolerance and intolerance without locating these processes in the context of the traumatogenic processes of failed dependency on our leaders and on structures of authority and power, which are primarily economic and generally political.

The chapters in this book are also imbued with an appreciation of the theory and concept of the "moral community", the study of which can be traced to the neglected work of Emile Durkheim (Hopper, 2024b). He was especially interested in the social conditions that breed a sense of collective identity: us and them as well as we and they. The boundaries of the moral community can be defined not only in terms of the shared beliefs, values, and norms of the members of them, but also in terms of the application of "judgment norms" to the actions of others. The members of a moral community both judge and are judged according to the same degree of relativism or absoluteness, and stringency or leniency (as I have tried to explain in my own contribution to this book).

Tolerance – A Concept in Crisis: Psychoanalytic, Group Analytic, and Socio-Cultural Perspectives will stimulate further exploration and debate concerning what I have come to call the "virtues" of Group Analysis and Relational Psychoanalysis. The flawed virtue of tolerance is essential to our professional formation and clinical practice, to our personal maturity, and to our ability and willingness to take the roles of citizenship.

Earl Hopper
Series Editor

References

Hopper, E. (2023). "Notes" on the Theory and Concept of the Fourth Basic Assumption in the Unconscious Life of Groups and Group-like social systems: Incohesion: Aggregation/Massification or (ba) I:A/M. In Traumatic experience. In C. Penna (ed.) *From Crowd Psychology to the Dynamics of Large Groups: Historical, Theoretical and Practical Considerations*. London: Routledge.

Hopper, E. (ed.) (2024a). *The Tripartite Matrix in the Developing Theory and Expanding Practice of Group Analysis: The Social Unconscious in Persons, Groups and Societies Volume 4*. London: Routledge.

Hopper, E. (2024b). The Social Unconscious, Trauma and Groups: A Constellation. In D. Finzi & J. W. Wolff Bernstein (eds.) *Thoughts for the Times on Groups and Masses. A Sigmund Freud Museum's Symposium*. Leuven: Leuven University Press.

Introduction

Gila Ofer and Avi Berman

On interpersonal, intersubjective, and societal levels, we are in the midst of denigration of the different. Insecurity, polarization, violent nationalism, and racism invade our public and private lives. It seems that maintaining tolerance, an attitude of integrity and restraint against impulsive anger and vengefulness, falsity and terror, has become increasingly challenging. Furthermore, we now live in a period of (post-)pandemic that only further stresses our abilities to contain personal fears, anxieties, and frustrations. By projecting inner anxieties on others, we may mark them as the cause of our misfortunes, creating antagonism towards them and diminishing tolerance and compassion.

The chapters that were returned to us by the authors in this book presented us with a picture of tolerance from many perspectives: from various countries and continents, and from diverse cultural and social environments. Though they had never spoken to one another on this issue, as we gathered their thoughts, it became clear that we were dealing with a concept in crisis. The idea of tolerance, once one of the pillars of a humanistic worldview, is experiencing an upheaval from several directions.

First, the existing concept of tolerance is perceived as unsatisfactory and even misleading. Being tolerated (Navaro, in this book) may be an expression of social stratification. The one who is tolerated remains hidden, their visibility and viability dictated by the privileged group who can be proud of their tolerant values while preserving their dominant status. According to Weinberg (in this book), tolerance may be experienced as "over-tolerance" within certain social groups and lead to a strong backlash. Moreover, while tolerance is still considered a value in some places, we are witnessing the development of an opposite value which we propose calling moral intolerance. Berman (in this book) suggests that tolerance might be taken too far and might result in over-adaptation to a painful situation. Thus, it presents a risk of identification with aggressors. It seems necessary to recognize the individual's subjective unbearable experience that limits over-adaptation. Dalal (2011) questions some of the beliefs and assumptions that have underwritten our understanding of tolerance, asking whether it is necessarily positive. He argues that there are occasions when

DOI: 10.4324/9781003200253-1

intolerance and conflict are ethical requirements. The corrective encounter between people requires engagement and mutual recognition, beyond declarations of tolerance or forgiveness (Ofer, 2017) and a distinction between those who are willing to carry this process and those who are not. Concepts like retributive justice (Spiro and Morgan) seem to replace the pursuit of tolerance in turbulent societies.

Thus, it seems, that the concept of tolerance requires, at the least, a reinvestigation, and likely an updated understanding. In this book, we offer an exploration of tolerance in terms of psychoanalytic and group-analytic ideas within the personal, interpersonal, and social realms through different perspectives, some of which are interwoven with personal experiences.

* * *

The Webster Merriam Dictionary provides these definitions of tolerance: 1) capacity to endure pain or hardship: endurance, fortitude, stamina; 2a) sympathy or indulgence for beliefs of practices differing from or conflicting with one's own; and 2b) the act of allowing something: toleration. Yet, other dictionaries prioritize the interpersonal dimension. The Oxford Dictionary understands tolerance as "the ability or willingness to tolerate the existence of opinions or behavior that one dislikes or disagrees with".

Tolerance is an outcome of developmental processes, emotional, intrapsychic and intersubjective. There is a difference between intra-psychic tolerance (for inner drives, one's ambivalence, frustrations, uncertainties, paradoxes, and vagueness) and tolerance of the Other (for other ideas, behaviors, people's emotions and attitudes). Nonetheless, they are interconnected, and one is the outcome of the other. The former is intrapersonal, the latter refers to containing disagreement as part of mutual belonging with others, or a sort of enlightened co-existence. Tolerance in society means agreeing to the existence of one's own otherness and of the other whose ideas and behavior are different from ours.

For Freud, love is associated with the ego's pleasure while hate is aimed to remove and expel the alien object that causes displeasure. Whereas love is an instinct directed at possessing a certain object, hate, its counter-form, represents the urge to evacuate and project those objects that cause suffering and unpleasant feelings. Hate is therefore intimately linked to instincts of self-preservation (*Instincts and their Vicissitudes*, 1915). We can conclude that, for Freud, intolerance represents self-preservation while tolerance can pose a danger to our existence.

Freud did not relate to tolerance developmentally. It was Winnicott who radically advanced our thinking about the role of tolerance in development. His notion of the "good enough mother" is connected to the child's cognitive and emotional development and their development of a healthy concept of external reality as well as a capacity to tolerate frustration. In discussing the mother's (or other caretakers') adaptation to the needs of the baby, he says that the mother allows the infant to experience small amounts of frustration. She is empathetic and caring. but does not immediately rush to the baby's every cry. She is not "perfect", but she is "good enough" in that the child is left only with a manageable amount of frustration (Winnicott, 1960). The child must develop tolerance to withstand the paradoxical situation where the mother is both good and bad at the same time. At this stage, the baby is in a magical world of illusion, although a necessary illusion. The ability to have an illusion is a pre-requisite to developing a sense of reality. According to Winnicott, it is neces-sary to develop the ability to withstand disillusionment in order to cope with reality. Through this gradual involvement with reality, the baby develops toler-ance for frustration, a capacity for being alone, and a capacity for concern (Winnicott, 1971). These are the antecedents of tolerance for others. Thus, despite its importance as a moral value, tolerance cannot be studied without attention to disillusion and intolerance.

* * *

It has been argued that tolerance for elements of the external world is condi-tioned by the development of tolerance for one's frustration. Tolerance of frus-tration is required to face unfulfilled wishes; illusions that are no longer supported by the environment; and mixed feelings of love and hate. We suggest that these intrapersonal aspects necessarily appear in the interpersonal realm and, consequently, in the social realm. There is a two-way interaction between the intrapersonal and the personal. The intrapersonal affects relationships and relationships may then be internalized to influence the intrapersonal realm.

As we attempt to outline the move from the personal to the social, Juliet Mitchell's concept of the "Law of the Mother" becomes relevant. According to Mitchell (2013), the Law of the Mother enables the infant to grow into the social. The mother emphasizes the passage from individual psyche to the social and to society, or, in other words, the need to tolerate inner drives and outer fears. The law forbids the infant from murdering their sibling and similarly forbids sexuality between siblings. This implies that each child is unique and equal at the same time. Forbearance, patience, and tolerance are then part of this law. In fact, Freud anticipated Mitchell's conceptualization of the Law of the Mother in *Totem and Taboo* (1912–1913) which is devoted to the topics of incest and murder and the ways by which society tries to cope with these tendencies which are the opposite of tolerance.

* * *

In fact, tolerance is not elaborated enough in psychology, psychoanalysis, and group analysis. Searching the psychoanalytic literature in Psychoanalytic Electronic Publishing (PEP) yields only a few papers that broach the topic. Until the final two decades of the last century, those papers that do relate to tolerance mention it in connection to frustration: tolerance as an intrapersonal quality, a capacity to bear something that is unpleasant, annoying, and frustrating despite the suffering that is involved, or tolerance as affect regulation.

In the last 20 years, the psychoanalytic literature has become less concerned with the developmental and more with relational aspects of tolerance. Rather than taking an intrapersonal perspective on tolerance (and intolerance), articles more often relate to tolerance through countertransference or enactments in analytic meetings. We argue that the changes that happened in the psychoanalytic literature mirror the individual's development of tolerance through the intrapersonal to the interpersonal and social.

Tolerance cannot exist in a void. It belongs not to an individual but to a relationship. The individual who aspires for tolerance thereby welcomes mutual tolerance. Tolerance, mutual recognition, and radical witnessing are the three constructs that Ullman focuses on, arguing that, together, they constitute a framework for relational psychoanalytic ethics. All three constructs assume a stance towards Otherness. Her chapter examines the meanings of these concepts for psychoanalytic work and in social-political contexts.

Berman elaborates on the concept of tolerance by placing it in a relational field. He depicts the significance and consequences of disillusioned tolerance that occurs through self-recognition of an unbearable experience. Combining group analytic and psychoanalytic perspective, Grossmark theorizes on tolerance through the lenses of Bion's theory of containment and the relational notion of multiple self-states and the centrality of enactment in the manifestation and healing of unrepresented states of pain, trauma, and fragmentation. The group becomes a containing, transformational matrix within which group members, together with the unobtrusive, yet present, analyst, can hold and know multiple self-states as well as the contradictory, sometimes abrasive, elements and sub-groups that may emerge. In this way, these can then be transformed from intolerable and indigestible – fit only for evacuation – into metabolizable, tolerable, and, most important, knowable others.

* * *

With the development of thinking about co-constructing the unconscious and about the social unconscious, the psychoanalytic and group analytic literature from the 1990s is ripe with references to tolerance in interpersonal processes, in patient-therapist encounters, and especially to social dimensions. This is even more evident from the beginning of the 20th century, with the expansion of discourse on gender and of crises related to refugees, racism, and non-democratic regimes. Social movements like Black Lives Matter and #MeToo that aim to bring awareness of abusive social situations and end suffering have also served to widen the scope and intensity of emotional expression. These trends, as well as the emergence of social organizations working against state discrimination and to correct political misinformation require public disillusionment and a cessation of tolerance for the status quo.

An important addition to this emerging image comes from the proliferation of social networks. It has become clear that these networks foster groups of Us and Them that act as mechanisms of Aggregation (Hopper, 2003). Within each group, the need for belonging (Foulkes, 1948) translates into attitudes of aversion and hatred toward other groups. In essence, intolerance becomes a social glue. Recently, suspicions about social networking media have been raised. Frances Haugen, a data engineer who has worked for Google and Facebook, among other social media giants, has asserted that the managers of these networks prioritize financial gain over all, resulting in the polarization we observe today. Haugen has testified to British and American lawmakers that Facebook would fuel more violent unrest worldwide unless it modified its algorithms which currently push extreme, divisive content and prey on vulnerable demographics to keep them scrolling. Moral intolerance and the polarization created within and by social networks together challenge the traditional sense of tolerance.

In this book, we include the individual perspective on tolerance alongside personal and social perspectives. Some chapters explore the socio-political aspects of tolerance and intolerance, written by authors who have all undergone personal processes related to political events and share with us their experiences and views.

Whether for intrapersonal or interpersonal reasons, the authors in this book describe social encounters where alienation is perceived as hostile and dangerous. Gadot and Hadar question the relevance of the concept of thirdness to tolerance. They examine the logic and dynamics of dyadic components of intractable conflict that are given to change and manipulation, thereby forming a basis for tolerance. They then examine the dialectic ties between the dyadic and the triadic consideration of tolerance and argue that each offers unique contributions, and that only through the continuous movement between dyadic and triadic positions can tolerance fully be understood and promoted. Hopper expands on the notion of intolerance by explaining his fourth basic assumption, massification versus aggregation. He argues that these processes are reactions to traumas and lead to nationalism, fanaticism, and fundamentalism. Levin explores several aspects of the complex dialectical relations between tolerance and intolerance in our clinical work, as well as in our role as citizens of societies and cultures. Trying to cope with the dialectics of tolerance versus intolerance, Weinberg suggests a circumplex model that is not contrasting tolerance with intolerance, but rather contrasting intolerance (which he suggests calling under-tolerance) with pseudo-over-tolerance. The model is helpful in determining when tolerance contributes to diversity and negates discrimination, dehumanization, repression, and violence, and when, in overdose, it paradoxically encourages more violence, discrimination, and divisiveness.

Ariel-Ganor focuses on the clinical encounter between Jewish-Israeli therapists and patients who are Palestinian citizens of Israel. While tolerance in a multicultural society is often taken to be the acceptance of different religious and cultural practices, her chapter is on a specific kind of tolerance that calls upon the therapist to maintain a capacity to withstand ambiguity and ambivalence in a clinical setting in which the Other is identified as a member of the opposite group involved in a violent political conflict. Mahler expands on the limitations of tolerance within a psychoanalytic process, during which the patient moves away from freely associating and provides material which stimulates action in an enactment rather than interpretation. Relating to the myth of Oedipus and through a clinical vignette, he demonstrates that tolerance stops being useful and justified if it is not part of the process of exploring what it is we are trying to tolerate. Blind tolerance leads to catastrophic consequences and dead ends. However, writes Mahler, the clash of intolerances between analyst and patient can foster intense analytic work and can reconcile but not diminish mutual differences. Through a social, personal, and professional personal history that stem from her experience being raised in the Soviet Union, Stolper looks at tolerance from a group analytic perspective and writes about the development of tolerance in what she calls the "prisoner matrix". The personal life journey of Wahrhaftig, who is a granddaughter of a religious political leader and comes from religious settler family, is also implicated in the development of her concept of "public tolerance" and the question of how to foster tolerance in her analytic group.

It is notable that the authors who highlight the contribution of group analysis to the process of tolerance use their own history and enactments to further develop our understanding of tolerance. Navaro questions the experience of being tolerated as a minority and argues that it has transformed her into a submissive, second-class vassal, distancing her from the power of assertion, open criticism, and resistance to intolerable governmental policies and actions. She suggests an alternative concept of acceptance. The South African experience of presupposed tolerance in a country suffused with traumas is narrated and conceptualized by Morgan and Spiro. They examine tolerance and how the concept may be used to engage in difficult interpersonal and intergroup exchanges. These exchanges may challenge the limits of tolerance as we conceptualize it. However, they posit that we may need to tolerate the intolerable as a route toward authentic integration. Drawing on social and psychological examples, Urlić explores tolerance and forgiveness as strategies of survival. Hornung Ziff and Ziff question whether the implementation of state-sanctioned political "forgiveness mandates" in Central America, South Africa, Colombia, and Spain, undertaken through amnesties and/or truth and reconciliation commissions, can realistically transform an injured and fractured society. Atrocities can be forgiven and the conflicting parties can replace their conflict narratives with a shared vision of society in coexistence. However, such attempts can also entrench feelings of mutual threat and generate resentment and resistance.

We believe that what applies to psychoanalytic schools of thought and to training institutes is also applicable to other areas and types of institutes. The importance of tolerance in organizations of all sorts is indisputable. Two papers approach the issue in relation to psychoanalytic training institutes.

The late Aron, who always encouraged plurality in thinking, argues for approaching contemporary psychoanalytic multiplicity with an attitude of "reflexive skepticism" and "critical pluralism". Diversity of psychoanalytic theories can enrich our knowledge. Other schools, viewpoints, or orientations can provide a function that no model can do for itself alone. He prefers a genuine appreciation of others and a perspective that others can offer to us and that we can offer to others. In this view, criticism from outside becomes a unique gift. Berman and Ofer detail the establishment of two psychoanalytic institutes and the slow and painful process of transitioning from resistance, rejection, and intolerance toward constructive competition and sources of inspiration for all involved.

* * *

The process of tolerance proves a difficult undertaking and may give rise to an ambivalent, contradictory, or even hostile attitude. This reality is captured in the two quotes from Voltaire and Thomas Mann that open this book. Where the first appreciates and even praises tolerance, the latter cautions us against its dangers.

Ambivalence toward the concept of tolerance has been discussed in the past. In *The Open Society and Its Enemies*, Karl Popper (2002) introduces three social paradoxes. In a footnote to Chapter 7, Popper describes what he calls the "Paradox of Democracy", the possibility that a majority can elect a tyrant. This is the lesser-known of the three paradoxes to which he pays attention, the other two being the "Paradox of Freedom", the idea that total freedom leads to suppression of the weak by the strong, and the "Paradox of Tolerance", that unlimited tolerance leads to the disappearance of tolerance. That is, unlimited tolerance may lead to tolerance toward the intolerant and thus bring about the defeat of tolerance.

In *Theory of Justice* (1971), John Rawls defends the right of the tolerant to stop the intolerant when the latter endangers their existence. The right to self-defense is proposed by Rawls as just. It is possible, then, that tolerance requires an element of intolerance in order to survive the paradoxes outlined by Popper. It is also possible that society periodically oscillates between poles of tolerance and intolerance, and that the pendulum today veers toward the intolerant.

Writing during what we know call the Age of Enlightenment of the 18th century, Voltaire's quote captures a specific moment in human history. The victories over oppressive autocracies; the development of medicine and eradication of great plagues; and the replacement of religious dogmas with scientific knowledge were considered the shared accomplishments of all human beings. This was the century when values of equality and tolerance were established. It is possible that things are repeating themselves in our time. Humanity has been confronted by the COVID-19 plague and continues to bear the consequences of a climate in crisis. It is possible that, in the face of these dangers, all human beings become equal again. It is possible that, in our time, there is still room for the pendulum to move toward tolerance.

Tolerance is crucial for the continuity of interpersonal relationships. It has an immense impact on the development of personal, group, and social-emotional functioning and growth. It affects our creativity, vitality, and many other aspects of life. Although in its interpersonal function, tolerance has been absent from psychoanalytic discourse for many years, the ability to tolerate plays an important role in fostering mutual respect and a genuine acceptance and appreciation of others and otherness. It offers a function that we provide cannot for ourselves (Aron, 2017, and in this book). These qualities make tolerance, and intolerance, of central importance to psychoanalytic theory and practice.

The readers of this book have an opportunity to further acquaint themselves with the vicissitudes of tolerance and intolerance from psychoanalytic and group analytic perspectives and to promote the exchange of points of view, concepts, and therapeutic contributions between group analysis and psychoanalysis, social and organizational bodies of theory.

***

When we started the joint journey of this book, it seemed that the idea of tolerance was already in crisis. Since we started, this crisis is only getting worse. This book comes out at a time when severe wars and terrorism are taking place in the world, which harms the humanity of all of us. It has been two years since Russia's brutal invasion of Ukraine, and most recently on October 7, a massacre took place, followed by a war in Gaza that resulted in the death of many civilians, women and children. In the current reality of killing of innocent people it seems that the humanity of all of us, and not just human life, is in existential danger.

It turns out that the encounter with the other and the different may be charged with hatred and hostile negativity. Humanity may become polarized into antagonized groups of the similar and the "others". In the absence of the potential space of containing the different and the discovery of the richness of others, war may replace dialogue. We hope that this book will contribute to preserving the discourse between all of us.

Avi Berman and Gila Ofer March 2024

References

Aron, L. (2017). Beyond tolerance in psychoanalytic communities: Reflexive skepticism and critical pluralism. *Psychoanal. Persp.*, 14(3): 271–282.

Dalal, F. (2011). Tolerating discrimination: Discriminating tolerance. In: Laurence Gould, Aideen Lucey, & Lionel Stapley (eds), *Reflective Citizen – Organizational and Social Dynamics*, pp. 19–41. London: Karnac.

Foulkes, S. H. (1948). *Introduction to Group-Analysis Psychotherapy*. London: Heinemann.

Hopper, E. (2003). *The Social Unconscious: Selected Papers*. London: Jessica Kingsley Publications.

Mitchell, J. (2013). The law of the mother: Sibling trauma and the brotherhood of war. *Canadian Journal of Psychoanalysis*, 21(1): 145–159.

Ofer, G. (2017). Forgiving and non-forgiving in group analysis. In: G. Ofer (ed.), *A Bridge over Troubled Water*, pp. 53–68. London: Karnac.

Popper, K. (2002) [1959]. *The Logic of Scientific Discovery*. Abingdon-on-Thames: Routledge.

Rawls, J. (1971). *The Theory of Justice*. Harvard University Press.

Winnicott, D. W. (1960). The theory of the parent-infant relationship. *IJPA*, 41: 585–595.

Winnicott, D. W. (1971). *Playing and Reality*. London: Tavistock.

The Emotional Challenge of Tolerance

Between Disillusionment and Forgiveness

Chapter 1

The Unbearable and the Emergence of Disillusioned Tolerance

Avi Berman

Tolerance is sometimes formulated in soft optimistic terms such as "containing differences", "co-existence despite disagreements", and "containing the mistake and the mistaken other". All of these terms are suffused with the humanistic values of universal solidarity, compassion and the gracious expansion of one's "Us" group by inviting and including people who represent the "Them" group as one's diametric opposition. I suggest that the Winnicott's term of transitional space (1958) serve as a containing concept for the inclusion of inter-personal differences. One can live with contradictions and the frustration they evoke, without losing closeness in relationships. Recognizing differences may challenge the relationship but does not destroy it or any of the partners in it. Relationships in which there are two attitudes without one imposing itself on the other may survive possible tensions and become mutually inspiring. In that sense tolerance is a consciously chosen and active presence in front of groups, or individuals that represent disagreements and differences of attitudes, beliefs and behaviors.

Intolerance, on the other hand, is a personal and group position that involves resisting attitudes that oppose those of the group and sometimes includes willingness to use force against those holding opposing views. This power might entail denial of civil rights, deliberate discrimination, exclusion and even personal harm and ostracism by state institutions. In situations of social conflict, Intolerant attitudes, may reflect Freud's description of Le Bon's mob behavior (1921) and the social aggregation within it (Hopper, 2003).

The disillusioned tolerance I address in the current chapter recognizes the threats and dangers of intolerant attitudes and strives to cope with them. Disillusioned tolerance takes into account the danger of the collapse of tolerant transitional space and the difficulty of preserving hope. I suggest that disillusioned tolerance is that which survives a crisis.

DOI: 10.4324/9781003200253-3

Disillusionment: Tolerance in Crisis

Illusion, according to Winnicott, is a crucial aspect of the transitional space. The mother supports the baby's illusion:

> Initially the mother gives the baby, by almost one hundred percent match, the opportunity for the illusion that her breast is part of the baby [....] The role of the mother is, in the end, to gradually bring the baby to disillusionment, but she has no hope to succeed in this, unless she has been able to give him a sufficient illusion opportunity first.
>
> (1971, p. 44)

Yet, the word disillusionment indicates that there had once been an illusion, which has now given way to some painful truth. Our conventional professional terminology presents illusion as a dangerous deviation from normal reality-testing. From this point of view illusion is denounced, while disillusionment is encouraged as it restores one's connection with reality and keeps one out of danger. Indeed, one of the entries in Webster's Dictionary reads "freedom from illusion". Here, illusion is considered to be seductive and dangerous. One might be captured by it.

As opposed to Winnicott's optimistic view, disillusionment might be the shattering of the dream. I suggest that it may also involve a traumatic experience in one's overall engagement with dreams, visions and hope. This includes being disappointed by people and, sometimes, even experiencing a profound rupture in one's belief in humanity and humanness. This includes an experience of loneliness and offence and evokes paranoid fears.

Disillusionment can result from a devastating encounter with experiences of exclusion, disregard for rights, racism or exploitation of weaknesses, in instances such as men's desecration of women's bodies and souls, or the abuse of minorities, or depriving the right to social mobility. We can assume that the disillusionment and the painful (sometimes traumatic) experience results in an emotional storm dominated by feelings of disappointment, fear and anger. This emotional jolt can eradicate a person's intention of tolerance, even if it has been constructed over years and has become a cherished attitude.

Traumatic disillusionment might interfere with social activism, or even bring it to a halt. Sometimes the optimism of the dream period turns into despair and cynicism. Disillusionment may lead to withdrawal. It drives people away from the social sphere and shrinks their inter-personal world down to their most intimate friends – those who have not yet let them down. I propose that some of those who are bystanders today have undergone a process of disillusionment.

Rage and vengefulness also threaten to eliminate tolerance. Unlike the submissiveness that results from fear and identification with the aggressor, anger seeks out company and might lead to the establishment of a mutual hostile alliance within the "Us" group. The most dangerous development, however, is the formation of collective vengeful wishes arising from anger. In these cases, people who once hoped that tolerance would be answered by tolerance may become active enemies. Schizo-paranoid positions might take over: the world can be divided in to good and bad, friends and enemies.

It seems that the crisis that causes disillusionment might be a vulnerable and fateful moment that requires special attention. As therapists, we ought to respond empathically to the experience of rupture that accompanies disillusionment. By providing a therapeutic space for the crisis, the therapist may facilitate its transformation into disillusioned tolerance. Since disillusionment is accompanied by a potent sense of reality, its elaboration may result in creating realistic hopes.

* * *

One of my most painful moments of disillusionment happened in the midst of my intensive social involvement period. During the 1990s, I was an adamant advocate of rapprochement through tolerance. Together with some of my colleagues, I established an organization called "Besod Siach" (translatable to 'in intimate dialogue'), which sought to bring together people who normally avoided each other and rejected any possibility of mutual understanding (the name was inspired by the Hebrew title of Martin Buber's collected chapters which, in turn, draws on the saying in Jewish Hassidic tradition: "In intimate dialogue with holy angels").

The assassination of former Israeli Prime Minister Yitzhak Rabin was the ultimate crisis in my hopes for tolerance. It sharply disrupted my experience of the tolerant co-existence of different peoples. For me, the murder of a peace-seeking prime minister in my own country was horrible and unbearable. My red lines had been crossed. Nor was I willing to keep quiet about it. In an assembly meeting of the Besod Siach organization, I announced that I refused to share this space with anyone who saw Rabin's assassination as justified. The right-wingers present at the meeting were astounded. Not only had they not expected such radical exclusionary statements in the inclusive tolerance-promoting organization we had co-founded, some of them – as I found out at the time – did view the assassination as justified. Indeed, I suspended my activity in the organization for an extended period and only gradually renewed it after I discovered a new meaning for tolerance – the meaning I hereby present of disillusioned tolerance.

Not long after the assassination, while we were still trying to heal our wounds and Israel was still engaged in efforts to achieve peace, Palestinian terrorist launched a series of attacks against the Israeli people. Suicide bombers blew themselves up on buses and in restaurants, scattering body parts all around them. One bus exploded in my childhood neighborhood, killing dozens and traumatizing many others, including myself. Something was broken in my peaceful belief in tolerance as I had previously understood it. For me, from that moment on, Israeli supporters of Rabin's assassination and the suicide bombers and their supporters belonged in the same category – the bottom of the garbage can of humanity.

My experience of the unbearable was a powerful and indelible one. In the presence of empathic witnesses and within a fraternity of others who shared my feelings, the unbearable experience could be formulated and shared, eventually reaching mutual recognition. The understanding that crossing people's boundaries of what is bearable causes rifts was illuminating. It helped me understand the radicalization of the political views of the Israeli (and, naturally, the Palestinian) public and explained crises that arise in relationships everywhere, whether in families or organizations.

The Unbearable

The "unbearable" is the term I suggest to describe a subjective experience of excess, of "too muchness", an accumulation of distress that becomes full to the brim. This experience brings the individual to their subjective limit, beyond which their long-standing adaptation comes to an end. It marks a boundary to tolerance by introducing a counter-component of intolerance.

The relations between the unbearable experience and disillusionment are discussed in the psychoanalytic literature. Gerson (2016) suggests that this link could lead to terrorism. Tillman (2018) sees suicide as a possible result of such a painful process. Turner, on the other hand, suggest that "wrestle creative meaning out of an unbearable anxiety that causes disillusionment" may become possible (Turner, 1984, p. 120).

Along with this possibility, I suggest that the experience of the unbearable and the disillusionment that follows may emerge within a painful interpersonal relationship and may bring about a further integration of the self and uncompromising selectiveness in one's human environment derived from it. The experience of the unbearable is simultaneously the result of a growing differentiation of self-perception and its empowerment. The person going through it recognize her/his needs and feelings with a new and powerful clarity and distinctness.

Often the unbearable experience is raw, regressive and unformulated (Stern, 1997) and pushes for spontaneous, sometimes uncontrollable expressions of emotional behavior. At first it may be non-communicative and requires processing and wording. In some cases, there may moments of conscious decision-making followed by change, cessation of something (including suicide in extreme cases of unbearable suffering), change in relationships or separation from people and places.

We could hope that the experience of the unbearable might result immediate transformation in one's life, like the uprising of a hero or heroine in fairy tales. In reality this is not the case. Even though I have come to know that in many cases real change is indeed achieved in the end, usually it takes a (long) period of going back and forth between rebellion and surrender, between anger and apology, between taking steps and regretful humble undoing. While some people eventually manage to reach necessary insights on their own, it seems that for most people such processing requires an intersubjective presence of another person who is willing to become an empathic witness to the emotional storm that is raging and helps in creating new meanings out of it.

* * *

Sexual harassment of women by men, everywhere, has been silenced until recent years. Dina tells her therapist the following painful memory: Some years ago, at the age of 22, she returned home with her boss, whom she mistakenly trusted as a father figure, from an important meeting on a dark winter evening. On the way, he reached out to stroke her thigh but she removed his hands. She refused verbally, too. But her refusal was unacceptable to him. He was hurt and angry. From his perspective, she should have been grateful for the opportunity to join him, an opportunity that might be rewarded with promotion (someday, if she cooperated). But now she has spoiled everything. Indeed, when he made another pass and she continued to refuse, he stopped the car and ordered her to get out. On the highway, traffic buzzed by. No one stopped. Finally, a slow truck stopped for her. She was completely dependent on the driver's mercy. Luckily for her he was fatherly and kind and likely saved her from further disaster.

A few years later, she shared the experience in an emotional conversation with her friends. Women only. The women exchanged distressing memories of similar events. One woman told of a friend's friend who showed up at her apartment, stuck his foot in the door and entered forcefully. He almost raped her but then she convinced him to let her go. She told him she was pregnant. Another woman shared a memory about her drama teacher who demonstrated emotional openness and expressiveness by stroking her buttocks in the class-room. Thus, they huddled for a long time. They shared fear and pain and anger. They took comfort in saying that not all men were like that. When they were exhausted, the conversation waned. They felt embraced and relieved. However, they did not launch a public campaign.

Years later, following the exposure of the widespread sexual-abuse allegations against Harvey Weinstein in early October 2017, the "Me too" movement began to spread virally as a hashtag on social media. On October 15, 2017, American actress Alyssa Milano posted on Twitter, "If all the women who have been sexually harassed or assaulted wrote 'Me too' as a status, we might give people a sense of the magnitude of the problem".

The phrase "Me too" was initially used in this context on social media in 2006, on Myspace, by sexual harassment survivor and activist Tarana Burke. At a certain moment sexual harassment became unbearable for some women. When communicated, it resonated with many other women. It stopped short their over-adaptation to oppressive behavior patterns and replaced it with a new-born intolerance to an intolerant situation. Burke has more recently referred to it as an international movement for justice for marginalized people in marginalized communities.

The combination of affiliation and belonging are essential to such social change. Selfhood that emerges out of an unbearable experience is conditioned upon an inner experience of entitlement (White, 1963). The female sisterhood that evolved especially in recent decades with the spread of feminist protest, has empowered women's sense of entitlement. At a certain moment, a member of the larger group like Tarana Burke could have formulated the collective experience of The Unbearable. In retrospect, it turns out to be a moment of leadership. It is likely that until it became clear that her self-disclosure represented many, and before others echoed her assertions, this moment entailed taking a crucial risk in the face of the dominant and powerful patriarchic culture. I would like to suggest that any stable group affiliation reinforces the experience of entitlement for its members. Group processes of resonance, mirroring and exchange (Foulkes, 1948) may rehabilitate individual's and collective self-esteem.

The "Me too" protests made waves everywhere. It also resonated in Dina's sessions. At one meeting, she arrived agitated. It had come to light that her 12-year-old daughter's drama teacher had demonstrated his guidance by touching girls without their permission (he too). Dina was furious. Abusive behavior towards her daughter was unbearable for her. The next morning, she arrived at her daughter's school and barged into the principal's office. She demanded that he investigate the case and inform the parents of the results of the investigation. She organized the mothers in the WhatsApp group and they united. "I can no longer bear humiliation by men".

The Me-too movement has affected us all. I would speculate that few of us would describe the position of those young women, who shared their harrowing stories of sexual harassment two decades ago, without organizing in opposition, as "tolerance". However, we should recognize that adaptation, and especially over-adaptation, can be presented as tolerance. Over-adaptation depicted as tolerance may characterize both sexes. It might serve as a consolation for the helpless, whose dignity is trampled in abusive and denigrating ways. The term "tolerance" may be invoked by some privileged groups to pink-wash the experience of choice to whom choice had been denied.

Ferenczi's concept of "identification with the aggressor" (1933/1980) may describe the psychodynamics of this euphemism as blurring the distinction between tolerance and submissive over-adaptation. According to Ferenczi, abuse or oppression may evoke the victims' dismay and helplessness and "compels them to subordinate themselves like automata to the will of the aggressor, [....] completely oblivious of themselves they identify themselves with the aggressor" (p. 162). This terror may lead one to placate the aggressor. According to Frankel (2002), placating behavior can be a defense mechanism, as it appeases the aggressor and reduces his dangerous behavior. It is my contention that appeasement of the aggressor, especially when it is the result of identification, may result in tolerance-like attitudes and behaviors, while unconsciously it may express frightened flattery. That is, identification with the aggressor breaks the victim's spirit and harms his or her reality-testing and inter-personal judgement. It may lead to the emergence of subjugator-subjugated relations.

The importance of the unbearable experience that stems from disillusionment lies in the fact that it marks a rescue from submissive identification with an aggressor. Disillusionment restores selfhood and sanity. Self-blame ceases, and anger at injustice may take its place. A better orientation of human relations distinguishes between victim and wrongdoer. Thus, the unbearable experience leads the victim to recognize reality; it relies on disillusionment and becomes a boundary to over-adaptation.

Dina says "I can no longer bear the humiliation". Another patient says of his wife's outbursts of rage: "I can't go on like this. I suffer too much". He goes to sleep in the living room because the Coronavirus lockdown compels him to remain at home. And someone else says of his partner who arrives one evening in the wee hours of the night: "Sorry. That's not what I meant. We talked about giving each other freedom. But this is not freedom. It's loneliness. Not his. Mine. So that's it. I told him we have to split up". But, wait. They are not yet separated. Often as a result of disillusionment and the experience of the unbearable, a mutual influence is created, followed by negotiation and reparation that allows the construction of a better new space. If that does not work, there may be a breakup.

The unbearable experience may create a crossroads between mutual recognition and the severance of a relationship. Disillusioned tolerance is based on the distinction between people with whom mutual recognition can be established and those with whom it cannot. The conditions for such mutual recognition are clarified and can be discussed. I suggest that precisely as a result of the formation of disillusioned tolerance, and within the limits of mutual recognition, a person's ability to bear disturbing differences and to feel empathy for the pain of others increases. Moreover, disillusioned tolerance does not exclude compassion or deny it. It facilitates it as a choice. Oftentimes, mutual influence is created, followed by negotiation and reparation.

Rachel

Rachel is a head of a department at a government office. She is eagerly awaiting to finish her current position, which ends in 18 months. In the past four years, she has been accredited with many achievements. She has been able to increase her department's funding and manpower as well as to expand its scope of operation.

But things have not always been like that. Rachel came to see me after having been shamefully turned down for the very same position she now holds so successfully. She began working as a temporary stand-in for the previous department head, who had retired. Due to a harsh competition between two men candidates over the position, none of them had been able to get themselves chosen at the time. Rachel was the solution to this administrative deadlock.

She loved the job. In the remaining time before the end of her term, department relations have improved. She led her co-workers in conducting orderly meetings and implementing transparent and pleasant communication. Disagreements were discussed in an attentive and tolerant way. She accepted useful initiatives no matter who suggested them. Her management was efficient, fair and mindful of others. The many praises she received convinced her to apply for a permanent position.

When the men candidates heard of her decision, her world came crashing down. They immediately stopped talking to her and began protesting her candidacy before the sector chief. The latter generally liked Rachel but his support of her became hesitant and unassertive. Instead of actively standing by her side and recognizing her achievements, he offered nothing more than comforting words. Moreover, the worst was yet to come, lurking in the shadows. One day, she found anonymous slanders on the internet. Her shaming was horrible. She was being publicly insulted in a dreadful manner: they said she was weak, not "militant" enough for the political challenges of the task; they mentioned her nasty divorce and hinted that she was responsible for the crisis in her family. She was certain that she knew which one of them had done it, but was unable to prove anything.

Rachel was broken. She just could not believe that people could be so mean. She had never encountered such profound ingratitude. The ambitions and the politics of ambitious men hungry for power and control have trampled the different atmosphere she had created with such dedication and good intentions. Disillusionment was forced upon her and was threatening to knock her down both literally and figuratively. She got into bed, called in sick and did not go back to work for two whole weeks. She was a battered woman. This was just unbearable for her.

She came to see me as a last resort, though her female friends and therapist suggested that she should be content with what she had achieved and set aside the wrongs she has suffered at the hands of her co-workers. Her women friends wanted to keep her away from the toxic environment in which she would spend hours on end every day. She sought out a male therapist, "because maybe he would understand how things work in this despicable male world".

As a male therapist in "this despicable male world", her transference towards me had an ambivalent starting point. I was both a beacon of hope and an enemy territory for her. I acknowledged this duality and helped her express it. Inside, I felt for her and identified with her pain and rage. I felt I knew people like her offenders from my own personal experience. Drawing on my memories I felt we were more alike than different. I, too, have been a victim of overpowering and discrimination. I remembered that in my internship I was actually afraid of women in positions of authority, rightly so, in some cases, until finding my personal style in dealing with injustice.

And I also felt her soft appeal to be understood and protected by me. Her anger at men sought a place for expression and containment. She needed empathic witnessing on my part and my participation in her first attempts of confrontation with people whose response was unpredictable.

I told her that maybe she feels as standing at a crossroads between choosing to return home from the battlefield and shut the door behind her or confronting the injustice. I said that each option had its own advantages and that she should assume that I could help her maximize these advantages as soon as she felt she was able to make a choice.

My attempt to express empathy towards any of her choices has not been experienced as empathic. Precisely because of my balanced expression, it became clear to me that Rachel felt that I was not actually inviting her to the Winners Club and leaving her isolated as a woman.

"If it was a male patient, you would guide him and not just point at his crossroad". And immediately afterwards she said, "I cannot stand the humiliation of coming every day feeling excluded in the company of these". She could not finish the phrase and say "these ass holes".

I said: "You say in a very touching way that you cannot bear the injustice and immediately afterwards cannot call them "ass holes" as you feel. And what if the struggle for justice is conditioned upon your willingness to attack back? It is very difficult for you to fight back and hurt someone. In your circumstances, this inability can be used against you".

She agreed with me. In our next session, she said that she preferred to face her enemies: "Actually, I want to get back everything I had created here and, if possible, take my revenge on them". Our next sessions were personal, emotional and ethical. She had to rearrange her values system and include within key concepts in her opinion such as "the right to react" or "the right to self-defense".

I will briefly describe a therapeutic process that went on for 18 months. After having chosen to face her enemies, Rachel stepped into the heart of darkness. The emotional abuse she had suffered came up and was acknowledged and witnessed by me. This was followed by the surfacing of ghosts from her past, including her father's dismissive and belittling attitude towards her and her mother lack of support. Rachel had never heard a single word of love and appreciation from him. Her father was a military man, a junior officer who admired his senior commanders, speaking their language and embracing their values. She stayed closed to her mother founding an alliance of the underprivileged. Rachel arrived at the origins of her rage and her humiliation.

At night, she began having dreams about terrorism and terrorists. Then, she dreamt of being a guerilla fighter and shooting bad guys. Rachel – a very feminine woman in her fifties, soft spoken and tastefully dressed – now discovered she had tough, combative aspects. Her murderous fantasies were worked through in the therapy and gave rise to practical next steps. For some months she had been oscillating between hope and despair, trying to be assertive and talk back in new conflictual situations. One of these eventually led her to approach one of the two men she suspected of spreading the slanderous emails about her on the internet. She told him that she suspected him of being the source of these offences and informed him that she had complained to the disciplinary committee and that if one more shaming email is published, she will demand a police investigation. The man reacted by alternately blushing and denying. No further actions were required.

Rachel felt she was changing: she learned to be suspicious. She learned to advance her own agenda by making dynamic alliances with her supporters. The decent people among her supporters were kindly rewarded and did not forget this. To her complete surprise, the candidate chosen in her stead began seeking her support. He had no one he could trust in this nest of vipers, which he himself had helped create, and Rachel was the most effective choice. He relied on her decency. A year later, he was offered another position and recommended Rachel as his replacement; among other things, to keep his old rival from taking his place. With full support from her environment, Rachel was once again appointed to the position from which she had been ousted.

By choosing to face her enemies, Rachel began a process that forever changed her. She confronted others when she needed to; she won when she had to. She brought some different tones home with her and recovering her tenderness towards her loved ones now required taking some time to relax. She adopted both disillusioned tolerance and vision. Yet her newly acquired disillusionment had taken away a part of her experience of innocence. She also gained a lot from her experience. She became firmer and more self-confident while confronting injustice. Something of this forgotten innocence was restored when her granddaughter was born. She found herself weeping emotionally while watching children's movies on a toddler channel on television – a relic of the kind moments of her childhood.

Disillusioned Tolerance

I suggest that disillusionment is a fundamental and necessary experience when encountering the otherness of people from the opposite pole. Disillusionment may stem out of suffering a severe emotional blow, disappointment and despair. When the experience of disillusionment is not worked through, it may bring an end to one's good intentions and motivations to act. The capacity to withstand traumatic disillusionment experiences cannot be taken for granted. It requires containment, discourse and working through. This process of working through can be significantly supported by therapy. When such working through is successful, it brings about a change which includes, in my view, a transition from rage and combativeness into an attitude of willingness and the ability to communicate it.

I suggest that the profound meaning of tolerance is, hence, disillusioned tolerance; the kind of tolerance which had survived the rupture (in Winnicottian sense of survival of the subject's destructiveness, 1968). Disillusioned tolerance consists of an ongoing negotiation between the experience of the unbearable and the effort to come to know the opposing perspective. This negotiation can only have favorable results when the people on the other side are willing to make a similar effort. It is based on the mutual empathic intention of each party not to trample on the unbearable experience of others. Disillusionment compels us to distinguish between tolerance and identification with the aggressor. Otherwise, one may run the risk of responding with false appeasement to people and attitudes who have prefer maintaining their privileged position to mutual understanding and negotiation.

I suggest that the prerequisite for tolerance is reciprocity. Tolerance cannot exist in a void; it belongs not to an individual but to a relationship. The search for interlocutors from the other side becomes more pronounced and there emerges a clear and painful distinction between rivals who can still be engaged in dialogue and those whose views and actions are experienced as offensive and harmful. Therefore, disillusioned tolerance may exclude those who do not accept mutuality.

Hope is needed too, hope that in the right circumstances, it is possible that one will be able to become the person one believes she/he can be and find the person with whom it is possible. The disillusioned hope is the one that has met reality, survived the disappointment and preferred the more appropriate other.

In my view, only the combination of disillusionment and hope can validate a vision and bring one closer to its attainment. Disillusioned people, those who have been broken and were able to repair the rupture and move forward, may become the most effective proponents of social and inter-personal agendas.

References

Ferenczi, S. (1933 (1980)). Confusion of tongues between adults and the child. In M. Balint, *Final Contributions to the Problems and Methods of Psycho-Analysis*. London: Karnac Books: 156–167.

Frankel, J. (2002). Exploring Ferenczi's concept of identification with the aggressor. *Psychoanalytic Dialogues* 12: 101–139.

Freud, S. (1921 (1958)). Group psychology and the analysis of the ego. In *Standard Edition*. London: Hogarth Press. 18: 67–134.

Gerson, S. (2016). The Anxious Amalgam of the Wish for "Recognition/Revenge/Reparation": Discussion of Rina Lazar's "What Are We Doing There? A Therapeutic Tale". *Psychoanalytic Dialogues* 26: 267–272.

Hopper, E. (2003). *The Social Unconscious: Selected Papers*. London and Philadelphia: Jessica Kingsley.

Stern, D. B. (1997). *Unformulated Experience: From Dissociation to Imagination in Psychoanalysis*. Hillsdale, NJ: The Analytic Press.

Tillman, J. G. (2018). Disillusionment and Suicidality: When a Developmental Necessity Becomes a Clinical Challenge. *Journal of the American Psychoanalytic Association* 66: 225–242.

Turner, B. S. (1984). *The body and society: Explorations in social theory*. Oxford and New York: Basil Blackwell.

Turner, J. F. (2002). A Brief History of Illusion: Milner, Winnicott and Rycroft. *International Journal of Psychoanalysis* 83: 1063–1082.

White, R. (1963). *Ego and Reality in Psychoanalytic Theory*. New York: International University Press.

Winnicott, D. W. (1958). Transitional Objects and Transitional Phenomena. *Through Paediatrics to Psychoanalysis*. London: Tavistock Publications.

Winnicott, D. W. (1968 (1974)). The use of an object and relating through identification. *Playing and Reality*. London: Pelican.

Winnicott, D. W. (1971). *Playing and Reality*. Tavistock Publications Ltd.

Chapter 2

Tolerance and Forgiveness

Theoretical and Clinical Perspectives on Coping with Painful Otherness

Gila Ofer

Introduction

Forgiving – and not forgiving – is both a process and an action that may follow an offense that has caused injury, emotional or physical. Tolerance is part of this process. It is, in fact, necessary for the possibility of forgiveness. Tolerance is the ability or willingness to endure the existence of opinions or behaviors with which one does not necessarily agree. It is to bear otherness within oneself or within others. In this paper, I discuss the process of forgiveness and the place of tolerance in this process.

Forgiveness is the discontinuation of a demand for punitive or restorative actions against the offender. Forgiveness can be seen as a decision to let go of the past, i.e., to accept the fact that what is done is done and is now unalterable. These definitions are negative in the sense that they state what one must give up: a grudge, one's due after being offended, resentment. Forgiveness is most important for the continuity of interpersonal relationships and has an immense impact on the mental health, and possibly the physical health, of both victim and perpetrator (Thoresen et al., 2000). It likewise affects individuals' creativity, vitality, and myriad other aspects of their lives (McCullough et al., 2000). However, forgiveness may be difficult to accomplish and thus an ambivalent attitude toward it may emerge.

Throughout life, one is subjected to offenses, insults, or traumas at the hands of others. The feeling about the offense can either be realistic or it can represent an overreaction. The ability to deal effectively and adaptively with narcissistic and other injuries caused by another person is a lifelong challenge that begins in infancy. The infant and, later, the child must come to terms with the anger and rage that are the outcomes of frustration felt toward the caretakers.

Like forgiveness, the ability to tolerate is an outcome of developmental processes (emotional, intrapsychic, and intersubjective). It should be noted that there is a difference between tolerance of internal states and conflicts – of inner drives, ambivalence, frustrations, uncertainties, paradoxes, vagueness, and tolerance – and tolerance of the Other – their ideas, behaviors, emotions, and

DOI: 10.4324/9781003200253-4

attitudes. Nonetheless, tolerance of the internal and external are interconnected, and one is the outcome of the other. The first is intrapersonal: how one can tolerate their emotions. The latter interpersonal: to agree or contain disagreement as part of mutual belonging with others, a sort of compassionate neutrality. Tolerance as an intrapersonal quality is the capacity to bear something that is unpleasant, annoying, and frustrating, despite the suffering that is involved. This is tolerance as affect regulation. For tolerance to be developed within an individual, there must be an appropriate amount of attunement to their needs as an infant. This attunement by the caregiver in childhood is necessary for the establishment of a capacity to contain frustration and to acknowledge otherness within oneself and another. It is a capacity that can be developed alongside the move from illusion to reality; the capacity to be alone; and the capacity for concern. Tolerance gradually becomes more challenging to become an attitude of integrity and restraint against impulsive anger and vengefulness and at the same time it should not be taken too far to risk identification with aggressors.

As Leonard Horwitz (2005) writes, forgiveness is a capacity. This capacity is largely related to the degree to which a person has been able to overcome splitting tendencies and achieve integration of self and object representations. It is related more to relational capacities, such as those for concern, being alone, reparation, and mourning, than to ego capacities, such as reality testing, impulse control, and tolerance of anxiety. In this context, Horwitz also classifies mentalization as a relational capacity since it is defined as the ability to understand how motives and needs influence behavior. Mentalization encourages the individual to empathize with the emotional reactions of others, including perpetrators, therefore providing the infrastructure for the taxing process of forgiving.

The issue of forgiveness evokes a certain emotional ambivalence. Forgiveness often plays a role in restoring a relationship with a loved or once-loved object and in reclaiming the injured and often dissociated parts of the psyche. The capacity to forgive is tremendously important, indicating the existence of ego capabilities and a level of emotional maturity that facilitate deeper and more stable interpersonal relationships. However, when the offense is acute, the desire for vengeance often hinders or precludes forgiveness. Empirical studies have related the ability to forgive to better mental health, demonstrating that people who forgive are happier and healthier than those who withhold forgiveness and cultivate grudges (Thoresen, Harris, & Luskin, 2000, pp. 254–280). However, forgiveness can also be embedded within a pathological constellation. For example, forgiveness can sometimes be an expression of denial or disavowal of an internal or external traumatic reality, as if one were saying: "This never happened" or "This really has no significance". Some people even develop a chronic tendency to accept and forgive as quickly as possible. This is characteristic of placating, masochistic, or destructive personalities, which tend to view the offender as a victim and thus engender false and superficial forgiveness (Akhtar, 2009).

While the expression "I'm sorry" is one of the most often used phrases in our everyday vocabulary, until recently, the majority of conceptual material written about forgiveness was restricted to Christian or theological journals. Rather surprisingly, psychoanalytic literature has been silent on this matter. As Salman Akhtar writes, "Psychoanalysis has had little to say about forgiveness (2002, p. 175). Within the literature on group analysis, even fewer papers have addressed this topic (for example, see Van Noort, 2003; Urlich et al., 2010).

Some may argue that forgiveness is irrelevant to psychoanalysis (for elaboration of these arguments, see Akhtar, 2002; Smith, 2008). Those who do see it as relevant, however, claim that the ability to forgive is related to one's early development, as well as the inter-subjective sphere. Therefore, the current theory holds that the inability to forgive is primarily a developmental disorder related both to the fear of re-traumatization as a result of further offense and to the offended party's shame at letting themselves get hurt.

The relative absence of literature on forgiveness within psychoanalytic writing as well as the current endeavor to address the subject more thoroughly can be explained in several ways:

1. Forgiveness has always been a major element in many world religions and theological disputes. Therefore, it may have been perceived as "out-of-bounds" for psychoanalysis.
2. Asking for forgiveness and being forgiven are sometimes considered insincere or are thought to be reaction-formations. For example, turning the other cheek and suppressing anger, a form of masochism.
3. Throughout most of its history, psychoanalysis saw itself as a one-person psychology, focusing on intra-psychic processes. Forgiveness was viewed as a behavioral activity, belonging to the interpersonal realm, and thus having nothing to do with one's inner workings. Only recently has the emphasis on Relational and Intersubjective aspects of experience made room for a two-person psychology.
4. The feuds and bloodshed between and within groups, along with the longing to achieve peace, have brought to the fore the possibility of reconciliation. Most notably in this context are the truth and reconciliation committees established in South Africa according to Nelson Mandela's conciliatory vision. In this context, political events have spurred psychoanalytic theories to reconceptualize forgiveness and to consider its role in contemporary personal and social life.

(Volkan, 2001)

The Two Aspects of Forgiveness

I suggest that the process of forgiving includes two aspects Ofer (2017). The first involves intrapersonal reparation. For true forgiveness to take place, reparation must occur as a reflective, internal process, possibly on two sides, in both the offender and the offended. The second part involves an interpersonal process: contact between the offended and offending parties that includes an admission of the wrong that was committed. These elements are not separate. Rather, they depend on one another. For both, tolerance, or the ability to accept, experience, and survive something unpleasant or annoying within oneself and another, is essential.

The Internal Aspect

True forgiveness must entail a meaningful internal process that comes face-to-face with the depth of the emotions brought about by the offense. Pain and anger must be processed both consciously and unconsciously. If the anger, the need for vengeance, and the sorrow stemming from the offense are not given their proper place, true forgiveness is impossible and the grudge may even grow. The most difficult part of this process involves working through the anger and resentment consciously and unconsciously. It takes time to let go of resentment and other intense negative feelings. In addition, this inner process requires the ability to see the offender in a greater context as a complex person, both good and bad, weak and strong. It also involves overcoming defense mechanisms such as the good-bad object split and developing an integrated view of the other as a whole person. The purpose of forgiveness is not to replace hateful feelings with loving ones, but rather to provide a more realistic view of the other in their entirety.

The complexity of this process prevents us from guaranteeing complete forgiveness on every occasion. We may encounter anything in the range from utter forgiveness to the decision to hold on to intense accusations and the need for revenge. Several factors may contribute to preventing complete forgiveness: fear of re-traumatization; vengeful wishes; sadism; over-attachment (as hostility makes it impossible to let go of the object); shame; envy; and a sense of power over the offender.

In carrying out healthy reparations, the subject must make peace with deficiencies, narcissistic injuries, mental ruptures, qualities of themselves that they dislike, and imperfect objects. This is essentially the work of mourning: without real internal changes, no true forgiveness is possible. Reparation is what facilitates action in the external world, and, in this case, the act of forgiving.

The Interpersonal Aspect

The second stage is no less important. It is an intersubjective, relational stage, taking place between two people. In order for this to happen, the two must meet. They must come in contact with one another. The offender must admit the wrong they have committed and the offended must bear the offender's admission of guilt. They must meet with some empathy on both sides and be able to tolerate one another. Only then can the process of forgiveness be carried out in full or in part. When the meeting between the offender and the offended cannot happen for some reason, there is a possibility of achieving a vicarious forgiveness through an encounter between offended and another person (e.g., a therapist).

I will now present two examples from popular culture that illustrate the above points. The first portrays a true and full process of forgiveness. The second is an example of non-forgiving. With respect to showing the kind of forgiveness that follows internal reparations and interpersonal interaction seen in reality, the movie Invictus, directed by Clint Eastwood (2009), recounts the story of Nelson Mandela. As the newly elected president of South Africa, and despite having spent 30 terrible and painful years in prison, Mandela maintains a desire to forgive: "Throw those knives, those guns, those machetes to the ocean. This is where reconciliation begins". The movie relates much of Mandela's inner reparations through his accounts of reading "White" literature and poems. He decides and declares that he will be nothing like those men who have tortured him. He refuses to identify with them, to become one of them. In the movie, he decides to support the South African rugby team, composed primarily of white players and one Black player. The team is anathema to the Black population, for it represents Apartheid and the Afrikaners who subjugated and humiliated them for so many years. Early in the movie, the Black South Africans support a team from another country, cheering against the national team, which is, indeed, defeated. Against all odds, despite all counsel against it, and forced to confront the bad blood that remains between White and Black South Africans, Mandela decides to support the national rugby team. Within the year, the team wins the World Cup. The movie shows that he had not forgotten what he experienced – he even sends the team to visit the prison to which he was imprisoned – yet he is still willing to forgive and look forward. In his words, "Forgiveness sets the soul free. It drives fear away and therefore it is such a powerful weapon".

In this context, the Zulu notion of Ubuntu, humanity or compassion, becomes relevant. It is a broader African worldview that considers each person's humanity as derived from the humanity of others. Some say that it is this idea that greatly facilitated the work of the Truth and Reconciliation Committees that were established following the collapse of Apartheid in the first half of the 1990s.

The second example presents an attempt at forgiveness that yields no true forgiving. It is taken from a letter that Franz Kafka (1956) wrote to his father in November 1919. In the letter, Kafka tries to delve into the gaping chasm that had opened between him and his father in order to understand what caused it and to perhaps reach some kind of reconciliation or forgiveness. Kafka had asked his mother to deliver the letter to his father, hoping that it might help mend their broken relationship. The mother did not deliver the letter and, instead, sent it back to Kafka.

In my opinion, Kafka is unable to make amends not only because the letter failed to reach its destination. While Kafka does manage to consider the origins of the process that took place between him and his father, he attains no peace and no means of controlling his anger. His writing is suffused with despair. The process of reparation is incomplete and, naturally, no forgiveness is granted.

Kafka writes:

> Dearest Father, you asked me recently why I maintain that I am afraid of you. [...] Even in writing, this fear and its consequences hamper me in rela- tion to you [...] To you the matter always seemed very simple, at least in so far as you talked about it in front of me, and indiscriminately in front of many other people[..]. You have not expected any gratitude [...] but have expected at least some sort of obligingness, some sign of sympathy. Instead, I have always hidden from you, in my room [...] nor indeed ever shown any family feeling [... you] charge me with coldness, estrangements, and ingratitude.
>
> This, your usual way of representing it, I regard as accurate only in so far as I too believe you are entirely blameless in the matter of our estrangement. But I am equally entirely blameless. If I could get you to acknowledge this, then what would be possible is [...] a kind of peace; no cessation, but still, a diminution of your unceasing reproaches.

Kafka claims that his father is accusing him of ingratitude and conferring upon him full responsibility for the state of their relationship. He is, in fact, both accusing his father and demanding his father stop accusing him. He adds:

> It is also true that you hardly ever really gave me a beating. But the shouting, the way your face got red, the hasty undoing of the suspenders and laying them ready over the back of the chair, all that was almost worse for me. It is as if someone is going to be hanged. If he really is hanged, then he is dead and it is all over. But if he has to go through all the preliminaries to being hanged and he learns of his reprieve only when the noose is dangling before his face, he may suffer from it all his life.

This is a penetrating, score-settling, and touching appeal made by a son who has never received any recognition from his father, who was even repeatedly humiliated, and yet is still willing, though not eager, to forgive. Nevertheless, he is incapable of doing so. Without admitting it, Kafka clings to his accusations, feeling that his father is the only one who is still making charges. He cannot release himself from the hold that his father has on him, a destructive grip that leaves him with a sadistic inner object. Because the offending father does not acknowledge his role, the son becomes tangled up with his denied offense. The process of reparation is incomplete. Most of all, what is missing is the level of actual interpersonal interaction, including an admission of guilt or remorse that could enable the process of forgiveness.

Forgiveness in Group Analysis

If we consider the capacity to forgive a sign of health (though not at any cost and not in order to placate), it is important to examine the contribution of the therapeutic group to the development of this capacity. Group analysis is an excellent tool that offers multifaceted opportunities for dealing with the difficult task of forgiveness. Through the matrix of transferences and countertransference between individual members and between members and the therapist, there is a lot of exposure to the different paths by which one can moved toward forgiveness of oneself and others. In order to illustrate this, I shall begin with a tri-partite vignette from a group analysis session:

A Three-part Story of Group Forgiveness

Part I

Eli (58 years old) and Omer (32 years old) have been in group therapy for several years. The group has eight members. Omer is single and obese. He tells the group that even though he would have liked to lose weight for his wedding, set to take place a year from then, he feels that it isn't worth the effort. The members try to explain, each in their own way and with great sensitivity, why weight loss is so important. They also refer to the meaning of being fat. Omer rejects every claim. It is apparent that in his momentary unwillingness to listen, he is being defensive and is thus unapproachable. Eli, quite the obsessive type and still not tuned in to emotional nuance, stubbornly keeps explaining that weight loss is vital. Eventually, he loses his temper and, with a reddening face, says: "Look at yourself! You have to lose weight! You're not well! Go see a doctor who'll tell you about your high blood pressure! About the heart condition, you could have any minute! You have to lose weight!"

Omer, who was already struggling to accept the group's concerns and interpretations (even though he asked for them), becomes upset and responds with rage: "You can't tell me what to do! Mister strict and spineless!" and continues with other similar statements. The group remains silent for several minutes.

Someone then addresses Omer and says: "But he only wants what is best for you, even if he put it the way he did."

Omer replies: "I won't have him humiliate me like this. I'm not his puppet. I don't want him to think he can control me. I had enough of that with my father and I barely talk with him ever since, nothing more than hellos and how do you dos".

Eli apologizes to Omer, saying that he might have overreacted, but he has nothing but his well-being in mind.

Omer replies with "Mach nisht kein toives (Yiddish for 'Don't do me any favors'). I can understand all that myself".

They both relax a bit and their faces return to normal coloring. The group then discusses their interaction. They say to Eli that, if he wants to influence someone, it has to be through empathy, through understanding where that person is, and not by lecturing. Omer then talks about his father's strict and harsh treatment of him and of how, up until his late adolescence, he never dared stand up to him. He did, however, receive an apology from Eli.

Part II

Two weeks later, Eli recounts a difficult fight he had with his son. The son, a 28-year-old student, took Eli's car without asking while Eli was asleep. He came back two hours later, with the car slightly dented. Eli says that he ordered his son to get the car fixed at his own expense, even though the cost was several thousand Israeli shekels. During the session, he is having second thoughts, as his son obviously did not mean for any harm to come to the car and such things rarely happen with him. The members are trying to understand and express their different opinions on the matter. Omer is the only one to insist, with great anger, that there is no room for debate and that the son must pay up, no matter what. He repeats this several times and Eli is at a loss for words to answer him.

Someone from the group then tells Omer that he is addressing Eli in the exact same way that Eli spoke to him several weeks ago: "Boy, you two are alike!"

The group discusses their notion that Eli and Omer's relationship shares much resemblance with those between Eli and his son and between Omer and his father in both these instances. Omer is embarrassed, admitting that he has indeed been acting like his father and that he might suddenly be able to understand him.

Part III

About one month later, Omer shows up and says that he is no longer speaking to his father. He says that he was greatly offended by his father who had asked for Omer's opinion regarding his new office. When Omer said to him "You picked out one ugly office", his father replied that he has no intention of minding Omer's unaesthetic opinion and that he was being insolent. Some of the members sympathize with Omer's anger.

However, Itay, another member whom Omer holds in great reverence and for whose responses Omer often waits to hear before contributing to the group, calls out: "But you hurt him first!"

Now, after hearing Itay, Omer becomes silent for a minute and then asks him why he would say such a thing. After Itay explains his point, Omer says that he suddenly understands that he hurts his father, too, and that his father still tries to get close to him. At the next meeting, he tells everyone that he and his father are talking again.

This example shows how the group helps Omer forgive his father for both current and previous offenses. The process of forgiveness takes place over several stages through the group process. In the first stage, Omer receives an apology from Eli, enabling him to relax. Though he meant no harm, the offender asks for forgiveness. In this instance, the group helps Omer mourn the fact that the father he has is not the one he wished for, but it does nothing to induce him to forgive. In the second stage, Omer discovers that he shares similar behaviors with Eli (or his father). The group helps him perform the inner work that leads him to stop seeing things in black and white, to discover that no one is either a complete villain or a complete saint, that there are no part-objects, but rather only whole objects that have both good and bad qualities. Here, too, the group is supportive, accepting, and not advocating any forgiveness. The third stage entails a kind of regression, by which Omer again sees his father as a bad object, mindless of the intricacies of their interaction. The group, as an active witness, helps him realize that he was an offender. Nevertheless, he is not sentenced or condemned. This process helps him understand his father. His need to forgive increases and he is able to forgive. In this manner, he can apply the interactions that took place in the group to his relationship with his father.

Vicarious Individual Forgiveness in Intergroup Meetings

Here is another vignette from a workshop of Germans and Israelis who have been working together once a year for more than five years:

In this workshop, the German participants, sons and daughters of Nazis, worked through feelings of guilt associated with the history of the Holocaust while the Israelis dealt with their experience of being children to parents victimized by the Nazis. Feelings of enmity between the two subgroups were sometimes hidden for the sake of friendship. At other times, they came to the surface. In one of the meetings, a German analyst placed in front of the members two thick photo albums. On their covers was an insignia of a helmet with the Nazi swastika.

"I found the albums hidden in the attic of my parent's house", he tells the participants with tears in his eyes.

An undisguised horror filled the room. The group felt frozen and para-lyzed. After a long silence, one of the Israeli analyst-participants sud-denly remembered her father's request before she went to Germany.

He had told her: "When you meet with the Germans, I would like you to tell them the following story."

Her father was 16 when the Germans occupied Holland and dismissed all the Jewish teachers from school. At that point, he decided to leave Holland. He got on his bicycle, intending to go to the unoccupied part of France. On the Belgian border, he was stopped by two German soldiers. One of the soldiers was a young man, about 20 years old, and the other was around 45. They asked him to stop and searched his bag. On top of everything in the bag was his stamp collection and some clothes. At the bottom of the bag was a small case embroidered with the Star of David. Inside that case were the *tallit*, a prayer shawl, and *tefillin*, or phylacter-ies, that he had received on his bar mitzvah. These were, of course, indi-cations of his being a Jew. The young soldier immediately realized the boy was Jewish. He quickly repacked the bag, covering the religious objects with the stamp collection and, instead of detaining him, waved him along.

The Israeli psychologist had been asked by her father to tell this story so that the whole group would know that, even in the most horrendous and monstrous times, there were individuals with conscience, a beacon of light in the darkness that enabled people to hold on to their belief in the existence of goodness in the world. It gave meaning to life.

The group needed this beacon of light to remind them that, at this shocking revelation of the photo album, that the German analyst was also a human being, full of pain and unbearable guilt.

The spontaneous reaction of an Israeli analyst within the matrix of this particular group enabled the German analyst to experience a human encounter that both acknowledged and recognized his tremendous pain. I believe that through the interpersonal interaction that the group provided; the sharing and empathy that the German analyst received; and the witnessing by the rest of the group, he was able to attain vicarious forgiveness and, thus, the relationship between the guilty and the righteous within the group changed.

The group provides a transitional space, one which enables play in its broader sense. This play-space allows for tolerance to develop and holds two elements that facilitate the process of forgiveness: one is the group's witnessing, a wit-nessing that corroborates the offense and the hurt it caused. The witnessing acts as a mirroring, a background that supports tolerance on both sides. Witnesses create a "live third", providing a kind of listening that gives confirmation to suffering while longing to understand its meaning (Poland, 2000; Ullman, 2008). The fact that Kafka's mother did not send the letter to his father deprived them of a "live third" who could see both of their perspectives and empathically serve as a witness for both. Mandela and the Truth and Reconciliation Committee had the third in the form of the world community that supported their efforts. For many dyads, mutual confessions and forgiveness may be too much to handle alone. The group's listening is by no means a neutral one, but rather one that takes a stand in order to enable the development of various forms of self-experience. This is done by inducing a positive yet flexible ethic, replacing a strict superego with social flexibility, and by creating, for the individual, tolerance toward inner parts that have been rejected, denied, or marked as shameful.

Another aspect of the group, and is perhaps most vital in facilitating forgiveness, is that it is comprised of a number of people who could represent different characters, both past and present, in the offended party's life. This multiplicity makes it possible to use another member as a substitute for the offensive primary object, through which the interpersonal process can be carried out. As referenced earlier, this forgiveness via a vicarious object could be termed vicarious forgiveness (Ofer, 2017).

In summary, the process of forgiveness is composed of two central elements: the process of reparation and the interpersonal process. As mentioned in the beginning, both can develop only when there is an ability to bear otherness, in other words, for tolerance. Reconciliation processes recognize that the past cannot change and that repair can happen only through acknowledgment (even if partial) of otherness, within us and others. In Nelson Mandela's case, we saw that his 30 years in prison included a deep internal process that freed him from anger. This process brought him to acknowledge the good and bad in everyone, granted him a capacity for tolerance and instilled in him the intense desire not to be like his captors and tormentors. This was followed by an interpersonal and public process after he was released and given an honorary position. He forgets nothing, sending the White team to visit the place where imprisoned Black South Africans were tortured, and yet attains full forgiveness that enables him to change reality. In Kafka's case, the absence of the interpersonal encounter that may have brought about remorse, admission of guilt, and a direct address of the offense, precluded the process of forgiveness to unfold.

The examples I cited from therapeutic groups demonstrated that the group was able to facilitate the full fruition of the forgiveness process, both on the concrete and symbolic levels. The group's support and its witnessing function made it possible for Omer to see that the parts that exist in a significant other, his father or Eli, exist in him as well. This was the first step toward tolerance and complete forgiveness. While the apology was not given from the primary offender, the process of witnessing and the group's transferential qualities permitted Omer to experience relief and to abandon the need for revenge.

References

Akhtar, S. (2002). Forgiveness: Origins, dynamics, psychopathology, and technical relevance. *Psychoanal Q.*, 71: 175–212.

Akhtar, S. (2009). *Good Feelings*. London: Karnac.

Horwitz, L. (2005). The capacity to forgive: Intrapsychic and developmental perspectives. *J. Amer. Psychoanal. Assoc.*, 553: 485–511.

Eastwood, Clint. (Director). (2009). *Invictus* [Motion picture]. USA: Warner Bros. Entertainment Inc.

Kafka, F. (1954). Dearest Father. In: *Wedding Preparations in the Country*, and other posthumous prose writings, Tr. E. Kaiser and E. Wilkins. London: Secker and Warburg.

McCullough, M. E. & Witvliet, C. V. (2002). The psychology of forgiveness. In *Handbook of Positive Psychology*, 2: 446–455.

McCullough, M. E., Thoresen, C. E., Harris, A. H. S. & Luskin, F. (2000). Forgiveness and Health: An unanswered question. In M. McCullough, K. Pargament & C. Thoresen (eds), *Forgiveness: Theory, Research, and Practice*. New York: Guilford Press, pp. 254–280.

Ofer, G. (2017). Forgiving and non-forgiving in group analysis. In G. Ofer (ed.), *A Bridge over Troubled Water*. London: Karnac, pp. 53–68.

Poland, W. S. (2000). The analyst's witnessing and otherness. *J. Amer. Psychoanal. Assn.*, 48: 17–34.

Smith, H. (2008). Leaps of faith: Is forgiveness a useful concept? *IJPA*, 89: 919–936.

Thoresen, C. E., Harris, A. H. S. & Luskin, F. (2000). Forgiveness and health: An unanswered question. In M. McCullough, K. Pargament & C. Thoresen (eds), *Forgiveness: Theory, Research, and Practice*. New York: Guilford Press, pp. 254–280.

Ullman, C. (2006). Bearing witness: Across the barriers in society and in the clinic. *Psychoanal. Dial.*, 16: 181–198.

Urlich, I. Berman, A. & Berger, M. (2010). *Forgiveness, Victimhood and Vengefulness*. New York: Nova Science Publishers Inc.

Van Noort, M. (2003). Revenge and forgiveness in group psychotherapy. *Group Analysis*, 36(4): 477–489.

Volkan, V. (2001). Transgenerational transmissions and chosen traumas: An aspect of large group identity. *Group Analysis*, 34(1): 79–97.

Chapter 3

Tolerance and Forgiveness as Survival Strategies

Ivan Urlić

On Tolerance

Tolerance as a subject is a multilayered concept that requires cautious approach from different sides. Since the difficulty in defining the notion, professionals rarely take the concept as a matter of research in depth of its meanings and interconnections with notions that complement its understandings, modes of perception and uses. Strange enough, because the concept is widely known as translating permissiveness, inclusiveness, patience with non-compliant diversity.

Fish (2014) describes tolerance as a fair, objective, and permissive attitude toward those whose opinions, practices, race, religion, nationality, etc., differ from one's own.

Tolerance is often described as a virtue. In that sense it is described as a version of the golden rule in that, insofar as we want others to treat us decently, we need to treat them decently as well. That stance corresponds to the general ethics present in all religions and ethical codes that, taken seriously, would prevent acts of open aggressivity, wars and crimes. Margalit (1998) wrote that what people are striving for is to live in a decent society. In spite of sounding as an idealization it is possible to see that level of functioning in the best organized societies in this world.

Fish tries to link another important notion which he connects with tolerance: the acceptance, that in human psychology is a person's assent to the reality of a situation, recognizing a process or condition (often a negative or uncomfortable situation) without attempting to change it, protest, or exit.

Shires (1983) defines tolerance as a fair and objective attitude toward those whose lifestyle differs from yours. The level of tolerance in your life can be attributed to levels of happiness and contentment, as many researchers have pointed out. However, researchers try to examine the paradoxical question of whether tolerant people are happier, or are happy people more tolerant. Shires quotes the results of neuroscientific researches that, on average, the human brain has the capacity to produce billions of thought processes per second, of which only around 2,000 could be brought into awareness. This means that

DOI: 10.4324/9781003200253-5

humans have the capacity to act and behave differently in all areas of their lives, bringing about upsetting and uncomfortable feelings in others. So, discussing brain activity allows us to gain a perspective on how important tolerance is in our lives and how common it can be for other people to focus differently on sensitive lifestyle choices.

Witenberg (2014) suggests that tolerance should be seen as a moral virtue that is best placed within the moral domain – but it is often confused with prejudice. The assumption made is that the absence of prejudice, by default, means a person is tolerant. Prejudice and tolerance are theoretically different concepts, and not the opposite of each other. In fact, they coexist. She links these thoughts with those of many recent philosophers who have linked tolerance with respect, equality and liberty, and argue that tolerance should be regarded as a positive civic and moral duty between individuals, irrespective of color, creed or culture. It should be a moral obligation or duty which involves respect for the individual, as well as mutual respect and consideration between people. Tolerance between people makes it possible for conflicting claims of beliefs, values and ideas to coexist as long as they fit within acceptable moral values.

I believe that in order to develop the capacity for tolerance it is first necessary to understand and evolve empathic attitudes toward our surroundings. In everyday life, empathic sharing of feelings brings our internal world very close to other people's worlds through deep emotional resonance. In psychotherapeutic situation this emotional complementarity is known as countertransference (concordant identification, Racker, 1968; Hunt & Issacharoff, 1977), and in everyday life as compassion. It is the very honest exchange of deep human feelings, since the beginning of life, that remain at the foundations of human emotional development. The longing for such a fundamental feeling that includes trust, protection, safety and calm remains as one of the basic searches throughout life. But, this idealization is difficult to attain, and when achieved it is difficult to sustain for some longer or shorter periods. In that sense, the search for an empathic relationship is always actual and frustrations in attempts to establish and preserve that quality of emotions is everlasting. Or, as Virginia Satir (1978) wrote, talking from perspective of human relationships, the essential elements of establishing and supporting human relationships are based on respect of differences, transformation of conflicts, development of possibilities, ability for undertaking the responsibility for one's own life, health, work and relationships.

Lessons on tolerance one starts to encounter from the age of 3–4. Some of them transmit authentic family memories, but they might appear like entering the mosaic of a family saga. I am recollecting one during WWI, when my grandfather was working for the court of justice in Northern Dalmatia, then part of Austrian-Hungarian empire that was contested by Italian nationalistic politics.

An Italian pharmacist lived in the same house with his wife. Whenever the pharmacist's wife was on cures in Italy my grandparents used to invite the pharmacist to eat with them. They shared many cultural values, but one topic was taboo: the political issue of belonging of Dalmatia. Under that condition the decent and respectful relationships could be maintained. After the fall of Austro-Hungarian empire Italian army occupied Dalmatia. My grandparents' family were protesting against Italy's territorial claims. One evening the pharmacist warned my grandfather to escape because they would come to arrest him the next morning. In that way he saved his life, but at the cost of leaving six members of his family unprotected for several months, until they succeeded in joining him in the non-occupied part of Dalmatia.

Obviously, the culture of that cultural circle could distinguish between other and otherness. Humanity and Christian ethics enabled people from different ethnic and political groups to respect each other, while their political points of view were completely opposite and untouchable. The mutual understanding and respect for otherness prevailed over the differences that could have been deadly to the weaker side.

Before WWII, the neighbors of my grandparents were a couple of prominent communist intellectuals. On the eve of WWII, that neighbor came to my grandmother's home to ask for some of her things to be stored with them because she was afraid of a police search. At that time, communists were persecuted, as well as those who were trying to protect them. My grandmother's family was aware of the risk but God's command was stronger, supported by life experiences. The police came to search the neighbors' home but didn't find any especially compromising material, which helped the activist to escape a longer stay in prison. Needless to say, during her imprisonment the husband was offered meals at my grandmother's home. Again, other and otherness were discerned. The tolerance of certain diversity was recognized and respected, amplifying the containing capacity for diversity.

Another story about other and otherness lived in the family as a deep scar from WWII. My uncle was a young physician, the son of Croatian father and Czech mother, and his wife was of mixed Serbian-Hungarian origin. By that time the young couple, with two small children, had decided to live in a Serbian provincial place. During night the uncle was asked to assist a woman in labor. Later his corpse was found in the woods – he had been shot dead. Despite that fact his wife was Serbian and he was not politically involved, his otherness in these heavily polarized societies cost him his life. In my grandmother's home an oil lamp was always lit under the portrait of the killed son. The price of otherness was extreme.

Obviously, these recollections contain some threads of the innocence of true believers in respectful relationships, dignifying the appreciation of others and otherness.

On a Forgiving Attitude, the Others and Otherness

One of the ways to preserve empathic connection with others and within our internal world is certainly the capacity to forgive. Practically, we ask for forgiveness permanently, in our daily contacts with people even many times without noticing it. Our excuses are presented to avoid conflicts, admitting some kinds of transgression. Starting from that point of view, forgiveness is not nebulous, unpractical or idealistic. It is, in fact, thoroughly realistic. In the long run, it's realpolitik (Durham, 2000; Urlić, 2013; Ofer, 2017).

I encountered difficulties in finding a definition of the culture of forgiveness. What I wrote was that the patient's attitude, actively waiting for the psychotherapeutic (individual or group) process to unfold, bringing about moving from victimhood (Berman, 2013), vengefulness (Berger, 2013), and other encapsulating behaviors, many times is not enough to approach the forgiving attitude. The bleeding wounds prevent its development. What can be found in these situations is the denial of the possibility to forgive, sometimes even "forever".

Unforgiveness has been defined by Worthington and Scherer (2004) as a combination of delayed and chronic negative thoughts and emotions (i.e., resentment, bitterness, hostility, hatred, anger, and fear) toward a transgressor. It occurs in situations that remain hurtful for extended periods, or permanently through continuing rumination. Forgiveness involves both the reduction of unforgiveness and an increase of positive emotions and perspectives, such as empathy, hope, or compassion. That involves the readiness to bear the pain caused by the offense (Kaufman, 1984). It is considered that healthy assertiveness in association with forgiveness is an important aspect when we are trying to enlarge the capacity to tolerate.

The Double-edged Sword of Facets of Tolerance and (Un)forgiveness: The Personal and Transpersonal Levels in Relationship with Otherness

Navigating between attitude and virtue I believe that tolerance manifests itself as a containing capacity for the retention of (quick) emotional and intellectual resonance, verbal or nonverbal or both, in order to weigh the response inside certain context. As an example, I would recollect an episode from a large group at a congress in Cairo.

At that time Egypt was going through turmoil caused by tensions due to the military coup overthrowing the government and bringing the army to govern the country, the Tahrir Square protests, that caused much violence and some casualties. Many were arrested. Several months later, at the congress, I was leading a large group that consisted of 400–500 participants, half men and half women. It was evident that there were more women in traditional costumes, many even with covered eyes, than two years earlier. The whole atmosphere was tense. One female participant wanted to speak up, but didn't dare and at the end she got sick. I was told that her husband and her son were arrested and that for more than three months she didn't have any notice of their destiny. I left the spot with the message – if you wish to be heard and helped you have to fight, speaking up about your fears, rights, and injustice.

The next evening she stood up and very dramatically told us about her worries and fears. The whole group divided in pros and cons, reflecting the social and political division of Egyptian public opinion between supporters of traditional values and those that were in favor of a more modern civil society. In that sense in the large group prevailed the atmosphere that didn't go in favor of the worried participant, what was voiced by several group members – if "they" were for the restauration of traditional values "it is right to suffer the consequences". But, in parallel, she should have been informed about destinies of her family members in the name of democracy. Many in the group expressed their consent and even the worried participant nodded. I underscored the brave exposition of the participant regarding her family drama in order to support freedom of speech and the tolerance in expressing different opinions without provoking violence. The reaction of the large group offered a mirror reflection of the recent and actual political situation of that society, the tensions and strivings of the society. At the same time the group was recognizing the wish for civil rights to be respected. For all the differences and otherness of the others, the respect of lawful attitude was acknowledged in the name of regulation of the social order. In other words, in the group it was discerned tolerable from intolerable attitudes of members of the two polarized groups.

The impossibility of attaining tolerance and the development of an unforgiving attitude brings bitterness, revenge and wars at a large scale from personal to international levels spectrum, talks about misery, destruction and death. The museum of Kobarid in Slovenia I remember as especially impressive in that respect.

During WWI, in southern Alps there was a place called the Isonzo Front, where some of the most important battles took place. In history books and films those most often named and presented are rulers and generals. This museum is specific about the soldiers and their destiny. There is the model of a dugout in the snow- and ice-covered landscape, with a reproduction of a letter, written under candle light in the freezing bunker, to the soldier's father. Remembering the family gathering, having the meals together, he writes about their desperate situation that evening – they haven't received anything to eat, not even a boiled potato.

This new way of expressing courage, to overcome the intolerant, belligerent, violent way of human behavior, was interwoven with the need for human comforting closeness and empathy, which is possible only in the frame of forgivingness and tolerance. Thinking of the associations mentioned here, it looks like the more we consider the meaning of these episodes, the more we feel that people were rendering their need for expressions of humanity and mutual empathy. May we say that empathic attitudes and tolerance represent the basic features of survival strategies?

Talking about others and otherness, are we taking into consideration survival strategies in the relational web? The question of permissiveness, tolerance, respect of other people, and the delimitation of otherness, which was not acceptable to the family moral values, is being transmitted through genera-tions. It has been shown that these values could have helped with survival and with other risks.

Personal Doubts and Dilemmas Mirrored in Survival Strategies Aiming at Achieving Tolerant Interpersonal Relationships

The long memories from the past can overshadow not only the present but also the future for indefinite duration. It pertains to recent events as well as to long histories reaching deep into centuries of painful memories. Among other recol-lections I am remembering the anecdote from Volkan's rich experiences in the psychopolitical field. He was taking part in an international group of psycholo-gists and psychiatrists whose task was to facilitate Palestinian-Israeli talks. These encounters were notoriously difficult and brought few results, if any.

The episode goes back in years of especially high tensions between negotia-tors. This time it was turn of Palestinians to start the negotiations. They started with the proposal of observing two minutes of silence for all those that had given their lives for the freedom of Palestine. Of course, in that circumstance it was not imaginable for the conference to continue. The facilitators proposed time out for consultations. In order to continue the conference, their proposal was that the negotiations start observing two minutes of silence in honor of all those that have given their lives for the freedom of their countries. The pro-posal was acceptable for both sides and negotiations could continue.

The capacity of the formulation of recognition of the high price of the sub-lime aim of freedom as worthwhile and acknowledgement of the sacrifice could not be rejected when purified from the direct aggressive arrow. Tolerance in interpersonal relationships means the possibility to neutralize the conflict-ual, offensive elements in relationships. That possibility might be understood as survival tool when aggressive confrontations are in question.

Tolerance is required not only in interpersonal, social and political relation-ships, but in the intrapersonal field as well. This includes primarily coping with raw urges from one side and superego attacks from the other. The first ones can be unleashed in decompensated persons suffering from psychosis, or socio-paths, borderline personality structures and malignant narcissistic structures manifesting great difficulties or temporary impossibilities of controlling their aggressive impulses, fears and other difficult feelings. On the other side, people who are inclined to superego attacks may feel at the mercy and disfavor of its rigid claims.

From many clinical cases the following remained in my memory as deeply dramatic. The veteran of war 1991–1995 was my patient immediately after the end of that war. He was very anxious and showing high psychomotor tension, complaining of insomnia with nightmares. The treatment, that included indi-vidual and group psychotherapy in an homogenous group of war veterans, and some anxiolitic medications, was helping him to overcome emotional difficulties and to regain psychic stability. After more than 20 years of his undergoing the mentioned therapy, he reappeared with complaints of insomnia, nightmares, high tension and anxiety, connected with recollections of the most traumatic episodes from war times. The enemy brought heavy weaponry to where the defense lines of the Croatian army could be attacked and destroyed. The small group of defenders for special tasks had to liquidate the enemy soldiers who were guardians of the weaponry. The special task consisted in silent liquidation of these guardians. Years later, his boys were growing up and he became occupied with worries if one day his sons would have to go to the army and whether the destiny of enemy soldiers might become the destiny of his sons. Nightmares started again, bringing him at the edge of suicide.

The war veteran wanted to try psychotherapy with me because the two of us were sharing the terrible secrets of the years he was repressing, until he couldn't avoid the transposition of it in the frame of reference of his own family.

The shared secret bore heavily on his transference, provoking deep resonance in my countertransferential response, especially as I had feelings of responsibility for the veteran's life. Psychotherapists dealing with heavy psychological trauma are divided about the question whether it is possible to identify with the person who killed another human being. I would say that it is possible, but requires emotional strain to understand the context and its changes during time. In that sense, both the patient and his therapist have to make special efforts in elaborating the unusual circumstances, roles and deeds.

Here I would like to recollect one patient of mine, a war veteran with severe PTSD symptoms that discontinued his psychotherapy and, before committing suicide, wounded three of his best friends and fellow soldiers. When I visited them in the hospital, one of them told me that he had already forgiven him because the war has taken his soul away. Usually, the encapsulation of heavy traumatic experiences does not give satisfactory long term solutions and sooner or later the repression and holding of their weight ceases to function. I would say that the "inner inocence", the idealisations lost, have to be thoroughly mourned for the new beginning to be taken into consideration, including past traumatic experiences (Urlić, 2013).

Therapeutic sharing becomes necessary in order to confront the traumatic deeds to enable the patient to pass through the process of mourning. Garland (1999) would say that some of that mourning must be for the patient himself – for his own lost world, his own pre-trauma life and identity.

You will never hear (from many Serbian politicians, church dignitaries or public workers in Serbia or Croatia) what Milan Babic, the president of the so-called SAO Krajina [s.c. Serbian Autonomous Region – in Croatia] in his closing remarks at The Hague Tribunal said, among other things:

> he participated in the worst kind of killing and persecution of people just because they were Croats, that a crime was committed that has no

justification, that only the truth opens the possibility for the Serbian people to be released from collective guilt and that he has no words to express remorse, with a request to Croats to forgive their Serbian brothers.

He could not express enough his remorse in words, so he killed himself in 2006. There is a key point of manipulation, lies and misunderstandings, but also reconciliation, writes journalist Jović (2018).

In order to continue to cope with repressed traumatic experiences it is necessary not only to encounter others with their character traits and behavioral modes, but also our internal world's capacities to bear tolerant and intolerant aspects of our experiences, feelings and evaluations. In that sense I suggest that there is no possibility of developing tolerance unless, first, the possibility of the process of forgiving has been developed. "If only all people could remember that they are brothers!" wrote Voltaire (2002) in his treatise on tolerance in 1763, considering intolerance as evil. He distinguished cautious, rational and moral arguments for tolerance. As a matter of fact, we are, every day, in the everlasting process of asking for excuses, pardoning, trying to avoid conflicts for being inattentive, distraught over, not cautious enough towards others. Ofer (2017) writes that in everyday lives the expression "I'm sorry" is one of the most often used part of our vocabulary.

To cope with painful otherness the notion of tolerance, as a "fair, objective, and permissive attitude toward the opinions, practices, race, religion, nationality, etc., that differ from one's own", or as a virtue, is interconnected with capacity to forgive. To heal the undeserved wounds on personal, social and ethnic-national levels there is a path that I understand as the five stages process that should unfold on both sides of the conflict:

1. becoming conscious of the complexity of the problem (confrontation with many diverse realities and experiences);
2. developing a deeper understanding of its manifest and especially latent contents (the mourning process);
3. working through the newly gained insight;
4. renouncing vengeance and making forgiveness possible;
5. creating the space for reconciliatory processes to unfold, with oneself and other(s), (i.e., restoration of the capacity to believe).

In order to attain the empathic civilization the process of tolerance through the capacity of mourning losses and injustice and to develop the capacity of tolerance as a survival strategy I would like to recollect the story of Eva Mozes Kor (Devčić, 2019).

Aleksandar Reljić, a journalist from Radio Television of Vojvodina (Serbia), made a documentary of global significance, one of those great stories which it is important remains recorded. He made documentary film "ENKEL" – "Grandson" (in German). About the film he said: "When I heard on CNN the story of the grandson of Commander of Auschwitz and the surviving inmates, I had to make a film about it."

Eva Mozes Kor, who lost her parents and two sisters in the concentration camp, adopted Höss's grandson, a man who lives haunted by the past, by the crimes committed by his grandfather.

What is it like to live with the knowledge that your own grandfather ran Auschwitz, that your grandmother and many close relatives knew about the gas chambers, even from the terrace of the villa that literally only a few meters high wall separated from the camp, watched the prisoners, knew about the crimes?

What is it like to be the grandson of Rudolf Höss, the man who commanded Auschwitz, whom the surviving inmates called an animal?

Another essential part of the narrative, which runs parallel to Höss's, is narrated by Eva Mozes Kor, a Jewish woman who, as a child, along with her twin sister, was imprisoned in Auschwitz; she lost her parents and two sisters in the camp, she and the twin survived. Thirty years later, dedicated to finding people who survived the experiments of Nazi doctors, she founded the Candles Holocaust Museum in America. Moses Kor, a woman with an impressive, strong personality, says what it's like to forgive Dr. Mengele, a notorious Nazi doctor known for his cruel experiments on twins. Because Eva Moses Kor found the strength to forgive Dr. Mengele. Forgiving the criminal, she says, she stopped being a victim, as she did not want to remain a victim of the Holocaust all her life.

Moses Kor symbolically adopted Höss's grandson, a man living haunted by the past, the crimes committed by his grandfather, and who, after surviving a stroke in his late 30s, devoted himself entirely to the fight against Nazism and the contemporary, ever louder, radical right. With a smile on her face, Moses Kor says that now she, not the criminal Höss, is enjoying his, now her, grandson.

With this last example I would like to underscore how important it is to understand in depth the notion of tolerance – nevertheless its content and significance can be ambiguous and ambivalent, as well as sincere.

There are countless testimonies that to cope successfully with painful otherness the whole human organism reacts in physiological and psychological ways. Survival strategies regarding all kinds of demanding circumstances and situations value the capacity of tolerance, which is intertwined with the capacity to forgive in order to reconcile with oneself and others.

The Recent Experiences of Some Radical Changes in Life Style and Tolerance Issues

In 2019/2020 a new threat started to spread from China and, in a couple of months, encompassed the entire world. The new coronavirus time had begun and the usual functioning of global life was forced to slow down in quarantine.

On my smartphone I received from an unknown author the following message:

We fell asleep in one world and woke up in another. Suddenly, Disney no longer has the magic. Paris is no longer romantic, New York is no longer a city that never sleeps, the Great Wall of China is no longer a fortress, and Mecca is empty. Hugs and kisses suddenly became weapons, and not visiting members of our families and friends an act of love. You suddenly realize that power, beauty, and money are worthless and can't provide you with the oxygen you're fighting for. The earth continues its life and it is beautiful. It only locked people in cages. I think it is sending us this message: "You are not necessary. Air, earth, water and sky without you are quite good. When you return, remember that you are my guests, not my masters."

Indeed, what is at stake? All of a sudden, the world we knew was turned upside down. As a global survival strategy, it looks like the Earth is sending us a question regarding the respect of ethical and moral values in organizing life in general. The ancient Romans used to say *sit modus in rebus, certi denique fines sunt* – there should be modes in things, there exist certain limits. This pristine wisdom our and following generations will have to think about profoundly, because the destiny of mankind is at stake. That means that the time has come to clearly distinguish what might be taken for tolerant and what should be defined as intolerant. Or, as Pat de Maré (1972) wrote: "the fate of our civilization must depend on a capacity to rise to 'One-ness', to achieve fellowship or koinonia", or the virtue and capacity of tolerance with proper reason.

References

Devčić, K. (2019). Enkel. Published in *Jutarnji list*, Zagreb (Croatian).

Durham, M. S. (2000). *The Therapist's Encounters with Revenge and Forgiveness*. London & Philadelphia: Jessica Kingsley Publishers.

Fish, J. M. (2014). Tolerance, acceptance, understanding … And how they differ in everyday life and in research. *Psychology Today*.

Garland, C. (1999). Thinking about trauma. In *Understanding Trauma. A Psychoanalytical Approach*. London & New York: Karnac.

Hunt, W. & Issacharoff, A. (1977). Heinrich Racker and Countertransference theory. *J. Amer. Acad. Psychoanalysis*, 5(1): 95–105.

Jović J. (2018). Sjećanje na Milana Babića (Croatian). (Memory of Milan Babić). Slobodna Dalmacija, Split, Hrvatska, (Croatia).

Kaufman, M. E. (1984). The courage to forgive. *Isr J Psychiatry Relat Sci.* 21(3): 177–187.

de Maré, P. B. (1972). *Perspectives in Group Psychotherapy. A Theoretical Background*. New York: Science House, Inc.

Margalit, A. (1998). *The Decent Society*. Harvard University Press.

Ofer, G. (2017). Forgiving and non-forgiving in group analysis. In G. Ofer (ed.) *A Bridge over Troubled Water. Conflicts and Reconciliation in Groups and Society*. London: Karnac Books Ltd.

Racker, H. (1968). *Transference and Countertransference*. New York: International Universities Press.

Satir, V. (1978). *Peoplemaking*. London: Souvenir Press.

Shires, Q. (1983). *Human Growth and Development: Tutoring Solution*. Ch. 9, Lesson 20 transcript.

Urlić, I., Berger, M. & Berman, A. (2013). *Victimhood, Vengefulness, and the Culture of Forgiveness*. New York: Novascience Publishers, Inc.

Voltaire (2002). *Trattato sulla tolleranza* (4th edn) Milano: Feltrinelli (Italian).

Witenberg, R. T. (2014, September 16). Tolerance is more than putting up with things – it's a moral virtue. *The Conversation*.

Worthington, E. L. & Scherer, M. (2004). Forgiveness is an emotion-focused coping strategy that can reduce health risks and promote health resilience: Theory, review, and hypotheses. *Psychology & Health* 19(3): 385–405.

Chapter 4

The Intolerable Narrative

How Politicizing Forgiveness Undermines Transitional Justice Processes

Anat Hornung Ziff and Tamar Ziff

Foreword

A significant challenge in the framework of transitional justice mechanisms is the balance of "justice" and "peace" (Uprimny & Saffon, 2017), with "justice" being shorthand for some form of criminal accountability and "peace" shorthand for the promise of an end to the immediate conflict. A successful balance can serve as a springboard for the country to move not only toward nonviolence but to a healthier society. However, an imbalance between justice and peace can be seen as mere political theater and add salt to the wound of bitter internecine divisions.

The country credited with creating the baseline model for transitional justice mechanisms is South Africa, with the Truth and Reconciliation Commission (TRC) set up to aid the transition from apartheid to democracy (Department of Justice and Constitutional Development, 2023). The TRC placed extensive emphasis on "forgiveness" as a key to national reconciliation and becoming a "rainbow" nation (Truth and Reconciliation Commission, 1998, p. 23). This emphasis embedded the concept of forgiveness as a primary element of transitional justice processes, although outside of what are commonly recognized as the "four pillars" of transitional justice: truth, justice, reparations, and guarantees of non-repetition (United Nations, 2010; UN Peacebuilding, 2008, p. 2).

This chapter argues that privileging forgiveness in transitional justice processes is misplaced and can impede efforts to repair a country after prolonged conflict. The initial part of the paper explains the theoretical basis for this view: first, that forgiveness is a subjective, discrete, and arbitrary act, and cannot be relied upon to direct or decide sociopolitical processes. Second, that in intergroup relations, the concept of forgiveness challenges identity narratives by creating a reified right-wrong dichotomy that angers and estranges groups in the conflict. The subsequent part of the paper applies these theoretical assumptions to an analysis of forgiveness in transitional justice processes in South Africa and Colombia.

Former Colombian President Juan Manuel Santos put the paradox succinctly: "In the end," he said, "it was a choice between justice and peace, and

DOI: 10.4324/9781003200253-6

I chose peace." Indeed, part of Santos' peace deal was amnesty for some of the FARC's brutal crimes. "I know," he added, "that many of my compatriots see me as a traitor," as he was accused then by many of sacrificing Colombia to the FARC, the insurgent group that fought against the Colombian state for five bloody decades. "There was no choice," Santos said. "We had to agree to the terms of the amnesty in order to secure peace." Yet much of the Colombian public saw such an amnesty and the implied forgiveness and reconciliation as unjustified, threatening, and, indeed, unforgivable.

The amnesty included in the peace agreement between the Colombian government and the FARC was not the first such agreement in history. Beginning in the 1990s other similar transitional justice processes intended to heal societies fractured by atrocities and institutionalized injustice conflated forgiveness with reconciliation, pardons, and amnesty – as in the South African context, "forgiveness was regularly associated with reconciliation, ubuntu, restorative justice and the abandonment of prosecutorial justice" (Saunders, 2011). Forgiveness, although vital for reconciliation, is nevertheless an individual and not a collective act. If so, can the politicized mandate practice of forgiveness in the context of post-conflict peace and reconciliation processes can make people truly forgive?

Forgiving in Transitional Justice

Forgiveness is an enigmatic concept, but it rests entirely on the personal sentiment. There is no such thing as "collective" forgiveness – the "nations do not have collective psyches which can be healed (Hamber & Wilson, 2002, p. 3). The United Nation (UN)'s "Question of the impunity of perpetrators of human rights violations, civil and political", written shortly after the establishment of the South African TRC, acknowledged that "forgiveness, insofar as it is a private act, implies that the victim must know the perpetrator and that the latter is willing to show repentance" (Joinet, 1997, p. 7). Hannah Arendt defined it as "an eminently personal affair" (Arendt, 1998, p. 241). Bishop Joseph Butler theorized that it is an "overcoming of resentment" (Garrett, 2018) by one individual towards another. Although broadly secularized, the concept is deeply rooted in religious thought and is often presented as a "Christian virtue", tied as it is to the practice of Catholic confession. Forgiveness is, therefore, a uniquely *subjective* process, reliant not only on one's personal relationship with another, but on preexisting feelings, attitudes, and even religious or spiritual beliefs. It is also entirely *discrete* and confined to the relationship between one person and another – just because one victim is willing to forgive one perpetrator, does not imply that another victim of the same perpetrator will do the same. The TRC, and subsequently the UN, attempted to introduce an element of conditionality into the process of forgiveness: that by "show[ing] repentance" (Joinet, 1997), or asking for forgiveness, the perpetrator can be forgiven by the victim. But forgiveness is not a mechanical process, and does not follow the logic of "if A, then B." It is entirely *arbitrary*, "act[ing] anew and unexpectedly, unconditioned by the act that provoked it" (Arendt, 1998, p. 241). Some victims may decide to forgive perpetrators that requested their forgiveness; some may not; and others may forgive even those that did not ask for forgiveness. Such a personal and emotional process is "not only apolitical but antipolitical" (ibid.). As a subjective, discrete, and arbitrary act and feeling, it should not serve as the basis for sociopolitical processes.

In intergroup relations, encouraging forgiveness through politicized "forgiveness mandates" can be detrimental to eventual reconciliation because it challenges group narratives and creates a reified right-wrong dichotomy which it never works to address. The "bad" group must ask for forgiveness from the "good" group, and the "good" group should, in return, forgive. This enforced dynamic is harmful for various reasons. First, if serious wrongs were committed why should they be forgiven? Second, members of the group required to forgive may, and are even likely to, reject this implicit label, and ask, why should we ask forgiveness? This dynamic is therefore pernicious for both parties, regardless of the actual effect or real harm committed, because it does not work to address the dynamic it establishes, unlike a judicial process that determines innocence or guilt. The roles, and the good/bad narratives attendant to those roles, are *assumed*, *imposed*, and therefore easily, and even reflexively, rejected.

For the parties, the attempt to impose such a forgiver/forgiven dynamic meant to deconstruct groups narratives and provoked resistance. Within a divided society, groups identity narratives, especially of the struggle, fostered strong identification between the individuals and the group. The Narratives, composed of realistic materials processed and designed in an idiosyncratic way, support and give meaning to the individual and the group, not only of "us" but also "who we are not", highlighting the persecuting "other". Concurrently, the reciprocal groups' projections of 'good' and 'bad' groups, bind the opposing groups in a systemic Gordian knot that, generating a tight, monolithic narrative of identity. The split within, embodied in the role of the 'Uncanny' (Freud, 2003), the villain, feeds the internal beliefs in the individual and group identity, fixating on the image of the "other." Such images accompanied by reciprocal feelings of existential threat deepen the distance between the groups and cannot be erased by any governmentally compelled forgiveness.

Forgiving in Transitional Justice Praxis

South Africa

Nowhere is this detrimental roleplaying more evident than in the context of South Africa's TRC, which misguidedly pushed the concept of forgiveness into the discourse of transitional justice. Overseen by Archbishop Desmond Tutu, the TRC invoked a "religious conception of reconciliation" (Seils, 2017, p. 7) which foregrounded the Christian virtue of forgiveness[1] as well as "ubuntu", or "humaneness" (Truth and Reconciliation Commission, 1998, p. 127).

In his foreword to the TRC final report, Chairperson Tutu conceded that the democratic transition, and the TRC, were a product of compromise (ibid., p. 1–23). In the four years prior to democratization, South Africa was on the brink of civil war, with various political groups with differing views on what the democratic transition should look like vying for power (Apartheid Museum, 2023). Hence, although there may have been some desire for a "Nuremberg-like" reckoning for apartheid crimes, the nascent democratic state lacked enough political capital to do so (Truth and Reconciliation Commission, 1998, p. 5). The report stated that attempting to bring perpetrators to trial was "extremely time-consuming and expensive" (ibid., p. 123), and that the "long-term objectives of national reconciliation and reconstruction of society" were not abetted by "prolonged litigation" over "gross human rights violations" (ibid.). As such, the TRC firmly equated "the reconstruction of society" (ibid., p. 124) with broad political amnesty and explicit calls for "forgiveness" in the name of future social harmony, citing the need to direct state resources to mitigate inequality "in the crucial areas of housing, education and healthcare" and provide reparations (ibid.).

Yet, almost thirty years after South Africa's democratic transition, "few would argue South Africa has achieved the reconciliation the TRC sought" (International Center for Transitional Justice, 2017). Post-hoc studies of South Africa's TRC found that victims were often dissatisfied with their experience. Those who came before the TRC to pronounce their forgiveness may have felt like "pawns in a national process over which they had little say" (Brankovic, 2013, p. 12) as their pronouncements were used to publicize the "success" of the TRC and South Africa's strides towards becoming a "rainbow nation". Meanwhile, perpetrators of human rights violations, if they sought forgiveness at all,[2] did so in some cases for the promise of political amnesty, although even those who were denied amnesty were generally not prosecuted.[3] The social aftermath was a country that remained divided along racial lines, with the process "not hav[ing] significantly changed attitudes of one race group towards another" (Brankovic, 2013, p. 7), while significant asymmetry in socioeconomic status between the black and white populations persisted along pre-apartheid lines, with many victims still waiting on promised reparations or having received very small sums.

The South African experience demonstrates how a focus on forgiveness and the attendant concepts of blame, guilt, and collective accountability errs in its maximalist conception of reconciliation (Keyes, 2019, p. 6). Despite the widespread tensions and political violence in the four years before democratization, in 1992, President F. W. De Klerk held a referendum to gauge public sentiment over the end of apartheid, and an overwhelming majority of the all-white vote – almost 70%, with a majority in 14 out of 15 country regions and 85% voter turnout – supported democratization efforts (Beresford, 1992). This indicates that, whatever their reasons, most white South Africans did not approve of apartheid, and wanted to grant equal rights to the black population. In 2000, two anti-apartheid activists launched a "Home for All" campaign (News24, 2000) which called on South Africa's white citizens "to sign a public apology for the sins of apartheid and to pledge themselves to redressing the racial wrongs of the past" (Hawthorne, 2001). Although some prominent white public figures signed on, the campaign was mostly met with derision, and even former President F. W. De Klerk, the architect of the transition to democracy, refused to sign, saying that "it represented an over-simplistic analysis which seeks to divide complex human interactions simply into good and evil" (Cauvin, 2000). One white liberal politician stated: "I've nothing to be apologetic about … I didn't initiate the system of apartheid I fought against. I don't need to join in a consolidated beating of the breast" (Hawthorne, 2001).

This initiative, coupled with the experience of victims and perpetrators during and after the TRC, exemplifies the shortcoming of a politicization of forgiveness. Only a small fraction of the thousands of amnesty applications submitted to the Amnesty Committee came from white members of the apartheid security forces, the majority coming from black members of black liberation movements (Brankovic, 2013, p. 5).[4] Meanwhile, there were 22,000 testimonial submissions from victims, and a "near lack of overlap" (Brankovic, 2013, p. 5) between these and the applications for amnesty. Victims who were hurt and sought justice not only did not receive it, but were made to bequeath forgiveness, some on live television; most of the "higher ups" in the apartheid regime, who oversaw the commitment of human rights violations, successfully claimed ignorance (Scheper-Hughes, 1998); and even the executors of human rights violations in the apartheid regime were generally not actively pursued or prosecuted.

Another example of detrimental politicized forgiveness was the response to an incident called the "Reitz Four", where four white students at the University of the Free State (UFS) filmed themselves humiliating black workers in protest against racial integration at the university (Duggar, 2008). The students were immediately banned from campus, but months later the university decided to drop any charges as a "gesture of racial reconciliation" (Jansen, 2009). The case nonetheless continued in criminal court, and the four men pleaded guilty and were made to pay fines in a settlement (Herskovitz, 2010).

The Chancellor's response was widely criticized, but it was seen as very much in line with South Africa's politics of forgiveness, where indemnity had become the reflexive response to acts of racial discrimination. The attitude of "reconciliation [as] dogma" (Msimang, 2022) continues to be damaging to conflict narratives in a society striving for legal equality and social symmetry by centralizing a discourse of blame and guilt which impairs concrete efforts toward a more equal society. Foregrounding forgiveness created an immutable moral dichotomy: the victims of apartheid – the black population – will be "good", benevolent, and forgiving while the white population will always be "bad" and should seek forgiveness, even if they opposed the regime. This dichotomy insults the group narratives of both populations. Being deemed somehow morally superior does little to improve the actual lived conditions of South Africa's black majority, nor does it necessarily provide closure for those deeply victimized under apartheid. Meanwhile, blanket censure of South Africa's whites challenges the narrative of white citizens who very much support an integrated, equal society. Politicized forgiveness in South Africa is therefore problematic because it is reductive and creates a simplistic good/bad dichotomy which does not leave space for the complicated feelings and realities surrounding the conflict.[5] It traps post-apartheid groups in the archetypical pre-apartheid roles of victim and oppressor.

The challenge posed by the TRC processes for both groups – blacks and whites – was that forgiveness for the sake of reconciliation without established relationships, compelled each to abandon their respective groups and self-identity. For Derrida (2001), this transcendence was impossible. He mentioned the testimony of a South African woman whose husband had been murdered. She contended that a commission or a government cannot forgive, only she could, and she was unwilling to do so. Forgiveness has nothing to do with judicial justice; representatives of a state body or any public institution can judge but they have no right, nor can they forgive.

In fact, according to Veraart (2012), allowing people to take legal action can counteract the possibility of historic injustice creating permanent victimhood. If victims are allowed vindication of their narrative, receive rightful compensation, and see their perpetrator punished, their victimhood is validated and they can escape it and seek broader identities. Victims who see no justice may continuously seek validation of crimes committed against them and be trapped, infinitely, in their victimhood. Such victimhood groups can be passed on from generation to generation as a powerful inter-generational unifying group narrative that reifies ongoing hostility and social conflict. South Africa's TRC aroused resistance from both black and white victims who decried being compelled to have their victimizers forgiven and, therefore, absolved of their crimes. Individual forgiveness became, in South Africa, a public and political display that at once acknowledged horrible crimes yet sacrificed the individual's right to grant or deny forgiveness. This transformed a personal and voluntary dynamic into one with an explicit political goal.

Colombia

Colombia provides an interesting contrast to South Africa's experience with transitional justice. While the historical contexts were very different, the Colombian process benefited from the South African experience as well as almost two decades of other transitional processes around the world. Furthermore, Colombia's division was not racial but political: the government had been fighting a left-wing insurgency group – the FARC (Revolutionary

Armed Forces of Colombia) – for over five decades and, as a result, a legitimate Colombian political left was virtually nonexistent, tainted by association with the FARC and other left-wing guerilla groups. The landscape of conflict was therefore divided into the right and the left, with the government and other paramilitary forces associated with the wealthy, landowning class on the right and the FARC and similar guerilla groups on the left. Despite serious violence committed by both sides, Colombia, similar to South Africa, sought to extend "the broadest possible amnesty" (Final Agreement, 2016, p. 48) to former combatants, but the Colombian peace process was more successful in accomplishing national reconciliation because it did not foreground forgiveness.

The Colombian Peace Accords were the product of four years of intense negotiations between the Colombian government, headed by President Juan Manuel Santos, and the FARC. The FARC began as a small militarized offshoot of the Colombian Communist Party in the late 1960s, and soon grew in size and strength with increased revenue from the expansion of the illegal drug market (Insight Crime, 2022). Throughout 70s and 80s, the FARC expanded operations and drew revenue streams from kidnapping and extortion, along with illegal drug trafficking, maintaining extensive strongholds in rural areas. Meanwhile, right-wing paramilitary organizations associated with Colombian state security forces, landowners and the conservative class were established to counter the FARC, and inevitably gained their own force and momentum as parties to the violent conflict (Semana, 2019). Attempted peace negotiations and ceasefires during the 1980's and 90's failed, and the FARC continued to grow in power and controlled territory, at one point controlling a swath of the country the size of Switzerland (Reuters, 2000) and presented a formidable military opponent to the Colombian government.

In 2002, the election of President Alvaro Uribe changed the game. With extensive financial and military assistance from the United States under Plan Colombia, the Colombian government doubled down on the FARC, decimated its forces, and saw national security increase markedly throughout his administrations as a result (Washington Office on Latin America, 2016). By 2012, the FARC was significantly weakened, and it was ready to come to the negotiating table of the newly elected President Santos, who had been Uribe's Defense Minister. By that point, the conflict, which had lasted for over five decades, had resulted in 450,000 deaths, tens of thousands of disappearances and kidnappings, and millions of internally displaced peoples (VOA, 2022).

The Colombian peace deal was very complex and included 578 stipulations – "concrete, observable and measurable commitments" (Peace Accords Matrix, 2020) – which addressed rural reform and land redistribution, guarantees of political participation, demobilization, the problem of illicit drugs, victim guarantees and reparations, and an overall monitoring mechanism (Government of Colombia, 2016). The Agreement explicitly stated that it would seek "the broadest possible" amnesty in accordance with International Human Rights Law (Final Agreement, 2016, p. 157). This meant it would pardon most low-level FARC fighters who agreed to demobilize and collaborate with the peace process, and for those who had committed "crimes against humanity" – i.e. kidnapping, torture, extrajudicial execution, among others – and could not be pardoned, they would, instead, go before the JEP (*Juridiccion Especial para la Paz*, or a Special Peace Tribunal) and serve an alternative punishment for their crimes, such as land mine removal or other community service (Acosta & Cobb, 2016). The goal was to avoid overly punitive measures or imprisonment and promote integration into society on all fronts, as well as focusing on "restorative justice" that prioritized the needs of victims (Final Agreement, 2016, p. 154).

The word "forgiveness" is mentioned only once in the over-300-page document, while discussing the hosting of public forums to discuss the impact of the conflict: these forums "may ... [enable] those who directly or indirectly took part in the conflict to engage in acts of acknowledgement of responsibility and ask for forgiveness" (ibid., p. 145).

Although internationally lauded, the peace deal was domestically divisive: an initial version was rejected in an October 2016 referendum by a slim 0.4% of the vote,[6] and the Santos administration scrambled to revise it in time for a Congressional debate in November (Reuters, 2016), after which it passed unanimously (politicians opposed to the deal boycotted the vote) (Murphy, 2016). At the helm of the hardline "no to peace" camp was former President Uribe and his Centro Democratico political party, who felt the deal was too lenient on the FARC. The victory of Uribe's acolyte, Ivan Duque, in the 2018 Colombian presidential election (Daniels, 2018) was perhaps a more telling second referendum on the peace deal, although Colombians faced a stark choice between Duque and Gustavo Petro, a former member of the M-19 leftist guerilla group who promised significant socioeconomic overhaul. The fact that Petro made it to the second round of voting, and garnered 41% of the final vote, was itself historic, and set the stage for President Petro's victory in the June 2022 presidential elections."[7] Considering the significant toll of the civil war, and severe and legitimate grievances on both the right and the left, how could this happen?

While a multitude of factors contributed to Petro's election, the peace deal, which demobilized thousands of former FARC combatants and legitimized a peaceful Colombian political left, certainly played a role. It could do so largely because it did not focus on interpersonal forgiveness, but emphasized productive, broad reform and unsentimental pragmatic social integration. Forgiveness certainly formed a part of the peace deal, but the 800-page final report of the peace deal's Truth Commission (Pozzebon, 2022) relayed episodes of perpetrators seeking forgiveness in a complex, philosophical light. In effect, the Truth Commission took forgiveness for what it was: a personal, reflective act that revealed the sentimental journeys and preconceptions of victims and perpetrators in a conflict, not a political panacea. The report also recognized that, when speaking of "reconciliation", they are in fact speaking of "(re)conciliation", parenthesized in order "to emphasize that it does not wish to return to relationships before the fracture of war, because many times [those relationships] were not equal and conciliatory. (Re)conciliation emphasizes a process that looks to a future with new modes of coexistence" (ibid., p. 85).

The peace deal did not confer a moral high ground – or low ground – on any party. It sought, among other things, to discover truth, create space for dialogue, and deliver tempered punishments in accord with international law and an aim toward restorative, rather than retributive, justice. In this manner, it avoided entrenching resentment and allowed for the construction of a narrative of deeds. This pragmatic and concrete focus of the Colombian transitional justice process – with less focus on the moral, "forgiveness" element and preserving groups' identity – made for more real social progression and a more likely shared, post-conflict societal meta-narrative of peace. Colombians reassured by their proper narratives were ready to move on into the future, to peace, inclusive, safe and prosperous. "If you ask a victim today, he will lean toward more justice, not forgiving," said President Santos, "but if you ask a future victim, he will lean more toward peace."

The Aftermath in Transitional Justice Processes, Towards a Tolerable Narrative of Peace

Transitional justice processes uncover a fundamental paradox within competing struggle narratives where what signifies "victory" for one party, signifies "loss" for the other. The question remains, writes Caruth (1996). in healing from a traumatic, violent past, how to know about it without betraying it, the narrative and the narrator?

In South Africa and Colombia society and people experienced traumas throughout years of violent civil conflict, and both attempted to end the conflicts through Transitional justice processes. Forgiveness, an eminent part of the processes, played a different role as both societies sought to construct a collective meta-narrative of peace.

Saunders (2011, p. 125) notes that the word "amnesty" comes to the English from the Greek 'amnestia' (forgetfulness). Truth and reconciliation commissions compiling public recollection of cruelty and pain processed neither trauma nor forgiveness in South Africa. A trauma is multi-faceted, and determining the truth, or truths, requires an attentive observation from a safe distance. That very intimate grace so crucial for the process of healing and freeing the past, was there replaced by a politicized process for the goal of social transformation and unity.

Only by acknowledging otherness, writes Gurevitch (1989) can we free ourselves from images and projections and allow us and them to be separate entities within one reality. And along these lines, Paul Ricoeur (1991) asserts that both the past and the future exist as potential narratives which we may choose to integrate into the wider structure of identity. He believes, and so was the case in Colombia, that an individual and a society can internalize a significant narrative through interpretation and what he calls "emplotment", thereby developing other possibilities of being in the world.

Transitional justice is no simple task. Beyond its four core pillars, the eventual aim is to create a society that is not merely a reflection of the conflict it experienced, but one that exists independently and can look forward as well as back. It should therefore serve as a springboard, not a trap: groups in conflict should be able to evolve into post-conflict roles, and not remain confined to the social roles they inhabited during the conflict. To mandate forgiveness, as occurred in South Africa, is to cage parties in their conflict roles, stunt social and political development, and make them incapable of imagining themselves beyond the reflection of their violent past.

Notes

1 Many black South Africans were "committed Christians" at the time of the TRC, and foregrounding a theological basis of forgiveness helped arguably helped it gain support (Gakunzi, 2000).
2 "Most [perpetrators] decided that testifying before the commission would be riskier than undergoing trial…and gambled that prosecutions would simply not occur in the majority of cases" (Brankovic, 2013, p. 5).
3 www.usip.org/publications/1995/12/truth-commission-south-africa.
4 "80% of those applying for amnesty are black" (Rosenfeld, 2001).
5 "Survivors … generally felt inhibited in expressing their legitimate rage and anger, and demanding just retribution" (Hamber, 2002, p. 18).
6 Many factors were raised to explain the result of the referendum, which saw a depressing 38% turnout: heavy rain caused by Hurricane Matthew in pro-peace areas had impeded turnout; supporters of peace were made complacent by polling prior to the deal and felt they did not need to vote; and poor rural areas, which tended to be hardest hit by the conflict, were not equipped with adequate polling stations (Anselma, 2016; Brodzinsky, 2016).
7 Duque left office with extremely low approval ratings, and public perceptions of Uribe became mostly unfavorable by a significant margin beginning in April 2021 (INVAMER S.A.S., 2022).

References

Acosta, N. and Cobb, J. S. (2016, November 12). Colombia, rebels agree revised peace deal to end 52-year war. *Reuters.* www.theguardian.com/world/2016/nov/13/colombias-government-and-rebel-movement-agree-new-peace-terms

Anselma, A. (2016, October 3). Colombia didn't really vote 'No' to peace, it mainly didn't vote at all. *Colombia Reports.* https://colombiareports.com/colombia-didnt-vote-no-peace-mainly-didnt-vote/

Apartheid Museum (2023a). *Negotiating a Settlement.* Apartheid Museum. www.apartheidmuseum.org/exhibitions/negotiating-a-settlement

Apartheid Museum (2023b). *On the Brink.* Apartheid Museum. www.apartheidmuseum.org/exhibitions/on-the-brink

Arendt, H. (1998). *The Human Condition*, 2nd edn. Chicago: The University of Chicago Press.

BBC (2021, February 18). Peace court: Colombia army behind 6,400 extrajudicial killings. *BBC*. www.bbc.com/news/world-latin-america-56112386

Beresford, D. (1992, March 18). Sweeping SA vote for reform. Even Afrikaners support De Klerk. *The Guardian*. www.theguardian.com/world/1992/mar/18/southafrica.davidberesford

Brankovic, J. (2013). *Accountability and National Reconciliation in South Africa*. Centre for the Study of Violence and Reconciliation. www.researchgate.net/publication/308330948_Accountability_and_National_Reconciliation_in_South_Africa

Brodzinsky, S. (2016, October 3). Colombia referendum: Voters reject peace deal with FARC guerillas. *The Guardian*. www.theguardian.com/world/2016/oct/02/colombia-referendum-rejects-peace-deal-with-farc

Caruth, C. (1996). *Unclaimed Experience: Trauma, Narrative and History*. John Hopkins University Press.

Cauvin, H. E. (2000, December 17). *In Africa, a mea culpa for apartheid tests whites*. *New York Times*. www.nytimes.com/2000/12/17/world/in-africa-a-mea-culpa-for-apartheid-tests-whites.html

Comisión de la Verdad (2022). *Hay futuro si hay verdad: Informe Final de la Comisión para el Esclarecimiento de la Verdad, la Convivencia y la No Repetición*. Comisión de la Verdad. www.comisiondelaverdad.co/hallazgos-y-recomendaciones-1

Daniels, J. P. (2018, June 18). Iván Duque wins election to become Colombia's president. *The Guardian*. www.theguardian.com/world/2018/jun/18/ivan-duque-wins-election-to-become-colombias-president

Department of Justice and Constitutional Development (2023). *Welcome to the official Truth and Reconciliation Committee Website*. www.justice.gov.za/trc/

Derrida, J. (2001). On forgiveness. In J. Derrida, *On Cosmopolitanism and Forgiveness*. New York: Routledge.

Dickinson, E. (2022, November 23). Colombia's last guerillas make first step toward "total peace". International Crisis Group. https://reliefweb.int/report/colombia/colombias-last-guerrillas-make-first-step-toward-total-peace

Duggar, C. M. (2008, March 10) On campus, a video reminder of apartheid's pain. *New York Times*. www.nytimes.com/2008/03/10/world/africa/10safrica.html

Final Agreement (2016, November 24.) *Final Agreement to End the Armed Conflict and Build a Stable and Lasting Peace*. University of Notre Dame Kroc Institute for International Peace Studies. https://peaceaccords.nd.edu/wp-content/uploads/2020/02/Colombian-Peace-Agreement-English-Translation.pdf

Freud, S. (2003). *The Uncanny*. Penguin Books.

Gakunzi, D. (2000, May). *The Truth and Reconciliation Commission of South Africa: An evaluation of Hugo Van der Merve, from the Center for the Study of Violence and Reconciliation (CSVR.)* https://base.d-p-h.info/fr/fiches/premierdph/fiche-premierdph-5487.html

Garrett, A. (2018). Joseph Butler's moral philosophy. In E. N. Zalta (ed.) *The Stanford Encyclopedia of Philosophy*. https://plato.stanford.edu/archives/spr2018/entries/butler-moral/

Government of Colombia (2016, 30 September). *Summary of Colombia's agreement to end conflict and build peace*. *Reliefweb*. https://reliefweb.int/report/colombia/summary-colombias-agreement-end-conflict-and-build-peace

Guardian Staff (2022, November 21). Colombian government and ELN rebels begin new effort to end 60 years of war. *The Guardian*. www.reuters.com/world/americas/colombia-eln-rebels-begin-peace-talks-monday-petro-2022-11-17/

Gurevitch, Z. D. (1989). The power of not understanding: The meeting of conflicting identities. *The Journal of Applied Behavioral Science*, 25 (2), 161–173.

Hamber, B. and Wilson, R. A. (2002). Symbolic closure through memory, reparation and revenge in post-conflict societies. *Research Papers: Human Rights Institute, University of Connecticut OpenCommons@UConn*, 5. https://opencommons.uconn.edu/hri_papers/5

Hawthorne, P. (2001, January 15). "The trouble with 'sorry'". *TIME Magazine*. https://content.time.com/time/world/article/0,8599,2048073,00.html

Herskovitz, J. (2010, July 28). Reitz Four fined over video furore. *IOL*. www.iol.co.za/news/south-africa/reitz-four-fined-over-video-furore-671236

IACHR (2023, January 30). Colombia is responsible for the elimination of the patriotic union political party. *Corteidh*. www.corteidh.or.cr/docs/comunicados/cp_09_2023_eng.pdf

International Center for Transitional Justice (2017, June 29). *After the Rupture: Understanding Transitional Justice and Reconciliation*. ICTJ. www.ictj.org/news/rupture-relationships-transitional-justice-reconciliation#:~:text=Thick%20and%20Thin%20Reconciliation&text=%E2%80%9CRestoring%20dignity%20in%20this%20sense,causes%20of%20marginalization%20and%20discrimination

Insight Crime (2022, July 15). FARC. *Insight Crime*. https://insightcrime.org/colombia-organized-crime-news/farc-profile/

INVAMER S.A.S. (2022, May). Colombia Opina #12. Valora Analitik. www.valoraanalitik.com/wp-content/uploads/2022/05/Encuesta-Invamer-mayo-2022.pdf

Jansen, J. (2009, October 18). Why we're withdrawing charges against Reitz Four – Jansen. *Politicsweb*. www.politicsweb.co.za/news-and-analysis/why-were-withdrawing-charges-against-reitz-four--j

Joinet, L. (1997). *Question of the impunity of perpetrators of human rights violations (civil and political): Final report / prepared by Mr. Joinet pursuant to Sub-Commission decision 1996/119*. United Nations Digital Library. p. 7. https://digitallibrary.un.org/record/240943?ln=en

Keyes, S. (2019, March). Mapping on approaches to reconciliation. *The Network for Religious and Traditional Peacemakers*. www.peacemakersnetwork.org/wp-content/uploads/2019/08/Mapping-on-Approaches-to-Reconciliation.pdf

Msimang, S. (2022, November 27). No justice. No peace. *Foreign Policy*. https://foreignpolicy.com/2022/11/27/south-africa-trc-reitz-ufs-jansen-race-justice-reconciliation/

Murphy, H. (2016, November 30). Colombian peace deal passed by Congress, ending 52-year war. *Reuters*. www.reuters.com/article/us-colombia-peace/colombian-peace-deal-passed-by-congress-ending-52-year-war-idUSKBN13P1D2

News24 (2000, December 16). 'Home for All' campaign launched. *News24*. www.news24.com/news24/home-for-all-campaign-launched-20001216

Peace Accords Matrix. (2020). *Methodology for Monitoring Implementation of the Colombian Peace Agreement*. University of Notre Dame Kroc Institute for International Peace Studies. https://peaceaccords.nd.edu/barometer/methodology

Pozzebon, S. (2022, June 28). Colombia's historic Truth Commission published its final report. Here are 5 key takeaways. *CNN*. https://edition.cnn.com/2022/06/28/americas/colombia-truth-commission-final-report-intl-latam/index.html

Reuters (2000, November 16). Pastrana urges rebels to give peace a chance. *CNN*. www.cnn.com/2000/WORLD/americas/11/16/colombia.peace.reut/index.html

Reuters (2016, November 19). Colombia's president to allow peace deal to be debated in Congress. *Reuters*. www.reuters.com/article/us-colombia-peace/colombias-president-to-allow-peace-deal-to-be-debated-in-congress-idUSKBN13E0LI

Ricoeur, P. (1991). Narrative identity. *Philosophy Today*, 35 (1), 73–80.

Rosenfeld, M. (2001, June 11). In South Africa, learning to forgive. *Washington Post*. www.washingtonpost.com/archive/lifestyle/2001/06/11/in-south-africa-learning-to-forgive/34aa33e1-32cc-425b-8253-57bb1fc48b16/

Saunders, R. (2011). Questionable associations: The role of forgiveness in transitional justice. *International Journal of Transitional Justice*, 5 (1), 119–141. https://doi.org/10.1093/ijtj/ijr003

Scheper-Hughes, N. (1998, December 22). *Undoing: Social suffering and the politics of remorse in the New South Africa*. The Free Library. www.thefreelibrary.com/Undoing%3a+social+suffering+and+the+politics+of+remorse+in+the+New...-a054169925

Seils, P. (2017, June 28). *The Place of Reconciliation in Transitional Justice: Conceptions and Misconceptions*. International Center for Transitional Justice. www.ictj.org/sites/default/files/ICTJ-Briefing-Paper-Reconciliation-TJ-2017.pdf

Semana (2019, August 29). ¿Cómo fue en inicio de las Farc? *Semana*. www.semana.com/educacion/articulo/la-historia-de-las-farc/467972/

Truth and Reconciliation Commission (1998). *Volume One: Truth and Reconciliation Commission of South Africa Report*. South Africa Department of Justice and Constitutional Development. www.justice.gov.za/trc/report/finalreport/volume%201.pdf

UN Peacebuilding (2008, February 20). *What Is Transitional Justice? A Backgrounder*. www.un.org/peacebuilding/sites/www.un.org.peacebuilding/files/documents/26_02_2008_background_note.pdf

United Nations (2010, March). *Guidance Note of the Secretary General: United Nations Approach to Transitional Justice*. www.securitycouncilreport.org/atf/cf/%7B65BFCF9B-6D27-4E9C-8CD3-CF6E4FF96FF9%7D/TJ_Guidance_Note_March_2010FINAL.pdf

United States Institute of Peace (1995). Truth Commission: South Africa. USIP. www.usip.org/publications/1995/12/truth-commission-south-africa

Uprimny, R. and Saffon, M. P. (2017). Transitional justice, restorative justice and reconciliation. Some Insights from the Colombian case. *DeJusticia*. www.dejusticia.org/wp-content/uploads/2017/04/fi_name_recurso_55.pdf

VOA (2022, June 28). Colombia Truth Commission gives scathing report on civil war. *VOA News*. www.voanews.com/a/colombia-truth-commission-gives-scathing-report-on-civil-war-/6637556.html

Veraart, W. (2012). Forgetting, remembering, forgiving, and the mundane legal order. In Bas Van Stokkom, Neelke Doorn & Paul Van Tongeren (eds), *Public Forgiveness in Post-Conflict Contexts*. Cambridge: Trinity House.

Washington Office on Latin America (2016, February 1). *15th Anniversary of Plan Colombia: Learning from Its Successes and Failures, Notable Improvements*. WOLA. www.wola.org/files/1602_plancol/

Part 2

Tolerance and Psychoanalysis

Chapter 5

The Stranger-Patient

Tolerance between a Jewish Therapist
and a Palestinian Patient in Israel[*,†]

Noga Ariel-Galor

In this chapter I will describe tolerance as the capacity to withstand ambiguity without collapsing to a dichotomizing stance towards the Other. To illustrate this idea, I will focus on a major challenge to tolerance in therapy, that is portrayed in the therapeutic encounter between Jewish therapists and Palestinian citizens of Israel patients. In these therapeutic dyads, the capacity for tolerance is severely challenged in the face of an intimate encounter with an Other whose large-group is in a violent conflict with one's own large-group. Such challenges will be described in this chapter through the case study of a Jewish-Israeli therapist, who had treated a young Palestinian-Israeli patient for five years. The details of this case study were given to me in an interview held with the therapist, as part of my doctoral research.

The Capacity to Tolerate Otherness

Tolerance is considered to be one of the beacons of the multicultural society (Brown, 2008), and a value that many resources have been dedicated to its education. But what does tolerance mean from a psychoanalytic lens? As Lacorne (2019) writes: "The Latin root for toleration, *tolerantia*, is derived from the verb *tolerare*: to accept, endure, put up with, support with courage a burden or a difficult condition of life" (p. 1). As opposed to existing literature considering multiculturalism, I contend that what we endure is not merely the cultural *differences* that lie between us and the other, but rather how these differences make us *feel* when we confront them. How we feel might differ according to our political and personal beliefs. It can include either positive or negative aspects of the way we view the other. Nonetheless, these feelings govern the

---

[*] This chapter is based on the doctoral dissertation titled "The Jewish-Arab dyad: Socio-political influences on psychotherapy between Jewish therapists and Arab patients in Israel", supervised by Prof. Aner Govrin and Prof. Alean Al-Krenawi, written in the Program for Psychoanalysis and Hermeneutics, at Bar-Ilan University, Israel.
[†] Translated to English as *The Uncanny*.

DOI: 10.4324/9781003200253-8

covert dialogues of our human encounters: they may determine who we push out, who we let in, and under what conditions.

Tolerance is thus defined in this context as the *capacity to regulate distress caused by otherness*. To delay action in situations that are ambiguous, and are therefore dysregulating and cause a great sense of vulnerability, in the presence of an Other. Therefore, I wish to draw attention to the idea that what we overcome through tolerance is not the cultural/ethnic/gender differences themselves, but rather the fear, loathing or idealization that these differences incite in us. Through tolerance we overcome the reflexes of either swallowing or spitting out the other from within us, the capacity to hold the tension between sameness and difference (Benjamin, 2018), between what is aversive and what is palatable. Hence, it is reflected in a suspension of action, and it is this suspension of action which is difficult the most in light of uncertainty.

In this chapter, I would like to address what I perceive to be a major challenge to tolerance in a therapeutic encounter, one that includes confronting an Other who is perceived not only as threatening in their different lifestyle and choices, but also possesses an imagined physical threat because of their affiliation with an enemy group, as is the case between Israeli Jews and Palestinian citizens of Israel. I contend that our capacity to tolerate is influenced by the level of closeness we feel, in other words how much we perceive the other as same or different; and this perceived closeness is fluid and dynamic. We are moving towards the other and away from them on a phantasmatic rail, their image constantly shifting in front of our unconscious mind's eye – *Perpetuum mobile*, always in motion. How can we tolerate this shiftiness, this ambiguity, in an intimate setting which holds both parties in radical mutual vulnerability (Aron, 2016)?

Israeli Jews and Palestinian Citizens of Israel: It's Complicated

The dynamics between Israeli-Jews and Palestinian citizens of Israel holds varied socio-political and historical factors at play, which act as inter-collective agents, defining and constructing relationships on both the collective and individual levels. It seems that every aspect of this encounter is multilayered, infused with inter-collective trauma and loss, the wish to come closer and the mutual fear of being hurt in this process, either physically or emotionally. In a space that holds the potential of being emotionally overwhelming, this encounter is a great source of discomfort, hope and dread.

The Jewish-Palestinian conflict is described by differing and conflicting narratives: For the Jewish people of Israel the 1948 war was a war of independence and liberation; while for the Arab population that was living in Palestine before Israel's inception it was a national disaster, the *Nakba*. The Palestinian large-group was split into two groups – refugees, now forming one of the largest populations of refugees in the world, and was pushed to the outskirts of the land; and the people who kept residing in Arab villages and mixed cities in Israel and were given Israeli citizenship. The occupation following the 1967 war, the violent uprisings (Intifadas) that took place, and further history of war and violence throughout the years have rendered the Jewish-Palestinian conflict the archetype of an intractable violent political conflict (Sharvit, 2016), and mutual relation of victim/aggressor was formed between the two peoples. The torn Palestinian population was thus split into two groups – one homeless, one unhomely – the former became refugees, while the latter group remained in their homeland, but their claim for it was put under question.

Yet the split in the Arab Palestinian population was more than just a demographic detail. For Israeli-Jews it split between the so-called "enemies", meaning the Palestinians living in the occupied territories, calling for the right to return to their homes (which are now populated by the Jewish majority); and the Palestinian citizens of Israel, who, by the power of the democratic state, were given what de jure is equal rights, and are therefore supposedly considered "friends".

I use the word advisedly, because while Palestinian citizens of Israel have been living side by side with Jewish Israelis since the inception of the state of Israel in relative calm, their affiliation with "the enemy" group – the Palestinians in the occupied territories – has rendered them potential aggressors. Thus, this artificial division left the status of the Palestinian citizens of Israel unclear – are they friends or enemies?

This sociopolitical ambiguity creates constant tension, which is reconstructed in the clinical encounter. Zygmunt Bauman's theory of The Stranger (1991) can be useful in understanding this tension. The stranger is first and foremost an *undecidable* – he is neither a friend nor enemy. Therefore, he or she hinders modernity's ability to classify and categorize; and creates a disturbing ambivalence. But according to Bauman, eventually every attempt to decipher whether the stranger is a friend or an enemy will expose the failure of this dichotomy. Therefore, strangers are perceived as a constant threat to the social order, and in the Israeli context – a threat to Israel as a Jewish state, thus evoking strong retaliation anxieties, and the enactment of annihilating impulses.

However, while both peoples have acted as aggressors and victims towards each other, one cannot say that the situation is symmetrical, since there is a clear differentiation between oppressor and oppressed, not only between Israelis and Palestinians in general, but also specifically between Israeli-Jews and Palestinian citizens of Israel, who have remained a weakened minority. Jewish therapists who are conscious of this will also feel a great deal of guilt and shame for being affiliated with the oppressive group, as well as fear of retaliation.

And so, the Palestinian-citizen-of-Israel's presence in the office will evoke intense emotions, shifting from feelings of guilt, responsibility and compassion (feelings one reserves for a friend), to feelings of threat, hostility and renunciation (feelings related to the enemy's presence). These are often triggered by both subtle and explicit messages, stemming from the mutual social traumas induced throughout the history of the Israeli-Palestinian conflict, as well as traumas related to Jewish history and the Holocaust, amalgamating past, present and future aggressors.

And so, the main motivation is to feel safe, and safety is related to the illusion of certainty. In the absence of certainty we exert tolerance, yet our capacity for it is constantly challenged. When it collapses, we turn to false certainty by using either extreme sameness or difference: prejudice, splitting or radical identification with the other. Thus, the capacity for tolerance can be framed as the ability to maintain this tension, without collapsing into one dichotomy or the other.

The Aporia in Culturally Sensitive Models for Psychotherapy

Strangers exist everywhere in modernity, as Bauman claims. And they even sometimes appear in the office, seeking to be viewed as subjects, longing to have their distress relieved. Yet in the office, they more often than not, encounter a therapist who is a member of the majority group, and has not only different cultural sets, but also a complex relationship with the socio-political representation of the stranger-patient themselves. I believe that this aspect of inter-ethnic psychotherapy is not discussed enough in the vast literature concerning cultural differences between therapists and patients, thus leaving the therapeutic dyad more vulnerable to unconscious influences, which when left unprocessed could lead to therapeutic impasses and premature termination. In other words, the ambiguity and the discomfort that stems from it are not only related to a lack of cultural knowledge, but to the psychic difficulty of lingering in a situation where the other's intentions are ambiguous, or their presence arouses emotional self-states which are difficult to tolerate.

In the multi-cultural psychotherapy literature, we see the tendency to present the characteristics of the "strange" culture to the Western therapist, for them to acknowledge the limitations of Western psychotherapy in comprehending this unique encounter. That kind of clarification could be seen as an attempt to create cognitive clarity, meaning to recognize the *observable aspects* of the cultural differences that could hinder therapeutic communication. Culturally sensitive theories were born out of the encounter with non-Western cultures and the therapeutic challenges these encounters produced. It is the result of a humanistic way of thinking, that understands there is cultural bias in therapy, which can cause damage by diagnosing mental pathologies with patients whose behavior stems from the socio-cultural norms from which they came; and also striving to create a more empathic therapeutic environment, assuming that with the help of determining mutual goals and personal connection one can create a more beneficial therapeutic alliance. This ongoing knowledge has gained more and more speed and many models for culturally sensitive therapy have been implemented in the therapist's training programs, mainly in the US (e.g. Gielen, 2008; Sodowsky, Kuo-Jackson & Loya, 1997; Sue, Arredondo & McDavis, 1992).

And indeed, Bauman (1991) claims that cognitive clarity is a prerequisite to behavioral certainty. When this certainty does not exist, it leads to a hermeneutic problem, which he compares to the difficulty one meets when they arrive at a foreign land and try to understand the strange language and culture. Following Wittgenstein, he claims that understanding means to know how to act, how to proceed. The hermeneutic problem arises when the ability to know for certain what this or that means is hindered, when the awareness starts sinking in that words and their meanings are not one and the same, and discomfort arises. Unresolved hermeneutic problems mean uncertainty regarding the right way to react. At best, this uncertainty is unpleasant, but at worst, it is perceived as dangerous.

Yet Bauman claims that the feeling of strangeness can never be solved as a hermeneutic problem, because this promotes the illusion that if we gained enough knowledge, we could classify the other and know how to respond to them. And as presented above, this rational knowledge does not assist us in solving the problem of the stranger, which is based on irrational mechanisms, that hinder the ability to cognitively decipher and create an untangled circular situation.

And so, although this understanding of cultural relativity is of utmost importance, focusing solely on cognitive/behavioral knowledge (cognitive knowledge regarding the differences between cultures, and its behavioral vicissitude for diagnosing patients and creating the right therapeutic interventions) could disguise something much more primal and irrational that arises in the therapeutic encounter, and eventually if we focus on cultural sensitivity alone we might find ourselves in the same place.

Considering this view, we can try to critically examine the vast theory which deals with culturally sensitive therapy with members of the Arab and Muslim society, and to discuss both its importance and limitations. Treating this from the perspective of a hermeneutic problem could go something like this: the Palestinian patient comes into therapy, and it is like a symbolic encounter between two residents of foreign countries – The sense of trouble created in this case stems from the mutual misunderstanding of the therapist and patient regarding the therapeutic goals and how to achieve them. This is real trouble, and it is important to deal with it. However, the attempt to reach a solution by resolving cultural differences alone, or sticking to the strict rules described in one model or another, is only an *illusion of a solution*. This is because the ability to contain the stranger is not dependent solely on knowledge, but on an internal stance. *We tolerate not only our overt knowledge or recognition of our differences, but mostly what we do not know about the other's intentions towards us.*

And so, solving hermeneutic problems does not replace the need to understand the unconscious mechanisms that come into action in the encounter with the stranger. Those can be expressed in politically-sensitive psychotherapy, which discusses the socio-political influences on the encounter. Furthermore, it can be asked why the vast literature that exists on the subject has not been implemented into training programs for therapists, which seldom include training in culturally sensitive psychotherapy nor in socio-political influences on it. It seems that also in constructing the training programs there exists a wish to avoid meeting the strangers in Israeli society, and thus another exclusion of Palestinian citizens of Israel is created, as well as other minorities, out of clinical thinking and practice.

Lilly and Ahlam

Ahlam was referred to Lilly during the final exams period of her high school diploma, for treating severe examination phobia and social difficulties. She was formerly treated by a man, an Arab therapist, but her mother had decided to move her under the care of a Jewish Woman therapist, Lilly, who was recommended to her by her own therapist. While first meeting with Lilly, Ahlam's mother had revealed that she had suffered from post-partum depression following Ahlam's birth because she had wished for a boy, and thus refused to acknowledge her daughter's existence. Ahlam had spent the first three years of her life under the care of her grandmother and paid help, even though she was still sharing her mother's home. Her mother recounted looking at Ahlam as a toddler, thinking that she was "bad" and withholding affection from her. It seemed to Lilly that even as the years went by the mother had still harbored feelings of resentment towards her child, and when she first brought her in for treatment, she declared to Lilly in front of Ahlam that "when she was born I hated her and wished for her to die". After Ahlam, her mother gave birth to a second daughter, this time a "better" one, to which she did not alienate but raised with love and warmth. Still, the dissonance between emotional alienation on the one hand, and lack of separation on the other, were evident – even as Ahlam got older her mother would come into the office with her, sit on the couch next to her, and complain to Lilly about her – urging her to fix her, to marry her. A couple of times Lilly caught her sitting outside her office window, attempting to listen to what was being said.

Ahlam had grown up in social exclusion and isolation that she had forced upon herself, and grew to be a thin and mousy girl, with a weak monotonous voice. She had isolated herself out of fear for social criticism because of her looks, personality and achievements, that were never considered sufficient by anyone. To her surrounding she seemed "weird", and the social reactions were concordant with her own sense of otherness and strangeness. The content she had brought into therapy was dull, and the absence of a mutual language hindered the therapeutic alliance. In many ways Ahlam seemed to Lilly like a zombie, neither dead nor fully alive. Despite this hardship their relationship was slowly built, and Ahlam had expressed her wish to stay longer in Lilly's presence, and it was more and more difficult to get her to leave after the hour was over. One day she had brought into therapy an abandoned kitten and asked Lilly to raise it in her backyard (the office was placed in her home). Lilly kept the cat as she was asked, and Ahlam would call him and pet him whenever she came into therapy. Through the abandoned, neglected kitten they could finally discuss Ahlam's own abandoned and neglected parts and her wish to become Lilly's adopted daughter.

During therapy, the subject of national otherness came up very rarely and hesitantly, but always aroused a great deal of sadness and a sense of deprivation. Ahlam was convinced that Lilly was charging her for missed hours only because she was Arab. She told her "you're not really going to give me what I need", when this need was endless availably on Lilly's side, total maternal preoccupation, and when she did not receive it, she attributed this lack to her Arabness. The sense of frustration brought her closer to the yearning of a complete container, a maternal figure that would give herself to her in totality, to want her in the same way and measure as she needed. Sometimes when she tried emphasizing a sense of misery, she would tell Lilly "You Jews", to distinguish between them, and insinuate that her coldness had to do with their different nationality. Other times she would bring in poems in Hebrew she had learned at school and ask Lilly to interpret them for her. Then she would complain that no Arab poets were part of the school program.

The years went by and Ahlam was accepted to university. During her studies, it seemed as if she was revived, and something in her had opened up both personally and socially. For the first time in her life, she had friends with whom she hung out. But as she started opening up, some of the content that she had not been able to touch upon for so many years was unleashed, and she admitted to Lilly and to herself that she was in love with one of her classmates, a woman. She could not bring herself to confess her love to her. Following that unrequited love, her mental state worsened. She would lay in her room, burning with desire to her friend, and deeply despaired that she could never be with her the way she wanted. She found it difficult to concentrate in school, and her fears of failing had increased. She asked Lilly if she could convert her, help her "go straight", but when Lilly tried suggesting that they could examine the possibility of following her desire and outing herself, no answer sufficed. She scolded Lilly of thinking that she could ever be with a woman like Jewish women can. In anger of the therapist whom she accused of betraying her, by making her feel and desire an unachievable life, she left therapy in a rush, never to return.

Six months later Lilly received a call from the colleague that had initially referred Ahlam to her, more than five years prior. That colleague was still treating Ahlam's mother. In the conversation it had turned out that Ahlam took her own life. Lilly was shocked and in pain, she arrived at Ahlam's family home to grieve with her family. The mother greeted her with tears, crying for never genuinely loving her daughter, condemning Lilly for not helping her daughter, but had quickly calmed down and never mentioned her anger again. During the interview Lilly confessed that the fear that Ahlam's family will avenge her death came to her mind, but did not concern her much after that visit. In grief, she came to talk with the colleague that had referred Ahlam, and learned that the mother suspected Ahlam was a lesbian, and that she, too, had lesbian encounters as a teenager. As a religious Muslim woman, she wanted Ahlam to marry a man as soon as possible and was fearful for her fate. She was sure that she gave birth to a "different" child as punishment for her own misdoings in her youth. Lilly summed it up saying that perhaps Ahlam manifested her mother's death wish for her, thus unconsciously compensating for her mother's "sins", and pleasing her, perhaps for the first and also last time.

This multi-layered encounter is extremely difficult to fathom, because of its dominantly tragic dimension. It shows how the capacity for tolerance is challenged in the face of otherness, in this case many forms of otherness. While this case study and the transference relationship between Lilly, Ahlam, the mother and her therapist can be analyzed from many different angles and through many theoretical perspectives, many of them useful, I would like to concentrate on the socio-political aspect as being enacted, because this aspect is so rarely taken into account.

When asking Lilly in the interview if she believed she could have acted differently, she said she regretted not turning to Ahlam's mother to reveal Ahlam's sexual tendency towards women, and explain to her that there is nothing to be done about it, and that therefore she should accept her as she was. That way, she said, she would have relieved Ahlam of her secret, while also clearing the path for her to live the life she wanted with her mother's blessing. Even though Lilly admitted that she would ordinarily never turn to an adult patient's parents to reveal such secrets, this fantasy haunted her and filled her with guilt and regret. She confessed that the guilt was for not feeling brave enough to confront the mother because she feared that the family would hurt her (Lilly) for bringing this up and considering it, for not changing Ahlam by "treating her pathology" but rather encouraging her "illness". She regretted not trying, for being a bystander, and also felt shame for her own ambivalence towards Ahlam which sometimes made her wish she would disappear from therapy because of her dullness and passivity.

Ahlam therefore had two mothers, both demanding, both rejecting, each asking to pledge her allegiance to one of them while leaving out parts of herself "that don't fit". I call this a *political enactment*, because in my view this is not only a transference/countertransference expression (though these aspects were also very much evident), but rather it can be viewed as reenacting the socio-political demands from the stranger, who is coerced to abandon the parts that threaten the majority group, and in this case the minority group as well. Ahlam's otherness for Lilly was not her being in love with a woman, but rather for not accepting that love because of her Muslim upbringing, and for rejecting Lilly's unconscious wish to "civilize" her into Western ideals. Both

Ahlam and Lilly failed to tolerate each other's ambiguous parts. As Dalal (2012) states, it is an error to claim that only the ones in power need to tolerate the less powerful, as is often described in multicultural tolerance. In reality, the less powerful are continually required to tolerate the ways the more powerful dictate. In the public sphere they are expected to put up with insults, to swallow hard and contain their rage. They realize that some reactions and behaviors are reserved for the members of the majority group and are denied from them. Ahlam too found it difficult to tolerate Lilly's attempts to make her question whether she could live as a lesbian or not. It was a mutual breaking point for both, which symbolized the breaking of trust, when the tension between sameness and difference they had fought to preserve was disturbed. And so, Lilly and Ahlam were both enacting a space in which there was no thinking – only power struggles, primal fears and unanswered wishes could take place. There was no room to pause, breathe and contemplate, no vantage point from which to observe things together like allies. And so, they parted ways, unable to pass the impassable.

Ahlam therefore represents the tragedy that is part of the impasse of having a hybrid identity, in which instead of accepting inner diversity there is a need to dichotomize, to have an "either/or" split in the self. This is the tragedy of the stranger – the promised land of Western freedom can be so seductive and tantalizing, yet Ahlam knew that she would never be Lilly's and Lilly would never be hers. For as Bauman noted, the stranger is never fully accepted. And so, she was facing a double-bind: If she were to be seduced by Lilly's words and follow her passion, she would be left defenseless; and if she were to forego her desires she would have to retreat to the familiar zombie state and turn off the glimpse of vitality that she had so briefly and painfully encountered.

She expressed her pain of never being fully accepted by Lilly through her lamenting that Lilly treated her differently than her Jewish sisters, in a way that was also familiar to her from the bias towards her own sister. She expressed her longing to belong by asking Lilly to interpret Hebrew poetry, and the ineffable secrets it holds that only an insider could know, and then expressed her pain that no one wanted to see and know her secrets, for Arab poetry is excluded from the colloquia, and perhaps also from treatment.

While Lilly cared for Ahlam, she admitted that it was difficult for her to tolerate her presence, which was always awkward. The difference in cultural values was not merely a hermeneutic problem, but rather was perceived as drawing the line between potential friend and enemy and raising it to the surface. Lilly felt the need to save Ahlam from her own group, by trying to convince them that it is acceptable and possible to be a lesbian, like one would try to talk to "friends"; while at the same time fearing going into "enemy turf" and knowing that she could never fully surrender to Ahlam's wishes to be emotionally adopted by her, if she were to choose to leave her family behind.

Another political enactment occurred when the fear of violence arose. As previously mentioned, the violent conflict between Jews and Palestinians can incite disavowed fear of violence. Lilly's fear from Ahlam's family's reaction could be viewed as the fear of discovering that they were in fact enemies, who would be violently rejecting her attempts to help them assimilate into Western values, and morally able to physically hurt her out of retaliation. And so, the fear of violence was split from Ahlam and projected onto her family, an act which can be viewed as a defense mechanism to rid the dyad from the disturbing ambiguity of the stranger in the office and keeping the therapeutic space "cleansed".

In conclusion, the capacity for tolerance is something we must all work to expand in our human encounters. It serves as a holding space in which we intentionally regulate ourselves in a way that slows things down, helps them linger, and perhaps open new paths of being. Bauman (1991) claimed that since the stranger is always an undecidable, what the member of the majority group must do is contain this ambiguity, tolerate it, because it could never be sufficiently resolved. But I also suggest that in therapy we do not only tolerate for the sake of endurance, but for the sake of being able to examine and observe ourselves and our patients through reflection, not reflex. Being aware of our own trigger points, whether intrapsychic, interpersonal or socio-political is an important part of this process.

References

Aron, L. (2016). Mutual vulnerability: An ethic of clinical practice. In D. M. Goodman & E. R. Severson (Eds), *The Ethical Turn: Otherness and Subjectivity in Contemporary Psychoanalysis* (pp. 19–41). New York: Routledge.

Aron, L. & Starr, K. (2013). *A Psychotherapy for the People: Toward a Progressive Psychoanalysis*. New York: Routledge.

Bauman, Z. (1991). *Modernity and Ambivalence*. Ithaca: C. U. Press.

Benjamin, J. (2018). *Beyond Doer and Done To: Recognition Theory, Intersubjectivity and the Third*. New York: Routledge.

Brown, W. (2008). *Regulating Aversion: Tolerance in the Age of Identity and Empire*. Princeton, NJ: Princeton University Press.

Dalal, F. (2008). Thought paralysis: Tolerance, and the fear of Islam. *Psychodynamic Practice*, *14*(1), 77–95.

Dalal, F. (2012). *Thought Paralysis: The Virtues of Discrimination*. London: Karnac Books.

Freud, S. (1919). The "Uncanny". In *The Complete Psychological Works*, Vol. XVII (pp. 217–256). London: Hogarth Press.

Ghent, E. (1990). Masochism, submission, surrender: Masochism as a perversion of surrender. *Contemporary Psychoanalysis*, *26*(1), 108–136.

Gielen, U. P., Draguns, J. G., & Fish, J. M. (2008). *Principles of Multicultural Counseling and Psychotherapy*. New York: Routledge.

Lacorne, D. (2019). *The Limits of Tolerance: Enlightenment Values and Religious Fanaticism*. New York: Columbia University Press.

Mintchev, N. & Hinshelwood, R. D. (2017). Introduction: The feeling of certainty, towards a psychosocial approach. In N. Mintchev & R. D. Hinshelwood (Eds), *The Feeling of uncertainty: Psychosocial perspectives on identity and difference* (pp. 1–10). London: Library of Congress.

Sharvit, K. (2016). Sociopsychological foundations of the Israeli-Palestinian conflict: Applying Daniel Bar-Tal's theorizing. In K. Sharvit & E. Halperin (Eds), *A Socio-Psychology Perspective on the Israeli-Palestinian Conflict: Celebrating the Legacy of Daniel Bar-Tal, Vol. II* (pp. 1–15). Switzerland: Springer International Publishing.

Sodowsky, G. R., Kuo-Jackson, P., & Loya, G. J. (1997). Outcome of training in the philosophy of assessment: Multicultural counseling competencies. In D. B. Pope-Davis & H. L. K. Coleman (Eds), *Assessment of Counseling Competence* (pp. 3–42). Thousand Oaks, CA: Sage Publications, Inc.

Sue, D. W., Arredondo, P., & McDavis, R. J. (1992). Multicultural counseling competencies and standards: A call to the profession. *Journal of Counseling & Development, 70*(4), 477–486.

Chapter 6

The Stranger on the Analytic Couch

Martin Mahler

In this paper I would like to explore the idea of tolerance in the context of psychoanalytic therapy. Tolerance clearly overlaps with other concepts that are part of psychoanalytic methodology and therefore it raises the question of its own specific value. I will present several parts of the sessions with one of my patients to demonstrate that the concept of tolerance can be useful and justified only if it is part of the process of mutual exploring and negotiating what it is we are actually ready to tolerate. Sometimes the analyst's capacity to tolerate the patient's conflictive contributions is compromised, causing him/her to violating the boundaries of the therapy (Cassorla, 2001) "which entails a shared vulnerability and co-suffering, in the faith that it will lead to repair" (Atlas & Aron, 2018). I want to coin here the idea that true tolerance can be re-established in some complicated treatments when standard analytic attitude is abandoned temporarily. It brings forward the risk of premature ending of these analyses, open meeting with analyst's and patient's antagonisms and vulnerabilities. It challenges working alliance and emotional closeness of this analytic couple. False tolerance functions to preserve unconscious collusion, hypocrisy and leads to anti-growth, dead ends or limited achievements. It could be disclosed via enactments and worked through.

I

The Latin word *tolerantia* implies enduring, suffering, bearing of something negative. The English term "toleration" implies the acceptance of something which one dislikes, disagrees with or is anxious of. In other words, we hold a negative judgement about certain persons or ideas and have the power to negate them, but we deliberately refrain from such negation. The reasons for such an attitude are varied, they stem from our respect for autonomy, pacifism, kindness, generosity, mutuality, modesty, and our pedagogical aims. I propose here to narrow the meaning of this concept to the following definition: tolerance is an act of our benevolent power (as we are endowed with sufficient competences either to accept and protect otherness of people, or to refuse and defend ourselves against it) as well as an act of our true concern in preserving

DOI: 10.4324/9781003200253-9

this otherness. Such encounters can provoke sometimes uncanny experiences and feelings of depersonalization, which does not necessarily have to be associated only with anxiety or anger, but also with curiosity, exaltation and fascination (de M'Uzan, 2013). Of course, tolerance is conditioned by our narcissistic capacity, by the need to maintain psychic integrity and safety. In non-threatening or partly threatening state of exaltation or fascination, the awareness of our uniqueness slowly fades and we open ourselves up to the influence of the new and the strange. The fascination may bring us closer to the experience of others and it might open the doors for tolerating them and for broadening our knowledge. In my understanding, the tolerance is a precondition for growing knowledge.

The psychoanalytic approach is designed to seek psychic truths and it involves almost all of the above-mentioned attributes of a developed tolerance. It is associated with neutrality, hospitality, empathy, trial identification, receptivity to another experience, enduring the paradox of many different perspectives, containment etc. Analytic tolerance is based on an exploratory, curious state of mind. It seems to me that general usage of this concept overemphasizes our willingness to accept while at the same time it somewhat bypasses our disagreement. Our tendency to smooth over differences, destroy otherness and find equality where it is not, is an antagonist of true tolerance. Sensitivity to disagreement is a key part of psychoanalytic tolerance and it's bypassing can disturb dialectic tension closeness/distance which is essential for truth seeking. To preserve specificity of the concept (originally related to the differences between people of various religions), I prefer to use the tolerance in psychoanalysis mainly in the context of collective or mass objects (political, religious, ideological, nationalist and gender beliefs, stereotypes, prejudices and "ghosts") people are (dis)identified with and that operate in their unconscious minds.

Of course, tolerance is not a one-way process, the patient has to endure the otherness of the analyst too. It is therefore preferable to view tolerance as a function of the psychoanalytic dyadic system rather than as the analyst's exclusive domain. Similarly, the analytic truth does not arise separately in the individual mind of the analyst or the patient, but emerges as the emotionally shared and lived experience. Under certain circumstances, when analytic couple loses from some reason their interest in seeking the truth and the analytic closeness/distance dialectics is compromised, it might be appropriate to leave the façade of understanding and risk open debate or even dispute to revive analytic collaboration.

II

My patient Denis lives in one of the post-Soviet republics and comes to me for shuttle analysis several times a year. We speak Russian together, even though neither of us speak the language as a mother tongue. For many people in Eastern and Central Europe the Russian language evokes ambivalent feelings due to the political history of the region. Of course, we realize that the language has a rich history in literature, art, film and science, but at the same time it is the language of imperialist invaders. In the communist world, this language served as a 'lingua franca' and it remains to this day the only common language between my patient and I. During the 20th century a vast territory in Central and Eastern Europe was destroyed by two world wars, the Holocaust, the Gulag, the expulsion of millions of people from their homes, and the era of the rise and fall of communism. The echo of these past collective experiences inevitably enters into our psychoanalytic discourse and can sometimes even capture it. It unites us, but at the same time divides us, because our collective identifications also diverge in many ways. During one of his sessions, Denis began to talk emotionally about his negative experience with Jewish neighbours living in the same building.

> These religious Jews were celebrating one of their festivals at the time. They even set up some kind of tent on the roof of our house, where they were singing and eating. They somehow irritate me, I don't trust them very much and they annoy me. After all, they're foreigners, they don't speak my language and never try to. They don't even speak Russian. But you see them everywhere, they're very active and self-confident. You often see them swarming around the synagogue, they look like creatures from another planet. Why are they in my country and why do they want to live there? They're obviously not aware they committed a sin when they crucified Jesus Christ! In my opinion, these people should behave more politely and discreetly when they're in my city and my country, and they should show some remorse for their crime! It also makes me very angry that one of my neighbours is called Judah. How can someone in this day and age be named after the man who betrayed Jesus? How can Jews give their children such a name? This name should be banned forever and deleted from the list of acceptable names! Are the Jews so ignorant, or do they just want to provoke us and test our patience? After all we were born here.

At first I felt no great emotion or interest in what the patient was saying, perhaps I felt like indifferent. I remained silent, as if there was nothing to add. In fact I wasn't able to talk or even think, just to accept it. Immediately after the patient's angry lament, perhaps I felt alienated and detached from what I had heard, as if it was told by someone else than Mr F. After a few minutes, when the patient had already changed the subject, I realized that I had never encountered such primitive anti-Semitism in my clinical practice and daily life ever before. It was like hearing a sinister, condemning voice coming from the dark European past or a scream from a culturally and geographically distant present. Vivid, fascinating images of pogroms, shouting and crying, escapes and beatings appeared in front of my eyes. Suddenly I was overwhelmed with strong affects of anxiety, anger and wish to stop any contact with this man.

After the session had ended, I shared this worrying experience with one analytic colleague, which helped me return temporarily to a more stable and reflective state. He suggested to direct my attention to transferential meanings in Denis' clinical material and he supported my analytic attitude. Still I felt disgust and revulsion for Denis: how could a patient *of mine* have such an anti-Semitic outburst? How could I continue to work with someone who identifies with such a primitive racist ideology? Does Denis want to confront me or possibly threaten me when knowing about my Jewish roots? Or perhaps he wants me to identify with his anti-Semitic prejudice to become his ally? Or maybe he doubts about my belonging to Jews? Or he pushes me to differentiate between various kinds of Jews? Should I feel lucky to stay on the "right" side? And did I have some part in provoking his condemning lament? What attribute imposed on me by this patient am I wearing? In any case, I felt angry and driven by a strong urge to say to Denis:

> Sir, you are an anti-Semite and I don't want to stay with a neighbour like you in one analytic house. Be aware of what you're saying to me, give me your immediate apology, or I won't be able to work with you further.

To spit these or other words at him would drag me down to street level and reduce our communication nearly to a primitive shouting match. But I found myself unable to approach his anti-Semitic statement in the same way as other creations of his inner world. Understanding and interpreting his momentary self-state in the context of the transference was simply out of the question, it seemed to me as hypocrisy, before I will express my open disagreement. It looked superficial to deal, for example, with his envy, fear of betrayal, fear of foreign occupiers etc. I felt as if I am caught in a kind of nightmare or more so in night terror (Ogden, 2005, pp. 3). This terror is described as a situation where:

> The child having a night terror "awakens" in great fear, but does not recognize the parent who has been awakened by his cries ... the next morning ... the child has little or no recollection of the night terror or having been comforted by his parents.

Like this child I found myself in a quasi-hallucinatory state, and found it difficult to differentiate my patient clearly from a pogromist. Hearing an aggressive impulse in his words and staying in the grip of persecutory fantasy, it was felt like the immediate impulse to defend myself and to leave. Partly I felt engaged also in an act of self-renunciation when protesting against this anti-Semitic prejudice considering it is also my moral duty. I was "less definitively myself" to paraphrase Ogden (2015). It was a matter of courage to let down analytic stance and to enter vulnerable situation without any certainty where it will lead us. Still, I believed that even street shouting could be an attempt to break the wall raised between us. The next day Denis mentioned he had a feeling that I had some kind of problem with him and he did not understand why. In spite of my hesitation, I spontaneously answered him:

> You know, it was hard for me to listen to what you said yesterday about Jewish people. I heard anti-Semitism in your words, and it's dangerous and unacceptable to myself and many other people. I have the impression you are repeating arguments that have been resurfacing for centuries. I realize it's you that's talking, but when I hear your words, it feels like a crowd of angry people have invaded and occupied our analytic space. I think we should talk about it because on this matter we don't agree with each other at all.

Denis was silent for a long time, but then he spoke while sobbing:

> It seems to me that you're out of your mind. Right now my only wish is that you would stop talking and just be silent. You see it in a completely different way than I do, and at this moment I just don't follow you, I simply don't understand you. It's confusing, you're actually forcing me to question who I am and where I belong. I feel like I'm being forced out, suddenly it seems like there's too much of you. I feel like I'm being dragged down into mud.

I was quite surprised that Denis was so taken aback by my claim that he professed anti-Semitic prejudice and that he had such a strong feeling of rejection. Obviously, we were both trapped in mutual misunderstanding and exclusion ruled by massive, dramatic enactment. This enactment was like turbulent event crashed through our analytic space similar to a large meteor, leaving us in a state of mutual isolation and shock. The previously mentioned "night terror" that the patient and I experienced together, could have been related to an aggressive, traumatic fantasy that became more central to our unconscious dynamics and only throughout this enactment it could be formulated. As if we both were in a hole filled with mud-ness/madness. To pull ourselves out of this hole, soon we both started to talk and think about the misunderstanding we had and seek an explanation for it. We both shared the embarrassment and growing concern that our mutual closeness was immediately lost. Denis was shocked at what I heard in his words and I was surprised at how he understood mine. Even in the midst of our "confusion of tongues" and mutual exclusion, there was a call for recognition, a need to listen each other and to dream up our shared experience. Denis felt hurt and was totally unaware of any of his racist prejudice. He said he just wanted to criticize religious Jews, but he knows very little about them and has no idea how to interact with them. He feels not so much like an anti-Semite, but more like a naive person watching strangely dressed creatures from another planet. Last but not least, his criticism was not consciously addressed to me, he did not think I had anything to do with these religious Jews.

> All of a sudden a lot of Jews moved to our country, there was just so many Jews! They come from a completely different environment, they have a

completely different culture and they make a point of showing their difference. Some of them are friendly and nice, but others see themselves as superior and look down on us. How can I coexist with them when I don't even
know who I am myself? You might find this hard to believe, but I didn't
realize what I was saying and how it would affect you!

We were both astonished by multiple voices, more or less personalized, we
heard in our misunderstanding. We accept that there are the well-established
voices that we simply recognize as our own. And there also are other voices
that surprise us, but we still had to concede that they belong to us. But the
voices that we were hearing now were not easy to endorse, even though we
knew they came from us. These were voices belonging to our identifications
with powerful collective stereotype in which each of us presented its opposite
sides "we" and "they". We both became unconscious echoes of our protracted
collective histories. The subsequent sessions were filled with images and memories from his totalitarian past. For many years he lived in a Soviet military
town and his world was permeated by collective programs that were enforced
on him by his teachers, the public service media, youth leaders, peers, neighbours, and even his parents whose ideological role in this process was not (in
his view) so crucial. Our confrontation triggered a "dull feeling of shame,
despair and guilt" in Denis. He felt painfully confronted with his cultural and
political naivety and blindness. In this Communist town, he did not meet anyone to reveal to him the truth, instead he waded through borrowed thoughts
and stereotypes for years. Loyalty to the ruling ideology was the only option,
and all residents were indoctrinated by the belief that they lived in the best
country on earth and Russian was the world's leading language. Difference
between people was not tolerated: they were all supposed to look essentially
the same, inside as well as outside. The fact that this collective spirit eliminated
free thought and initiative was continuously denied, and the suffering caused
by this ideological terror was perversely turned into a social virtue. For example, people were proud to have survived the murderous violence to which they
had been repeatedly subjected to by the regime. The more twisted the truth
they shared about the totalitarian regime the more loyalty they felt to it.
Ironically, even at that time Jews lived in Denis' neighbourhood, but it meant
nothing to him then. They looked and behaved like all people. Open anti-
Semitism was suppressed by the totalitarian regime (it was concealed in anti-
Zionist propaganda) and things like the Holocaust were rarely talked about.
This epoch ended in the collapse of this collective "dream" and my patient, like
many others, was exposed to a deep disillusionment and a crisis of identity.
However, the demise of this previous world was not sufficiently mourned and
the nostalgia for this lost "Garden of Eden" remains in the minds of some
survivors. It seems that other ideologies have filled the void, some of which
have re-surfaced after decades of communist propaganda and repression.
Denis mentioned to me that he was reading a heroic novel about his nation's
history written in his mother tongue. He tried to satisfy his desire for a valid

national identity through national history, myths and half-truths about its heroes. In these stories the Jews often refrained from committing to the cause and sometimes were even hostile to it. It seems that in these vastly shared stories Denis found the springboard for his anti-Semitic stereotype. During our sessions he was unknowingly alternating between Russian and his mother tongue. He told me that his nation had been persecuted for centuries, and his homeland was repeatedly occupied by various invaders. He also mentioned that his mother tongue was blacklisted and in danger of extinction. The personal and collective experiences played into an underlying fear that people could lose their homes any moment and that they could somehow end up being evicted by the newcomers.

Slowly our mutual misunderstanding became clearer and we could make sense of it in the light of our re-established dialogue. I have got more aware of the "ghosts" from my family history which intensified the victim – perpetrator scenario enacted between us. Also the traumatic memories re-emerged related to Soviet military invasion during so called Prague Spring. It seems to me that Denis' incomplete mourning for his lost unity with the communist collective identity has paved the way for Denis to establish himself as a frail individual lacking a home in which he could recognize and nurture his own personalized identity. At the same time, this mourning summoned the "spirits" of this lost world, and they again colonized the patient's imagination and emotions, while remaining disconnected from their deeper symbolic representations. Perhaps this re-colonization was enhanced by many difficult experiences with cultural and economic otherness met by Denis during his analytic visits in the city of Prague. (By the way, I often met in the foreign patients seeking psychoanalytic treatment with me unstable sense of a psychic home or unsafe internal place for building personal identity. As we know, this identity is "a dual structure with individual and collective parts in mutual interactions and shifts" (Kennedy, 2014).) In the therapy with Denis we were faced with the task of transforming his frail identity in his new "Western" home. Necessarily, it brought forward also alienating and persecutory experiences provoked by cultural, political and economic differences between our countries. It could strengthen also our unconscious collusion and denial of mutual differences. When the collusion broke up, it reopened doors for these hidden differences and persecution anxieties.

We investigated what other multi-layered truths might have been behind his anti-Semitic clichés. For example, to what extent these clichés concealed the denial of collective hatred, the fear of diversity and envy of other communities, and to what extent these clichés were hiding his individual fears of our own contact and the treatment itself. Gradually we could explore transferential – counter-transferential meaning of our enactment. Denis brought up his feeling of insecurity and loneliness in our relationship, self-suppression and withdrawal from his own wishes and positions, as well as his pain from a vague identity. He had begun to feel incompetent and somehow lost, complained about difficulties to think clearly and consistently. He felt he was just bringing his "psychic apparatus" into the therapy and by stating this he was asking for our therapy to become a place where he could become himself. During one of the subsequent sessions Denis mentioned the following dream which brought more light into his emotional situation in our relationship:

> He lived in a glass cube fixed to a large, multi-storey building that looked like a fortress. Someone had decided that he should live in this apartment that was protruding beyond the outside wall of the building. The ceiling of the cube was also made of glass and there was a constant danger of something falling from the roof of the building above. Mr. F. felt very nervous in the apartment and wanted to leave.

Finally we could approach the threatening, intolerant moment in our relationship that we had kept apart with help of unconscious collusion. It had protected us from meeting archaic anxieties of invasion, exploitation and possible destruction. Among other things we focused on strong ambivalence regarding achieving greater mutual closeness versus maintaining clearly defined distance between us (fragile glass cube associated loosely to compact multi-storey fortress). It became clearer that Denis felt my presence as hardly "metabolized": superior, parasitic, alienating or self-consumed with my own needs and wishes. He felt very lonely and, in the dream, he expressed also his craving for closeness and belonging. For a long period of our analysis his pain had stayed mute, until the conditions for its externalization and "performance" developed. Although he had verbalized his experiences of envy, betrayal and alienating otherness several times, it had previously rather awkward and superficial impact on me: perhaps I tolerated his experiences blindly, defending myself from threatening identifications with selfish and expansive religious man "celebrating one of his festivals" on the patient's "roof"? It seems probable that I returned the projective contents back to him without metabolizing them and it could lead to crossed projective identification (Cassorla, 2001) and acute enactment.

III

Of course, it is questionable whether true tolerance could have been achieved only via personal clash. In my opinion, standard analytic approach lost, though temporarily, its therapeutic function in the work with Denis. In retrospect, the clash of our mutual antagonisms that interrupted a period of false tolerance prompted us to resume intense analytic work and to reconcile but not diminish our differences. Once we have understood them more, I tried to separate my conflictive contributions from that of the patient and take my responsibility for them. It helped to re-establish the psychoanalytic dialectics of our closeness/distance. Paradoxically, my negative reaction opened up space not only for pain, but also for the influx of new material that we could process and dream together.

I believe that the jump from analytic discourse to "street talk", which dragged to the surface a layer of established collective prejudices and ideologies, proved to be a productive event – even though it ran the risk of our therapy failing. I crossed the usual boundary of the patient – analyst relationship to communicate with him from a position of identifying with my collective internal objects, and as a result I was not able to avoid open personal conflict. I emphasized my personal disagreement, but later I/we also offered my/our good will to try and understand what the patient was telling me. At first the patient focused mainly on my disapproval of what he had said, however after our uncomfortable confrontation some of our "ghosts" were repatriated instead of being forced back to the margins of our discourse. I am aware that our conflict could have killed the therapy, and it is possible that this was the unconscious goal of my patient (and perhaps myself?) all along. But ongoing analysis has shown that after sufficient elaboration of these violently projected collective introjects, we were able to re-focus on an individual and more personalized range of topics. We proved our readiness to stay together even in very painful areas and moments of analytic exploration. Without previously build positive, loving relationship our work could not survive such a severe accident. Even if it concerned things that were difficult to accept, we were achieving now fresh knowledge about them with emerging unity, kindness (Civitarese, 2016) and true tolerance. Deeper closeness was formed as we succeeded to bridge the alienating gaps between us. Our work began to focus more so on ontological aspects (Ogden, 2019), it shifted partly from associative contents and we started to concentrate on the way things were communicated and shared. In other words, besides just analyzing thoughts and emotions, we began to notice both their authors, Denis and myself, or to be more exact the place where these authors happened to be in that moment in their vulnerable, co-created relationship.

References

Atlas, Galit & Aron, Lewis (2018). *Dramatic Dialogue. Contemporary Clinical Practice.* Routledge.

Cassorla, Roosevelt M. S. (2001). Acute enactment as a "resource" in disclosing a collusion between the analytical dyad. *IJPA*, 82(6): 1155–1170.

Civitarese, Giuseppe (2016). Truth as immediacy and unison: A new common ground in psychoanalysis? *The Psychoanalytic Quarterly*, 85(2).

Kennedy, Roger (2014). *The Psychic Home: Psychoanalysis, Consciousness and the Human Soul*. Routledge.

de M'Uzan, Michel (2013). *Death and Identity. Being and Psycho-Sexual Drama.* Karnac.

Ogden, Thomas (2005). *This Art of Psychoanalysis: Dreaming Undreamt Dreams and Interrupted Cries*. Routledge.

Ogden, Thomas (2015). Intuiting the truth of what's happening: On Bion's "Notes on Memory and Desire". *Psychoanalytic Quarterly*, 84: 285–306.

Ogden, Thomas (2019). Ontological psychoanalysis or "What do you want to be when you grow up"? *Psychoanalytic Quarterly*, 88(4): 661–684.

Chapter 7

Tolerance, Mutual Recognition and Radical Witnessing

Three Degrees of Separation

Chana Ullman

This chapter focuses on three constructs which together constitute a framework for a relational psychoanalytic ethics: Tolerance, mutual recognition, and radical witnessing. All three constructs assume a stance towards Otherness. I will argue that each places a different demand on the subject and depends on a different distance in relation to the other. The chapter will examine the meanings of these concepts in social-political contexts and in psychoanalytic work.

Tolerance – When Does it Fail?

I begin with an attempt to give meaning to a failure: The failure of a year-long effort to organize a workshop, with Palestinian Israeli and international professionals, on the grounds of the Talitha Kumi guesthouse in the occupied West Bank.

Following IARPP's decision to hold their 17th international conference in Tel Aviv, we at the executive board of IARPP and members of the organization received letters protesting the decision.

The protesters argued that having a conference in Tel Aviv means supporting the Israeli government's policies of occupation and violation of human rights and demanded a change of location for the conference. The point was also made in the original letter as well as others that followed, that Palestinians and others who are openly BDS supporters will not be allowed entry into Israel and therefore will not be able to participate. It was argued that one cannot hold a scientific meeting in a place that might deny entry to some who might wish to come, on the basis of their political affiliation and identity.

The board's attempt to address the protest by explaining the decision and IARPP's policies as a non-profit professional membership organization, supporting the large and active chapter in Israel, and inviting to a dialogue including the acknowledgment of the violations of human rights and of Palestinian suffering, did not help. The protest intensified with calls to boycott the conference and withdraw IARPP memberships flooded the social media.

In the context of this heated debate, at the preliminary stages of organizing the conference in Tel Aviv I was joined by four colleagues (Sharon Ziv

DOI: 10.4324/9781003200253-10

Beiman, Tamar Barnea, Uri Hadar and Yitzchak Mendelson) to plan an Israeli-Palestinian workshop entitled: "The occupation, mental health and relationality."

We had three purposes in mind: First, we wished to ascertain that the reality of the Israeli occupation of the West bank and Gaza is present at the conference and included in the program.

Second, we intended to witness, listen and meet Palestinian colleagues, mental health professionals, with whom we can discuss and from whom we can learn about the impact of the occupation on their lives and their work.

Third, we wished to create an event outside Tel-Aviv and in fact outside Israel in the occupied territories, in a location that would be relatively easily accessible to Palestinians as well as to Israelis and any other interested professionals.

In an effort to address the reality that Palestinian professionals from the West Bank and Gaza may indeed be denied entry to the conference in TA, even if they wished to do so, and, moreover, from our standpoint as Israelis who oppose our government's policies and try to resist the Occupation, we were resolved to respond with a concrete endeavor that will allow a meaningful participation of Palestinians and an acknowledgment of their lives under occupation.

We found what we thought was the perfect location for this workshop – Talitha Kumi Guest House in Beit-Jalah which is on Palestinian territory close to the checkpoint and easy access from Jerusalem, and often hosts workshops including Palestinian and Israeli participants.

Talitha Kumi Guest House was happy to host us. We visited the place and our reservation was accepted. Palestinian and Israeli colleagues who had established an ongoing psychotherapy workshop for Palestinian and Israeli professionals in Jerusalem accepted our invitation to participate. We were pleased and hopeful to get some enthusiastic responses to our invitation from Palestinian speakers in Gaza and the West bank.

Our first obstacle came when an Israeli Palestinian colleague bluntly refused our invitation to join our steering committee.

The next obstacle came about when one of our colleagues felt that he would not be able to continue participating in the workshop's steering committee. Some of his closest friends and colleagues reacted with pain and outrage to what they saw as his betrayal of his solidarity with them.

At the same time, we dealt with various objections and obstacles from our Jewish-Israeli friends who opposed the inclusion of a "political pre-conference workshop" in a "professional" conference. These disagreements within the group of Israeli conference organizers were resolved and the workshop at TK was scheduled for the opening day in parallel to the other pre-conference events.

We continued to correspond with our Gazan and other guests to create the content and topics to be discussed in the workshop. We had the program titles and abstracts from all the presenters and all the logistics figured out. In January

2019, when our program was set, we wrote to several colleagues in NY who we thought would be interested in this event despite their objections to holding the conference in Tel Aviv. We described the workshop – its purpose, its location and its program.

Within a few days (we do not know whether the timing is related to the above letters), Talitha Kumi Guest House surprisingly and unilaterally canceled our reservation leaving no room for any negotiation. Immediately thereafter, our main speaker from Gaza canceled his participation. Other Palestinian-Israeli speakers also retracted their acceptance of our invitation.

While we could probably find another venue and possibly other speakers, we decided to cancel the workshop with sorrow and pain.

I believe this is a story of misguided and thwarted tolerance. One can argue that our Palestinian partners were intolerant. On the other hand, there can be no doubt that our own proposal reflected tolerance. From our perspective, we were acting in an attempt to respect the Other – the Palestinians who called not to attend the conference in Tel Aviv. Although we felt differently about the boycott, we wished to acknowledge it, and enable a meeting on their territory.

From our perspective, then, we were trying to remove some obstacles that stood in a way of a meeting and dialogue with the Other. However, in retro- spect it seems to me that our well-intentioned tolerance of Palestinian's protest was steeped in blindness. In retrospect, I realized that for the Palestinians our invitation was experienced as another act of "occupation" from a position of the superiority of the organizers – Jews who are willing to confer tolerance and interest on the oppressed Other, but are not willing to join them, and in fact even negate their struggle by offering a token of a compromise. We were acting in tolerance as we understood it, while ignoring the subjectivity of the Other.

A dictionary definition of tolerance includes: Willingness to accept behav- ior and beliefs that are different from your own, although you might not agree with or approve of them. Tolerance is also defined as endurance, the ability to endure adverse or difficult situations (from the Cambridge dictionary). In psy- choanalytic terms, tolerance is therefore a one-person state. It is the state of one person who is strong enough or resilient enough to endure otherness or adversity. It does not require a relationship, nor does it have to involve a desire for closeness or affinity with the other.

In clinical settings tolerance is often a prerequisite. Our endurance and abil- ity to accept opinions and behavior different than our own are often required in the consulting room. While tolerance of differences is a necessary prerequi- site for a therapeutic encounter, it seems to me that it is not sufficient, and may even result in pain and disappointment, as in the failed workshop described above. In the Israeli context, differences of political opinions between patient and analyst often become a challenge. This is ubiquitous – patients and ana- lysts everywhere may differ in their politics. However, the differences may become unbearable when the political is inextricably and immediately tied with daily existential fears, terrible losses and traumas and when the stakes are high.

Such was the case with my patient (see Ullman 2011) who is a woman about my age. She comes from, and in turn has raised, an Orthodox Jewish family, committed to a rightwing ideology. Her first-born son lived in a remote settlement in the occupied Palestinian territories with his wife and small children, when he was killed by a Palestinian terrorist who barged into their house while they were having their Shabbat dinner. All her other married children live in similar settlements, places which are usually inhabited by the most extreme rightwing groups. While my patient and I could not be further apart in terms of our politics, I like her and I can empathize and feel her horrible loss and suffering. While our politics are worlds apart, other self-states of mine completely identify with her as a first-born daughter (which I am too) to Holocaust survivors (which my parents are) from the same east European regions where my parents were born. We worked together for a few months in which she mourned the loss of her son and her sense of estrangement and dissociation from the rest of her life and her need to protect her parents from her agony. I felt our work proceeded well despite my well concealed but deep disagreements with her world view. Following about 6 months of therapy, my patient cancelled an appointment, did not ask to reschedule and then avoided my calls. After several attempts to invite her to talk to me, I get hold of her husband who tells me that she saw a sticker on my car which clearly identifies me as a "leftist". She cannot bear this and cannot continue therapy with me. I understand that continuing her sessions with me feels to her like a betrayal of her son and all that was sacred to him, and that she feels deceived by me. I realize in retrospect that my tolerance was necessary but not sufficient. Despite my genuine empathy towards her loss, my tolerance of the views she expressed was rightfully experienced as inauthentic. While working hard to conceal our differences, I was unconsciously critical. I was left experiencing sadness over this rupture that could not be repaired. The empathic bond and many similarities between us could not bridge the gap. At that moment of discovering the gap I became a unidimensional "leftist" for her and alliance was no longer possible. I wonder: Had I been able to directly address the political difference between us at the onset, rather than trying to tolerate and endure it, could the outcome have been different?

In inevitable situations of impasse and enactments, tolerance cannot be sufficient. In fact, it may involve concealment of genuine self-states that become dissociated and likely disruptive. It may hinge on inauthenticity and denial of self. Here is where mutual recognition becomes the relevant stance.

Recognition, Acknowledgement and Mutuality

In the work of Jessica Benjamin mutual recognition replaces autonomy as the ideal goal of development (Benjamin 1995). Mutual recognition is a developmental achievement in which the child discovers the other as a subject who is a center of consciousness independent of one's own and who is not in one's control. In her later work, Benjamin develops an intersubjective theory of psychoanalysis organized around the idea of recognition. (Benjamin 2018). Recognition is conceptualized "first as a psychic position in which we know the other's mind as an equal source of intention and agency ... second, as a process of action, the essence of responsiveness in interaction" (2018, p. 3). It is then a position that rests on two persons and describes a relationship that involves not only endurance, but responsiveness to the Other. Moreover, it is not a relationship in which only one person is assumed to be tolerant, more resilient and therefore better able to interpret the other, but a relationship in which two subjects can know and not know, each can destabilize the other at any moment. In analysis and in development, the second meaning of recognition is of utmost importance – it confirms that I am seen, known, I have an impact on you and therefore I matter to you. Furthermore, in contrast to tolerance, recognition is not an effort or a test of endurance, it is a motivating need and a desire for intersubjective relatedness for its own sake.

Assuming an intersubjective relationship in which two partners confront and negotiate otherness (Bromberg 1998), implies that ruptures of recognition are inevitable and repairs are essential in the developmental, the analytic and social settings. Repairs are contingent on our ability to reflect on our contribution to the impasse and to acknowledge harm, it is a dual responsibility to admit failure and acknowledge the other's hurt, which paradoxically avoids the repetition of original wounds (Ferenczi 1988). The repair also requires that the stronger party "goes first": In Benjamin's terms, the therapist assumes the responsibility of reinstituting a lawful world.

The attempt to remain in an ideal place where we are a "complete container", perhaps similar to my honest but failed attempt to be with my bereaved patient, renders us a "failed witness". It keeps us from validating for the patient the fact that we have hurt them or even negated their most precious self-state. We thus become unable to bring the world back to its lawful and moral state – especially with patients who have experienced trauma.

Recognition and mutuality however have their own potential for "potholes" (Bromberg 2003). Moving back to the social arena, in the middle of the second *intifada*, Benjamin initiated a project of "acknowledgement" that brought together Israelis, Palestinians and international 'mediators,' in an attempt to implement her notions about mutual recognition as a platform for reconciliation and reparation. (see Benjamin 2018, pp. 236) It was a heroic attempt, which led to several meaningful encounters and precious moments of meeting; still, as an encounter designed to facilitate mutual recognition, the project was a failure. A failure we can learn from. It seems that the heroic effort to achieve mutual acknowledgment cannot succeed in situations of ongoing trauma and extreme power imbalance. It would be akin to expecting tolerance, mutual acknowledgement and reconciliation between a child and an abusive parent while the abuse is ongoing.

Relational Trauma, Moral Witnessing and the Radical Witness

I wish to suggest that the position of the radical witness is an important alternative to tolerance and to mutual recognition under such conditions of chronic trauma and power imbalance. Radical witnessing entails no expectation for mutuality, nor reparation, but attempts to see the other in her alterity, without the claim for transformation, justice or reconciliation. In fact, as claimed by Oliver (2001), it is a position which includes victims right to an existence outside "our" definition or construction of them.

The concept of witnessing as used in contemporary psychoanalysis is founded on our understanding of the nature and impact of relational trauma on the mind.

In contemporary relational literature, trauma is given a central place as a cause of distress and ongoing suffering and as distorting development. The accumulating knowledge about the prevalence of sexual or other abuse in the family environment and the psychic injuries this causes has brought trauma back into psychoanalytic discourse. Actual injuries in one's actual relationships with parental figures and the exploitation of attachment become woven into one's psyche. Unlike other traumas, that are not man-made and which do not take place in the context of attachment, such relational traumas occur within unequal power-relations (whether between parent and child, man and woman, therapist and patient or anyone in a position of authority and their subordinates), through ongoing relations of oppression and humiliation. This theoretical change forces us to address the broader cultural-political context in which we act. This is a paradigm shift within psychoanalysis, in the understanding of common pathological phenomena, emphasizing the role of actual harm as distorting the psyche.

Relational trauma (meaning, traumas that are man-made and occur within a relationship) leads to fixed self-states and two paradoxical reactions: one is dissociation, which detaches one from the intolerable traumatic situations; the other is repetition-compulsion, which leads one to repeatedly retell the same story through action. A neutral, interpretation-oriented position is ill-suited for working with dissociative states; it only makes things worse (Ferenczi 1988; Bromberg 1998). Tolerance is irrelevant here as well, as it does not require engagement with the other's anguish, only the endurance of it. It is only when the therapist relinquishes attempts to understand or endure the patient, and surrenders herself to the intersubjective experience as also taking place within herself, that words and thoughts are able to symbolize the experience rather than replace it, thus allowing the patient to experience being recognized and not only tolerated or understood by the other. Furthermore, at the wake of extreme trauma, dissociation takes hold and our search for maintaining a connection can be obscured by the patient distancing maneuvers.

Recently, a young woman therapist working in a community-based setting for holocaust survivors told me the following story – a new patient was referred to her; this man is an elderly holocaust survivor who has been bouncing between therapists at the community clinics, evoking resistance in everyone through the compulsive manner in which he repeatedly tries to describe how he had been wronged, years beforehand, when he was fired from his job. Everywhere he goes, he carries papers that support his claims, asking to show them to people. He typically leaves therapy soon after it had started. Her first session with him began in this same manner, with the young therapist finding it difficult to listen and feeling disquiet and bored in the face of his repetitive claims. However, at some point in the session, she suddenly pictured this patient as a parentless child in a concentration camp, looking for someone to listen to him. She felt as if she was there too, a forlorn child where no one was able to listen. She did not share this profound experience with the patient but something shifted in her and the atmosphere in the session changed. At the end of the session, the patient said: "I think you understand me. I want to come again to see you."

Alongside dissociation, trauma is characterized by what Freud called repetition compulsion. One is compelled to repeat the situation in which the trauma took place, which keeps recurring as the story of a gaping, screaming wound. Ferenczi (1988) views analysis as the domain where trauma inevitably both claims its place and hides from sight, turning us therapists into unwilling colluders with the crime of abuse. In treating relational trauma and betrayed attachment – it is vital for us to assume responsibility and acknowledge the injuries. The therapeutic session inevitably becomes difficult and hurtful. We cannot just tolerate differences, we must fight for the relationship and negotiate our presence as a hurtful figure, who forces the patient to experience the agonizing events in her life. This means being willing to dwell in a field where no one likes to dwell, to talk to dissociated infantile and adult parts.

Recently, I believe we are in the midst of yet another paradigm shift in psychoanalytic discourse – one which takes us back to Freud's blind spot when rejecting his trauma/seduction theory. Trauma involves not only the individual's inner world and their specific history of attachments, but also social power structures, socio-political world history, forces and structures that enable and maintain oppression and social violence. These traumas are insidious (see Efi Ziv 2012) as well as chronic and collective. The impact of such forces and structures is ongoing and powerful, though often enough both we as therapists and those who experience this impact remain blind to its psychic consequences. We are not talking about symptoms of hysteria like Freud did, nor even PTSD nor complex PTSD – because there is no "post" here: there is no expiration date on traumas related to racism, poverty, misogyny, homophobia, etc.

Such as the daily living conditions of blacks in the United States, Palestinians here in Israel, women, migrant workers, people suffering from poverty. In such situations, collective context and individual trauma are indistinguishably interlaced.

What does this mean for us as psychoanalytic therapists?

We often view the social forces that come up in the consulting room as derivatives of individual dynamics, as if the social domain is clinically meaningless, but psychic life is inextricably interwoven with the interpersonal and social context.

Here is a brief vignette to illustrate this interwovenness and its implications.

A patient comes to see me because of difficulties in his marriage. He brings up feelings of guilt about his infidelities, a sense of worthlessness and irritability alongside a wish to hold everything, to be a protector and a savior of his wife and others. He unfolds a long history in the security forces, including various operations in which he operated heavy machinery and participated in demolishing city streets. His experiences include some which are better left unmentioned and he therefore speaks little of his days in the service and tends to minimize their importance. I join his silence.... I have thoughts about the unspeakable traumas he might have experienced, and inflicted on others, but I wish to protect him and me from what might surface, and of what he might experience as intolerable otherness ... and we go on talking about his intimate relationships. Until the moment when he shares a dream, a nightmare in which his house burns down. The image of curtains in flames and his fear that the fire will consume everything, while he is unable to put it out. The dream presented the question of who started the fire, who is to blame. The fire started in the basement and, in his associations to the dream, he links this to an explosion he witnessed in the basement of a building he was guarding in his military service.

I say: "There is a fire coming out of the basement that might consume everything ... this basement is your psyche, but this basement also actually existed, you've been in it ... you ask who is to blame for this fire? Are you to blame for this fire?"

We talk about his fear of losing his home because he has been leading a double life, having affairs ... this is then linked to the double life he had led in the service. Only then does he begin talking about the horror of this double life, allowing me to be a witness to tales of bravery and dread.

During these sessions he keeps saying: "I never realized it had a price."

It is with regard to individual and collective trauma that witnessing become a moral imperative and radical witnessing needs to replace understanding, tolerance as well as recognition.

Bearing witness to experiences of actual insidious ongoing trauma inevitably compels moral responsibility, forcing its addressee to assume a political position, in terms of understanding the power-relations underlying the trauma. I view witnessing as a distinct therapeutic quality which is not the same as containment, holding, interpretation or empathy. It is a function which entails both otherness (Poland 2002) and the witness' commitment to "walk the distance" to the Other (Ullman 2006). It therefore entails tolerance of differences, recognition of the traumas, but goes further to validate and to engage with the others' pain without expecting reciprocity. As Oliver (2001) claims, radical witnessing includes not only recognizing the identity or rights of victims but their subjectivity outside our definition or construction. It thus requires a radical acceptance of otherness as an end in and of itself.

I understand radical witnessing as ethical imperative (Boulanger 2012) in the clinic and beyond. This understanding is related to the definition offered by philosopher Avishai Margalit, in his book, *The Ethics of Memory*. Margalit (2002) describes moral witnessing as a social function which affects collective memory.

The moral witness is an eye-witness; she describes what she has seen with her own eyes. The moral aspect has to do with the content of her testimony: she bears witness to human suffering which had been caused by evil. In Margalit's definition, both these elements are necessary: evil alone (such as exposing a plan before it is carried out) or suffering alone (as that caused by natural disasters) do not constitute moral witnessing.

The testimony of someone who had remained safe and far removed from the events does not suffice as moral witnessing. This risk is the very fact of belonging to the category of people towards which evil is directed (e.g. holocaust survivors) or a consequence of the very attempt to record, to speak out or validate an event which is denied. The act of bearing witness entails hope – the hope that evil is not the way of the world and should not be accepted in silence.

As witnesses to our patients' traumas, we do not have to decide between different narratives or versions of the truth. Nor do we have to interpret their motivations. Most often, as in the brief vignette above, the thing is that there is no version of the truth; the reality of suffering and evil is being denied or disavowed. Bearing witness begins where denial or distortion hold sway.

The undoing of dissociation through witnessing is a crisis-laden process for both sides.

The crisis that emerges through witnessing also stems from the encounter with the inevitable otherness of the therapist, which is present not as an obstacle but as a therapeutic element. From this perspective differences are not only to be tolerated, they exist as an opportunity to be engaged with and negotiated in a way that reduces the patients' experience of alienated, dissociated not-me parts.

Radical witnessing as defined by Kelly Oliver (2001) adds another component – the position of the witness as enabling subjectivity and as an alternative to mutual recognition: Oliver proposes a significant distinction between "recognition" and witnessing as a process. She argues that recognition involves acknowledging similarities, the possibility of seeing the other as similar to me (For example, we might say – "they're a human being too, and they deserve to be respected"), and has to do with a tolerance which, in fact, reenacts Hegel's master and slave relation. According to Oliver, witnessing is more radical; it is recognition of something that is beyond the familiar, that is alien, not just different. Radical witnessing is essential for the formation of the subject. It entails more than an encounter with something similar or with historical truth. Witnessing confronts us with epistemological questions about the truth (did it happen or not?), about who is more deserving of our empathy (the migrant worker or our fellow citizens? The hysterical women or her respected relative?), about belonging and collective identity (where do I belong if I bear witness to Palestinian suffering?).

Tolerance or recognition do not require us to rethink these questions. Both pose less of a challenge for our subjectivity and do not necessarily involve an emotional reaction of love, touch, looking towards the other. Tolerance and recognition do not open us, as Oliver puts it, to the "adventure of otherness".

Conclusion – Towards a Relational Ethic

In a paper entitled "Beyond tolerance in psychoanalytic communities" (2017), the late Lew Aron challenges us to go beyond tolerance and respect of differences to a "critical pluralism", where the Other, in this case a different theoretical perspective, is appreciated for what it can uniquely contribute to us. His call is to recognize that the other view of psychoanalysis serves a valuable function that we cannot perform ourselves – it is an opportunity to disturb a balance and prevent stagnation, an opportunity to raise questions not in order to give up our perspective but to re-examine and refine it. Similarly, it seems to me that my analysis of tolerance, mutual recognition and radical witnessing presents different degrees of separation from the other, and calls for critical pluralism in our engagement and emotional distance from the other's subjectivity. In particular, in situations of evil and suffering inflicted on individuals or collectives, our tolerance and endurance is hardly sufficient, in fact may become a hinderance when we remain the resilient, privileged party. Mutual recognition takes us a step further towards the other in that it assumes not one-sided endurance, but a relationship in which both parties may be destabilized by their differences and there is an expectation of moral responsibility to repair harm. Finally, radical witnessing involves not only recognizing difference but cherishing the otherness and apprehending the other as a subject who fails to conform to our construction of their identity. This defines a new aspect of relational ethics in the consulting room and beyond.

References

Aron, L. (2017). Beyond tolerance in psychoanalytic communities: Reflexive skepticism and critical pluralism. *Psychoanal. Perspect.*, 14(3): 271–282.

Benjamin, J. (1990). An outline of intersubjectivity: The development of recognition. *Psychoanal. Psychol.*, 7S(Supplement): 33–46.

Benjamin, J. (2018). *Beyond Doer Done To: Recognition Theory, Intersubjectivity and the Third*. NY: Routledge.

Boulanger, G. (2012). Psychoanalytic witnessing: Professional obligation or moral imperative? *Psychoanal. Psychol.*, 29(3): 318–324.

Bromberg, P. (1998). *Standing in the Spaces. Essays on Clinical Process, Trauma and Dissociation*. Hillsdale, NJ: The Analytic Press.

Bromberg, P. (2003). Potholes on the royal road: Or is it an abyss? In *Awakening the Dreamer*, pp. 85–107. Hillsdale, NJ: The Analytic Press.

Ferenczi, S. (1988). Confusion of tongues between adults and the child. *Contemporary Psychoanalysis*, 24: 196–206.

Margalit, A. (2002). *The Ethics of Memory*. Cambridge, MA: Harvard University Press.

Oliver, K. (2001). *Witnessing: Beyond Recognition*. Minneapolis: University of Minnesota Press.

Poland, W.S. (2000). The analyst's witnessing and otherness. *J. Amer. Psychoanal. Assn.*, 48: 17–34.

Ullman, C. (2006). Across the barriers: Bearing witness in the clinic and beyond. *Psychoanal. Dial.*, 16(2): 181–198.

Ullman, C. (2011). Between denial and witnessing: Psychoanalysis and clinical practice in the Israeli context. *Psychoanal. Perspectives*, 8(2): 179–200.

Ziv, E. (2012). Insidious trauma. *Mafteach*, 5: 55–74 (Hebrew).

Part 3

Tolerance and Group Analysis

Chapter 8

The Transformation of Intolerance

Political Divide, Enactment and Containment in Group Analysis

Robert Grossmark

Prologue

One chilly Saturday night during the seventies, some friends and I were set upon by a group of somewhat drunken bullies. We, a group of North London Jewish teenagers, some wearing yarmulkes, were obviously regarded as easy prey for the ruffians who first surrounded us, then goaded us with the usual assortment of provocations and degradations. They saw Jewish kids as weak and coddled and no doubt, wealthier than them. And we, with resignation and our own condescension, saw them as "the goyim": what else did we expect from them? Reeking of alcohol and cigarettes with bad teeth and the loud accented voices that spoke of an ownership of the streets and the neighborhood where we were no more than trespassers. Our attempts to keep on walking and avoid eye contact, as we had been schooled, were of no use and they were quickly among us, pushing, shoving and blocking our path. I found myself up against a fence being punched and kicked. Not trained in fighting, I was ill equipped to give a good account of myself, and made hopeless attempts to fend off and avoid the blows. Turn the other cheek, I had been taught. For they know not what they do. They don't really hate us. They are just not educated. Once you get to know them. And so on and so on. At some point, enough was enough. I shouted and yelled and began punching the bastard with everything I had, surprising him almost as much as myself, and the fight was quickly over. They scurried off as a group with yelps and sneers, leaving us strewn all over the pavement, picking up and straightening yarmulkes and glasses and nursing cuts and bruises. I was left unsure whether I felt exultant that I had broken through the invisible wall of restraint and tolerance that had surrounded me or whether I had taken a beating and was once again – for there had been numerous versions of this incident before – going to have to recover with the meagre salve of moral superiority and higher aspirations.

I was reminded of this incident as I have struggled to write this chapter. Tolerance was always held up as something to aspire to, a Ghandi like state of transcendence, the path toward a world of greater meaning, understanding and cooperation between people. Recent experiences in our societies and

DOI: 10.4324/9781003200253-12

communities have forced upon us some questions we were quite comfortable ignoring and avoiding. Is there a limit to tolerance? Perhaps "tolerance" itself is the wrong word and the wrong concept for these times, itself pregnant with the dynamics of power, privilege and stigmatization.

When initially invited to write this chapter I had jumped at the chance. I had experienced a powerful sequence in one of my psychotherapy groups. A night after Donald Trump won the 2016 general election in the USA – now my home – the group of seven devastated members had to find a way to engage with a fervent and ecstatic Trump supporter. I felt that the work the group – and myself – had subsequently engaged in illustrated the power of the group to contain and metabolize rage, hatred and fear such that we could find a way to live and work together, if not harmoniously, then at least collaboratively and without lasting damage. In fact, I felt that the work had been helpful for all group members. The paper I was to write would extol the transformational capacities of the group – and no less, the almost saint-like capacities of the therapist to contain and hold the intense pain the whole sequence generated. I have had time to reflect on all of this and now offer a somewhat different rendition of that initial chapter. I will reflect on the events in that group during those first months following Trump's election and will consider the issue of tolerance in both group and individual treatment. At the center of my thinking is the analyst's capacity – or at least attempts – to contain unbearable psychic pain: a task that we can sometimes manage, and sometimes not. Knowing our limits is probably not such a bad thing.

The Group

So here's what happened that Wednesday evening in the group. This is an ongoing group where the members have known each other a long time, some of them for a number of years.

Seven of the eight members arrived on time and all were devastated by the election result, some still disbelieving that it could have happened, everyone appalled, and some scared. After about five minutes Dennis arrived. During the presidential campaign he had occasionally mentioned that he didn't think that the candidate Trump was so bad, but no one had taken the issue up with him, and mostly the group didn't seem to take him too seriously: there were always more pressing and urgent matters to be dealt with in the moment. But his arrival on this night was seismic.

He virtually danced into the room yelling "Yes: We did it!!" and attempted to high five the other group members.

Some were speechless and some immediately enraged. Voices were raised and insults thrown along with incredulity – "You can't believe what you're saying can you?" – and fury. People talked about how they don't recognize the country and certainly Dennis has lost his mind. Dennis responded with fury of his own. How dare you? For eight years he hasn't recognized this country!

"Don't you know how painful it has been for the last eight years (of Obama's presidency) for people like me? We have felt like our country was taken away from us! You can't deny us our turn".

Some members took up actual issues: immigration, walls, respect, the dignity of women and so forth. Dennis flew into the breach: like a mad wrestler and the group engaged.

I recognize such moments as the activation in real time of unmetabolized trauma, where little is talked *about* and everything is lived through in emotional actuality. My work in such situations is to hold the group and internally contain the unbearable pain that is emerging. One hopes to gradually help the group articulate the emotional experience so that the pain can be made real and graspable. When this works, the group can neutralize the toxicity of the trauma and affect and find a path to reality and relatedness. At the core of this position is the idea that such moments are not deviations from the work of the group, but are rather, the thing itself. Dennis was creating in the group – and most importantly, in me – an experience that he had gone through, but had yet to suffer and it was my work to find a place for it, to engage it and to not eradicate or dismiss it. The group, in its inevitable turmoil, disbelief and rage, was about to live through aspects of Dennis's life and mind that he had yet to be able to experience and symbolize in thought and feeling.

So it was with no little effort that I – like the majority in the group, greatly disturbed and appalled by Trump's election – was able to ground myself and actually *think* about what was happening and what might be helpful, and to pay great attention to my own and the group's experience.

I was active. I insisted to the group that diving into the issues of policy and politics – immigration, walls etc. – was not going to help us get the most out of this difficult moment in group. I suggested that we would do much better, and have to work much harder in fact, to try to understand where each of us – and especially Dennis – was coming from. I noticed Henry, usually an ally of Dennis's in the group, both of them being devout Catholics. He had fallen silent. His face had darkened and his temples were throbbing. I checked in with him.

He responded: "It's nothing. I don't give a shit".

Aware of Henry's violent and traumatic early years and his work in the group to find ways to be angry without causing damage to himself or others, I asked what feelings he was having toward Dennis.

Again, and now with anger toward me: "I told you, right now I really don't give a shit!"

Others had picked up on Henry's state and told him that he was clearly in a rage and that it would probably be helpful for him as well as everyone else if he could say what was going on. "Well", Henry ultimately said "I don't think I can look at him (Dennis) right now. If I do, I'll rip his fucking head off!" I should point out that Henry is huge and extremely strong, a regular in the gym and the weight room and has a history of assault and violence. Such comments are not simply metaphorical.

Dennis takes up an old theme of his with petulant justification: "See this is why I can't be in this group. No one understands me and everyone is against me." Dennis himself the middle child of five had spent his entire life in psychic pain, feeling unwanted and invisible and nursing a deep sense of righteous indignation, his lonely life punctuated by bursts of dissociated, sometimes dangerous, self-destructive acting out.

Beyond their shared Catholicism, both of these men share the psychic sequelae of trauma and neglect. Never having been soothed and regulated with consistent parental kindness and love, both lack a developed capacity for containment and are vulnerable to states of too-muchness that have to be evacuated and projected into others and both seek prosthetic regulation in internal sado-masochistic object relations that pervade their interpersonal relations. It is inevitable that such dynamics are repeated in group. The group's work is not simply to eradicate such behavior, but to find, understand and engage with the pain, longing and fear that drives these daunting repetitions, so that these fragmented shards of arousal and pain can be processed and modified within the group matrix. This is the work of building the capacity for containment in the group and in the members' minds as they internalize this quality of the group's functioning. The guiding principle is that these repetitions are not an avoidance of psychological work or remembering, but are a form of remembering and engagement in the register of enactment. They are an untelling (Grossmark, 2024), a narrative that is yet to have symbolization, and the expressing of a long-held need for containment and transformation. The great opportunity in group is to transform these pre-experiences into actual lived and shared experience via the promotion of dialogue and engagement between members, such that rather than being suppressed, these dynamics can find full expression and impact and the group can offer the rudimentary containing function that has been so painfully lacking.

I insisted to Dennis and Henry: "You guys have to find a way to talk to each other. Now!"

And gradually they talked.

"So why the hell do you think like you do?" asks Henry.

For Dennis it is clear that he is energized and inspired by Trump's lack of inhibition: he says whatever he feels, no matter whether, and often because, it is provocative and dangerous. Enough of this superficial and stifling political correctness. The group knows that Dennis was never seen or heard in his family and beyond and there is a slight shift in the sentiment in the room as his idealization of Trump begins to line up with his personal struggle to be recognized and felt. Hence his almost violent percussive entrance that night, emblematic of the conflation of pain and abrasion with human contact and aliveness.

And then when Dennis asks Henry why he is so enraged, Henry is both visibly touched and angrily reticent. He doesn't yet quite believe that Dennis truly wants to know and it takes some time before Dennis can assure him. He is troubled and upset by Henry's very palpable rage. Henry too is unfamiliar with real interest and concern.

He begins. "See you and I, we're mostly allies in here. You know how much I think of you".

And then he returns to the story of terrible trauma that he grew up with that the group knows well: he is also the middle child of five and grew up in a household of violence and fear. But what he talks about this time is new for us. He talks about the family struggle, his father losing his job and then losing his benefits due to Republican policy. He relates the family's struggles with addiction, violence and imprisonment in the eighties to Republican policies that affected unemployment benefits, government assistance and cuts in local programs. Henry's life had been organized around a flight from this painful upbringing and he had developed a remunerative career in financial services in an attempt to distance himself from that very background and from the inner pain and trauma embedded within him. In his work in the financial sector he has seen greed and selfishness. He absolutely sees the power and hates it. These people, he says with deep conviction, destroyed his family. Dennis says he really appreciates what's being said. The atmosphere in the room changes to one of shared melancholy and closeness. Other members, still reeling but now engaged in this sincere dialogue, seem thoughtful and express their appreciation for both men. They find a transitional space within which to hold the horror of Dennis's support for Trump.

An older woman member is able to joke with him about his support for Trump: "Oh now I get it, it's the hair. Irresistible!" And we all chuckle, including Dennis.

With five minutes remaining, Timothy speaks up. He is in Law enforcement. He says has to make an admission to the group. Oh no! Yep: he has to admit: he almost voted for Trump. He just couldn't vote for Hilary Clinton. He is an immigrant from a former Communist country, and cannot stand the pretense of democracy and the entitlement he sees all around. He sees the Clintons as manipulative and deeply untrustworthy. Why not try someone new, he had momentarily thought, ultimately opting to vote for neither. He had been planning to keep this a secret from the group. The other members are shocked again, but this time, the quality of his admission, containing within it some respect for the other members' sensibilities combined with their knowledge of his terrible experiences as a youngster in Communist Eastern Europe allow for an almost sympathetic response from the group. There is still shock, but some understanding that, indeed, many have viewed the Clintons with suspicion.

Over the following few weeks and months there were frequent returns to Dennis, Timothy and Trump. Anger, disgust and fear continued in the group as more cruelty, racism and inhumanity spilled out of the new administration in Washington.

"And now?"

"How are you feeling about him now?"

There were ripples of anger and skirmishes. By and large it seemed to me that the group was finding a way to live with and regulate itself in relation to a true insurmountable difference amongst its members. Yes: there was some understanding regarding Dennis and Timothy's decisions and there were attestations of a brotherhood within the group that could transcend and contain these differences. A family that could manage its splits and oppositions rather than fragment. I myself felt that we had found a way to live with this situation and not avoid it and that the group was providing a good enough holding environment for the anger, pain and potential fragmentation that the election had ignited. The trauma of the election itself and the evocation of early psychic pain and brutality was being held and recognized. No one was asked to disavow their position and there was a degree of empathy and understanding. There was also hurt, disgust and mistrust. But the group continued to do its work and there was a sense of living in a less than perfect reality that seemed honest and real. This felt like the work of tolerance: the holding and detoxification of opposites and combustion. We might say that the dangerously incendiary sub-groupings had found a way to speak to each other. Taking back their projections, they had enabled growth and maturation of the group-as-a-whole (Agazarian, 2010) and restored the unity of the common purpose of the group. Further we might conceptualize the group as having suffered a tremendous and destructive rupture where the moral and unifying third had been threatened and momentarily lost (Benjamin 2018). Lawlessness and destructiveness beckoned and was assuaged by the work of repair fueled by recognition and acknowledgement (Benjamin, 2018).

But …

About one year following the election, Dennis's employers decided to relocate him to another state. In part this was a consequence of difficult relationships with his colleagues in the New York office. Unsurprisingly, the group was not the only place where his internal world of sado-masochistic object relations determined that he would often find himself embroiled in abrasive and destructive interactions. It seemed clear to me that when the position out of state became open, his current managers were quite happy to suggest that he be considered. And thus he announced that he would be leaving the group. There were some weeks to process his leaving and he and the group discussed the many aspects of his time in the group returning on many occasions to the election and their differences. He often clung to the hurt and isolation he experienced in regard to the election and the group returned to their feelings of betrayal, rage and disgust that he could not see who Trump was. Some members talked about the value that Dennis had brought to the group and the loss that his leaving created. Others were unafraid to say that they would be relieved when he was gone. His views, they felt, had invaded the group and caused turmoil and strife. There was, however a shared agreement that they had shared a remarkable experience with Dennis and some suggested that the whole country needed a group experience like this where both sides of the political divide could be expressed and heard.

My feeling at the time was that this passage in the group's life had been beneficial. Pain, aggression and disgust had found recognition and engagement and had been leavened with some empathy, understanding and the solidifying agent of a shared endeavor. I had struggled with my revulsion at Dennis's views, and felt that I and the group had done the work of self-regulation and detoxification of the pain – we had stumbled into containment and had repaired a destructive rupture.

On Being Tolerated

Barry is a young man who first came to me for individual psychotherapy when in college. He was paralyzed by intense obsessions and compulsive habits and struggled with what he called intrusive thoughts. He was so highly anxious around other people that he was struggling with any social contact at his college and had retreated into a lonely life of study and composing electronic music alone. Initially at college, class-mates had invited him to parties and other gatherings, but he was so filled with panic on the few occasions that he did manage to attend that he was barely able to talk, found himself left out of conversations and would leave early and alone. He obsessively washed his hands and was meticulously neat and orderly and would spend hours devoting himself to the maintenance of his room and things. His intrusive thoughts were entirely negative and self-punishing: relentlessly assailing him with the idea that he was a nothing and that he would amount to nothing. He was in a constant state of agitation.

Barry was in despair and quickly engaged in the three times per week treatment. A massive trauma pervaded his and his family's life. Shortly after he was born his father suffered a terrible accident and suffered physical and neurological damage from which he never recovered. He was confined to a wheelchair and required constant attention and care for all his bodily functions. Barry's mother devoted herself entirely to her damaged husband's needs and care. Barry, an only child, was cared for adequately, but always seems to have understood that for his mother, he and his needs were always secondary to his father's. In the first years of the treatment, Barry was able to connect to the pain and anger he felt toward his mother and his father and the terrible guilt that accompanied such feelings. They were, after all, the victims of terrible misfortune. How could he feel anger toward his mother who was burdened by the care for her husband and toward his father, so terribly deprived himself of his prior life and vitality. His obsessive symptoms improved along with his greater emotional freedom and he was able to make some lasting friendships with other young men. However, his anxiety and panic would always resurface when in large social gatherings and when there was any hint of some interest in a young woman. He would retreat to his inner world of persecutory ideation and become awkward and terribly self-conscious. Who would want to hang out with me? I am so inadequate and useless.

But Barry was determined and forced himself to hang out with his friends at social gatherings and to be a part of the group. Things seemed to go well and it did appear that people liked him. He was kind and generous with his friends and revealed a gentle sense of humor. But the inner terror that he was defective like his father remained alongside and despite his progress. One session he appeared in an agitated state. He had discovered that one of the girls in the group had spoken negatively about him and his appearance to someone else. He had barely been able to maintain his calm whilst with the friends but burst into a loud and pained torrent of emotion in the session.

"See, they all think I'm defective! Just like I feared. And you know all this time I have felt that I was doing better, that they really liked me. They don't like me" he yelled "they are TOLERATING ME!! And it is the worst feeling in the world! To be tolerated"!

It was a challenging time in the treatment with Barry. He had taken a powerful blow and it would take some time to recover some equilibrium and to regain his feeling of acceptance with his friends. Furthermore, this incident opened up a painful channel to explore a long-suppressed feeling that, at best, he had always been tolerated, rather than unconditionally loved by his parents. The sessions were painful but he was able to name and face some previously unbearable thoughts and states. But I was struck by his words. To be tolerated is the worst feeling in the world. Why? Because he felt that being tolerated signified an insincerity and a secret hostility behind the veneer of acceptance. Hostility and erasure are wrapped in tolerance. Moreover, he could now see that he had been tolerating his own inner life and feelings. Tolerating rather than actually engaging with these feelings, knowing them for what they were and living them. While digesting these events with Barry, I realized that he was helping me understand something about the experience in the group with Dennis. I will return to this momentarily but first, I was to learn more from Barry.

Along with the hard work of his treatment, Barry developed an interest in, and a growing commitment to, a form of Brazilian jiu jitsu, an athletic and percussive from of martial arts. He attended daily classes and developed considerable competence and prowess. He was much liked by the other members of the club and was chosen to represent the club at tournaments. The benefits were manifold and his self esteem and sense of ownership of his body, now distinct from the damaged body of his father, offered him a path to freedom from the damage and claustrophobia of his parents' world. He also had a wonderful channel to sublimate his aggression and transform helpless and guilt-infused rage into agility and competence.

And then came Covid. We continued our work via Zoom sessions from his room at home. Like so many of us, working on Zoom has offered us a view into the private spaces of many of our patients. And what did Barry have on his wall behind him as we conducted our sessions? A poster of the notorious boxer Mike Tyson with the famous words inscribed under a close-up of his face:

"Everyone has a plan 'till they get punched in the mouth".

And Barry loved this poster. We spoke much about it from many angles. In some ways it summed up his life. There had been a plan for him and it had been derailed in the most violent and obdurate way when his father was injured. It also of course, affirmed a kind of masculinity and power that his father was unable to offer, however contentious such a position is. He gained a sense of strength, bodily coherence and presence that was entirely new for him.

But most compellingly, the Tyson quote captured a sense of grief which began to be palpable for Barry. Grief for the life he should have had, the father and mother he should have had, the body he should have had and the self-possession and self-confidence he should have had, the unborn younger siblings he should have had and that he now fantasized about. The terrible injustice. These sessions were barely tolerable for him and for me. There were many tears and at times over-powering physical symptoms of agitation, pains in his limbs, headaches and tremors as he and his body attempted to contain what had been uncontainable.

Reconsideration and Renewal

In this chapter I have related three separate stories. My personal teenage memory of violence and transformation, the struggle in my psychotherapy group with Dennis and his allegiance to Trump and Barry's painful journey of healing via psychic pain and mourning. Barry was able to utilize the holding environment of the treatment to mourn his parents and the life that was stolen from him when he was "punched in the mouth" by his father's terrible injury. The depressive position involves a deep inscription of the reality principle: life is full of obdurate and unkind truths many of which emanate from our own psyche. Unpleasure, mourning and finitude are the signature of a fully realized life. When my friends and I were attacked by the group of thugs, I had struggled to engage with the reality of hatred and the immutability of actual events and blows. I too was "punched in the mouth" and it took me a few seconds before I could re-arrange my psyche such that I could respond. I had learned what Barry was many years later teaching me: that there is a limit to tolerance; there is a grandiosity to tolerance. Of other and of self. To accept one's limits is to mourn our omnipotence and accept our place in reality.

Which brings me to the group and Dennis with his allegiance to Trump. Perhaps it is true to say that the group was also "punched in the mouth" by Dennis. To this day the group members refer to Dennis and that sequence on occasion with a mix of awe at the intensity of the hatred and fear that was held in the room, relief that Dennis left the group and sadness that the group was ultimately unable to help him sufficiently with the hurt and injury that he carried. Yes, he left because he was re-assigned at work, but the feeling is palpably that a larger narrative of limit and division was enacted. During this period of history in the USA we are living in a time of "cold civil war". People take sides and live in completely different realities, narratives and histories. It would seem that the social unconscious (Hopper & Weinberg, 2011) spoke louder than any personal or group work could comprehend and contain. History over-rides personal psychic containment. Perhaps some ruptures can be repaired at some times and at other times they both cannot be repaired by us and maybe should not be.

For Dennis and his political views to have been accepted with tolerance would have been, as Barry so poignantly said "the worst feeling in the world". What was required was a metabolization of trauma and hatred and I do believe that the group was able to accomplish meaningful work in that area. But we came up against a greater force. We had a plan and were "punched in the mouth" by history: a painful but ultimately realistic engagement with the depressive position and irreparable rupture. And we mourn and we are healed.

References

Agazarian, Y. M. (1989). Group-as-a-whole system theory and practice. *Group*, *13*, 131–154.

Benjamin, J. (2018) *Beyond Doer and Done To: Recognition Theory, Intersubjectivity and the Third*, Abingdon, UK & New York, NY: Routledge, Taylor & Francis.

Grossmark, R. (2024) The Untelling. *Psychoanalytic Dialogues*, *34*(1), 13–19.

Hopper, E. & Weinberg, H. (2011) *The Social Unconscious in Persons, Groups and Societies. Volume 1: Mainly Theory*, Abingdon, UK & New York, NY: Routledge, Taylor & Francis.

Chapter 9

The Development of Tolerance in a "Prisoners' Matrix"

Ella Stolper

The opportunity to teach in former USSR countries after my departure and not setting foot there for almost 30 years, brought to my memory an episode from my work as a probation officer 20 years ago. It brought me back to a frightening, moment in my life, perhaps as an attempt to warn me regarding the upcoming trip.

He and I sat together in a small windowless prison cell, a strait stone table dividing the space between us, and the steel door locked. I, who came to make a court ordered assessment, sat down first, and he, who was imprisoned for severe violence towards his ex-girlfriend, walked slowly towards the table. The guard explained to me about the button I should push at the end of the meeting or if I'm in distress, and he disappeared in the narrow hallway. The prisoner spoke in length, trying to convince me to recommend to the court to release him to house arrest subject to restrictions. I listened to his threats, to the stories of his tantrums against her and the hemorrhages left in her body. In an impulsive revelation, he also told me of a "pocket" with razor blade pieces that he sews to his palate to attack those who "talk back" to him at the prison.

"You have to watch your back, or you're screwed".

I, too, decided to be frank and when he asked me, "What will you recommend to the court?"

I answered, "Not to release you at the moment, because you are high risk".

He stared quietly at the floor when I collected the papers from the desk and was getting ready to leave, when suddenly the light had shut off and the room turned completely dark. I heard steps in the hallways and knocking on the door in an adjacent cell, and a guard's distant scream: power outage! I froze in my chair, this time without the ability to say anything. The steel door got locked, and I immediately felt paralyzed, covered with cold sweat. It's only him, me, and razor blade pieces sawn in his palate. I lost faith that the door would open; within seconds, I became a prisoner.

A memory in which I became a prisoner behind locked doors, behind the "Iron Curtain" and the country's metaphorical detention facility, hovering over the country's residents. The threat of imprisonment and of losing one's

DOI: 10.4324/9781003200253-13

freedom, even after the fall of Soviet regime, was formed through intergenerational transmission of the collective traumatic events.

In this paper, I discuss the development of tolerance in group analysis in the post-communist society of the USSR. For this purpose, I will discuss two concepts –"Prisoner Matrix" and "Tolerance" – present historical background, explore their mutual influences and interactions, discuss the social unconscious of post-communist societies in eastern Europe and use a seminar that I have led there as an example.

According to Foulkes, the matrix is the hypothetical web of communication and relationship in a given group which involves all levels of communication. "The individual takes part in its shaping and creation and at the same time rebuilds the conditions for his primary web as he experiences it" (Foulkes, 1964, p. 292). Hopper (2003) argues that the stronger the annihilation anxiety or the hope for fame are in a given matrix, the more people tend to identify with it – with both its positive and destructive aspects. Friedman suggests looking at cultures that exist in a state of war, as societies that exist in the "Soldier Matrix" where the identity of its members is affected by the level of their "mobilization" (Friedman, 2015).

I propose "Prisoner Matrix" as a definition of cultures with characteristic of communist and post-communist societies which can also be found in non-democratic regimes characterized by the ruling of a single leader or political party, prohibition of freedom of speech and persecution of dissidents. "Prisoner Matrix" is a dynamic matrix that describes the culture, structure and atmosphere in which the entire society functions as a prison for its citizens. People that live under such regimes are characterized by distrust, obedience and much suspicion of the government and authority figures as well as of each other, due to the snitching phenomenon among citizens. Arbitrary punishment, absence of fair trial, forced hospitalizations and executions create annihilation anxiety in this matrix.

Groups, like individuals, have an immune system with mechanisms of regulation, control and protection that keep it from attacking itself, but in rare instances, due to disruption in these mechanisms, a group – just like a body that does not recognize its own organs – destroys them as if they were foreign invaders (Goren, 2016). I believe that this definition can be applied also to societies that develop in a Prisoner Matrix. In my view, these societies have an autoimmune structure in which the government, through snitching mechanisms attack other citizens by recognizing them as foreign invaders. The imprisonment experience and its effects on the matrix do not only apply to the period of the dictatorial regime but remain decades after.

My Own Personal "Prisoner Matrix"

I was born in a Soviet regime country and witnessed the fall of the Iron Curtain in my adolescence. The end of the cold war and the dissolution of the Soviet

Union brought immense relief to countries that were under its political oppression. However, at the same time, they also led to a quick collapsing of the social and political structure, causing chaos that led to many new losses and much suffering. The radical metamorphosis from dictatorial communism to democracy created much uncertainty and instability that was hardly contained and processed emotionally.

At the age of 17, together with my family, I said goodbye to my home town, knowing that this goodbye is final, just like the death of a loved one. The night before the emigration to Israel, I went with my childhood friends to say goodbye to all the places, smells and buildings that were my home. I knew that there was a possibility – that was not unlikely at all – that I will never return to these places. I knew that that happened to my grandmother, who emigrated to Israel in the seventies with my mother's younger sister, and then the heavy door of the Iron Curtain was closed behind them for an unknown period of time. I grew up in the shadow of my mother's tears, as she read aloud her mother's letters every two months, letters that were delivered to our house half open after being inspected by the KGB. My mother's tears were a sign of a painful family rupture between my mother and her mother and young sister that were separated from her by the Iron Curtain, when for many years the prospect of union seemed like a surreal fantasy. In addition, like all relatives of people who "defected" to the West, our social status was lowered due to our relationship with people who were considered as traitors of the state. Family members who remained in touch with the "defectors" aroused suspicion in the environment and were sometimes even perceived as traitors themselves due to the contact with them.

My mother's painful separation from her family found expression in her fear of separation and when I reached adolescence, I encountered her panic of my need for separateness when she prohibited that I shut the door of my room. She experienced the shutting of the door as final detachment and separation between us, just like the locking of the Iron Curtain that separated her from her family for dozens of years until we finally emigrated to Israel in the nineties. Paradoxically, the wide-open door of my room in adolescence formed my own personal matrix of prisoners, which was intimately related to the closed door of the Iron Curtain.

Foundation Stones of the Social Unconscious

Foulkes, the founder of group analysis, held classic psychoanalytic views but also enriched them with new, radical terms such as the "social unconscious" (Foulkes, 1975).

According to Hopper, the pressure to conform and obey in societies that suffer from massive collective trauma is immense, and personal identity is expressed through belonging to a collective (Hopper, 2003). Personal and social identities were blurred in various ways in the Soviet Union's republics, when one of them was conquest through language. Russian became the official dominant language in the Soviet republics, with all formal communication from road signs to official documents done in Russian regardless of the mother tongue of that country.

Bohleber (2007) argues that a generation that experienced a collective trauma – without any recognition or processing of its traumatic experiences – embeds its wound in the social unconscious as a collective memory which then passes to the next generations in the form of traumatic object relations. In my view, living under the Soviet regime was traumatic, a collective trauma with no recognition, mourning or processing. More than that, the social, political, and financial crises caused by the collapse of the Soviet Union made people idealize the Soviet era and even miss it. Although *Perestroika* means re-building, it brought mainly chaos, instability, and poverty. The processing of collective trauma was inhibited remained socially unconscious.

Tolerance

Tolerance comes from the Latin word *tolerantia*, and is a sociological term and moral value that involves acceptance and respectful attitude towards people who are different socially, culturally and religiously. Disagreement is a necessary condition for tolerance, since it necessarily involves difference between the individual and the object of his tolerance. Tolerance is different from restraint, indifference and benefit in that it involves conscious choice, and thus is necessarily an active and not passive attitude. The values tolerance tries to protect are freedom and equal freedom of choice. On a social level, it requires caring for others' wellbeing, acceptance of others and refraining from use of power against values, opinions and behaviors that are inconsistent with its values.

In Hebrew, as opposed to English, tolerance ("Sovlanut") and patience ("Savlanut") are two different words that share the same root, and even though this shared root assumes conceptual resemblance, their meaning is different. In Russian, the word tolerance does not exist at all and it is replaced with the term "tolerance for otherness" and in that it emphasizes an aspect that is completely different from the term's meaning in English. Whereas in Russian, tolerance refers to a passive attitude towards otherness, the English definition of tolerance refers to an active attitude/action that is based on recognition of the right for otherness, which requires conscious investment in accepting the other. It seems that there is a conceptual link between Russian and Hebrew, in that both base the term on a similar root "suffer". In addition to this resemblance between Hebrew and Russian in the context of tolerance, I believe that there is also a resemblance in the perception of otherness. Israel's continuous conflict with the Palestinians generates a split-off view of between "us and them", of two nations that are found on two sides of the conflict and the "Prisoner Matrix" that splits the regime and its opposer-citizens. Borodizki argues that there is a close relationship between language and people's thinking and views.

She believes that language does not only reflect and structure our reality, but it also dictates basic dimensions of the whole human experience, including how others are treated. Thus, it can be concluded that the definition of tolerance in different societies is indicative of how they treat this issue (Borodizki, 2003).

Harban (2003) argues that tolerant cultures are characterized by openness to otherness, interactions with different cultures, a non-hierarchical internal cultural structure and high social mobility. The level of tolerance in societies is measured, among other things, through the level of physical, economic and cultural isolation of the society from other societies. Intolerance is more widespread in societies in which the regime holds on to an exclusive perception of the truth.

Aron (2017) argues that tolerance is not a polite coexistence, but willingness to be criticized by someone who is different from me. According to him, "reflective skepticism" and "critical pluralism" facilitate the development of tolerance that occurs in the form of balanced movement between the common and distinguishing features, not only for the sake of comparison and contrast or to achieve integration, but to learn from each other's opposite views. Aron believed that tolerance is vital for our mental development and that there is much to gain from expressing mutual respect in the encounter with otherness.

Is tolerance possible in a Prisoner Matrix? I would like to argue that a Prisoner Matrix that develops in the context of a dictatorial, hierarchic and castrating regime in its very essence blocks balancing movement between oppositions and represses pluralistic and critical thinking, thereby systematically hindering the development of tolerance in its population. Such regimes reinforce excellence, ambitiousness and obedience which are then intensified, and develop mechanisms that ensure single mindedness and cohesion as a basic condition for their existence. The regime's cruel punishment for expressions of otherness creates very challenging conditions for development of tolerance and resulted in traumatic stagnation.

Case Study

Below I describe a group that I have facilitated in one of the former Soviet republics (not Russia), in which the group and I got trapped in a Prisoner Matrix, and I will discuss the necessary conditions for development of tolerance in the group

The group that met as part of the seminar "Trauma, dissociation and psychological witnessing in therapy" included therapeutic professionals and took place in one of the former Soviet republics in recent years. The seminar's structure included theoretical lessons and supervision of the participants' clinical work.

"Are you recording?" Julia asked Rima, who sat next to her during the second day of the seminar.

"Me? No way", she answered hesitantly

"You are recording us! I can see the record button on your phone".

"Maybe I pressed it by accident", she replied embarrassedly

"I knew it", Julia continued passionately, "it wasn't by accident, I saw how you deliberately arranged your phone and how you reopened it after the recess. To tell the truth, I wasn't sure whether I should say something, I was afraid of exposing you, but since people are saying personal things about themselves, I decided that they have to know that they are being recorded".

Loud silence filled the room. I was surprised and angry with Rima. Her turning on a recording device secretly in the room hit me and elicited in me strong feelings about breaking the rules and attacking the supervisory setting. Even though I did not speak, the shock was evident on my face, and in my mind resurfaced the persecutory gaze of the big brother who penetrates private areas and listens secretly to the occurrences. I looked at the participants' faces and I could feel that a storm was coming.

The participants attacked Rima cruelly, their words becoming more and more humiliating, with threats of punishment and social exclusion. Rima sat in her chair paralyzed, ashamed and terrified and I had associations of a public execution. Nevertheless, I didn't rush to stop the attack and deep down I felt she deserved punishment for her actions. I remained silent for a long time, consumed in my reverie about my childhood. My mother used to punish me when I expressed opinions that were different from hers. I felt guilty about my fantasy to punish Rima, but through my reverie, I realized that I grew up in a similar matrix in which otherness threatens and is punished.

After a while the course coordinator threatened Rima with revoking her psychologist's license and when I saw that no one came to her rescue, I stopped the attack.

I was shaken by the intense aggression of the group and by my passive position that was expressed by my looking away from the attack until I finally stopped it. I thought about my silence, my anger at Rima and my identification with the attacking group in the moment of discovery. Grossmark's words on the therapist's active part in the enactment in the analytic situation came to my mind. (Grossmark, 2007). I suggested to the group to reflect together on the process that was taking place in the room.

"Recording without permission the seminar's facilitator and participants who are sharing clinical and personal materials is without a doubt a hurtful and unethical thing to do" – I told the group –

"but since for me it was obvious that recording in the seminar is forbidden, I did not mention this as part of the setting when we started the seminar. In addition, I believe that this occurrence is closely tied to the group dynamics and the subject of the seminar and I invite us to reflect on the occurrences in view of this specific context".

Rima, how did you learn about the seminar?" Valery asked insistently. "You are not a part of the psychoanalytic community, right?"

"That's true", Rima replied, "I belong to a different school, but why do you ask?"

"Perhaps in your school the rules are different", Valery replied arrogantly.

"We are trying to reject her because she is the only one who doesn't belong to this group in her professional training", Natalia suggested cautiously.

"Our psychoanalytic community is closed and it does not easily accept new people", Helena added.

"You speak Russian and not our language. Perhaps the fact that we all have to go back to speaking Russian for you and to put our language aside reminds us of the Soviet conquest", Olga dared to challenge me.

"I was disappointed with you, I expected you to punish Rima and not protect her", Svetlana added while looking at me. "She broke the psychoanalytic rules here and you didn't protect them, and thus you did not protect us. I don't understand all the talk about belongingness, what does it have to do with anything".

"Your courage to say things to me directly is important to me, I would like to hear more voices", I said to the group.

"You didn't punish Rima", Lera said. "Perhaps we attacked her instead of you; we came close to revoking her license to do psychotherapy. You are one of us, but you left, you emigrated to Israel and you are living there, it arouses envy".

"The rules regarding recording were not entirely clear, there were theoretical seminars in which recording was allowed", Helena remarked.

"I find it very confusing and stressful that every little mistake can cost me my license, and also that the entire therapy profession can be eliminated here in one arbitrary governmental decision", said Valery.

"The fear of the authority's attack and vengeance is intense", I said to the group. "You've attacked and sacrificed the person who broke the rules of the setting in the group. I believe that the scapegoating process related to a collective trauma in which a violation of the boundaries of the establishment is severely punished".

"Your reaction is different from our professors", said Inga, "they surely would have had a fierce reaction to such a situation".

"To say the truth", I suddenly heard Julia again,

"I need to make a confession. I, too, recorded in the first day of the seminar – only the lectures and not the supervision sessions – but I, too, did not ask for permission. I wanted to hear the recording later in quiet when I'm alone, to take something from you back home with me, and I was also afraid that I would not remember everything".

As the discussion continued, after the scapegoating process – that had been a traumatic repetition of prisoner matrix in which the breaking of rules and open criticism of the regime could end in catastrophe – had stopped, three other people raised their hands and told that they, too, recorded the seminar in the first day. The people who confessed doing so were Rima's main attackers, who wanted to expel her from the group and revoke her professional license.

In those moments, the recording didn't seem to me anymore an attack on the setting only; it was an appeal for my sympathetic witnessing of a trauma that they have experienced, that we have experienced. A cruel attack and denial of freedom and working license due to expressions of otherness and challenging of the setting were a repetition of the trauma, and the attempt to obtain recorded evidence, embodied a wish not to lose one's individuality in the annihilation performed by the collective or regime. The group asked that I, who, too, belonged to a prisoner matrix and knew it from inside – but was also a foreigner who had been living almost 30 years in a western society – validate, recognize, and serve as a empathic witness to the accumulated trauma of living under the Soviet regime.

The group stopped identifying me and Rima with "foreign invaders" who attacked it from inside and resorted from its attack to new areas of reflection and processing of traumatic experiences that were accumulated in the shared "Prisoner Matrix". We could all breathe again.

Analysis of the Example

The group and I were caught in a "Prisoner Matrix" that excluded and annihilated the other for rising against the structure (setting/regime). In the beginning, the group identified me as a foreigner and the discussion that took place in Russian – language that was forced by me – resonated in the group as conquest, perhaps since Russian (the only language that we shared) was experienced as the voice of the conqueror. The trauma, that held its grip on me along with the group, served as an "unthought known" (Bollas, 1989) and was repeated by displacing the anger at the conquest on my part to the "participant who recorded" the seminar against the rules that I did not clearly state.

"The public execution" of the participant who broke the rules of the setting demonstrated in the group the social trauma of people who lived in a prisoner matrix and internalized its principles. The participant who broke the rules by Recording in secret the supervised session represents the traumatic part of snitching mechanisms in the Prisoner Matrix. The participants attacked cruelly and relentlessly the "recording participant" in front of my wide shut eyes and with my silent agreement. The totalitarian and punitive authority took over me when the secretive recording act was revealed. I experienced the recording as an unforgivable breaching of the supervisory space and my silence served as permission to attack those who I experienced as attacking the psychoanalytic setting.

Later, my coming to the defense of the person who breached the group setting and the privacy of the group participants was for me a spontaneous movement of freedom and an expression of tolerance for otherness that until that moment I had experienced as intolerable. This act of freedom required me to break free from the ties of the conquering, totalitarian identity inside me and bestowed on me, and move towards a freer identity that can challenge conventions. My holding and recognition of multiple identities inside me allowed me to find in myself tolerance for the "other" who attacked the psychoanalytic structure and freedom to object to the policy of executing people who spoke against the system. Simington (1983) described the "act of freedom" as spontaneous, intuitive moment that stems from the therapist's choice to take a path that is different from what is accustomed or expected at that moment, a path that expresses his selfhood authentically.

I would like to argue that the therapist's "Act of Freedom" is vital but insufficient to facilitate and develop tolerance in a group process in general, and when working in the group with a "prisoner matrix" in particular; it is only the first step in the process. The second stage requires the group therapist's active encouragement and invitation to express directly anger and criticism towards the authority figure. As was shown in the case described above, this stage allowed participants to stop sacrificing the "recording participant", the scapegoat, and engage in an open, direct dialogue with the authority about the silenced and undiscussed aspects of their relationship.

And finally, as a third stage of the process, the group used me as an analytic third (Ogden, 1991) that could recognize and witness the collective trauma they have experienced in the Soviet regime. I believe that recognition and sympathetic witnessing alongside setting clear boundaries without "execution" policies allowed the group to step out of the "guard and prisoner" pattern, overcome the stagnation and dissociative barriers that the traumatic experiences left in the mind and move towards a real encounter with their own multiple identities and with the other inside them.

Act of Freedom as Promoting Tolerance in the Group

I argue that the processing of social traumas supports the development of tolerance in the analytic group and in society. Collective traumas are repressed to the social unconscious and could be reactivated, especially in situations of threat.

The therapist's entanglement and entrapment in the trauma experienced by the group is inevitable, since the therapist and group are enslaved, in Symington's words, by the personality-cultural illusion that turns them into a single communicative unit. In addition, I believe that the entrapment in traumatic personality-cultural materials is also necessary for reaching deep insight regarding the trauma that froze without processing or recognition.

The group therapist's or one of the participants' act of freedom allows being in touch with traumatic material that was forbidden for thinking. Act of freedom leads to insight and recognition of the trauma and to the development of tolerance.

The recognition and witnessing of traumatic experiences that are told in the group in the form of a mumbling symptom (Foulkes, 1964) or enactment (Grossmark, 2007) are necessary conditions for moving out of the traumatic repetition. However, my argument is that the main agent of change in the development of tolerance is the internal act performed by the analyst or members of the group, when he and the group get trapped together in the ties of prohibitions and limitations to thinking. The most internal mental act is significant; through it the therapist and members regain their freedom.

When the analyst is trapped in the enactment and cannot free himself, sometimes one of the group members can be the one who performs an act of freedom in the group, and allow the entire group, including the therapist, to free itself. This situation requires from the therapist willingness to be in a state of unknowing, trust the power of the group and encourage the participants' act of freedom without vengeance.

Summary

In conclusion, I would like to argue that to develop tolerance in general, and in a Prisoner Matrix – in which the group and therapist are trapped in an enactment – the analyst and the participants must find inside them internal freedom to challenge the conventions of the controlling structure that they sometimes identify with and to process their collective trauma. Act of freedom entails meeting their multiple identities, overcoming the entrapment and dissociation, and moving towards an experience of freedom and healing. This intrapsychic process of meeting multiplicity of voices, including those who challenge conventions, can develop freer interpersonal communication free of dangers of execution and exclusion and promote a culture of tolerance in the group associated with mental health.

References

Aron, L. (2017). Beyond Tolerance in Psychoanalytic Communities: Reflexive Skepticism and Critical Pluralism. *Psychoanalytic Perspectives*, 14(3).

Bohleber, W. (2007) Remembrance, trauma and collective memory – The battle for memory in psychoanalysis. Paper presented at the *45th International Psychoanalytical Association Congress*, Berlin, Germany (71–282).

Bollas, C. (1989). *Shadow of the Object*. New York: Columbia University Press.

Boroditsky, L. (2003). Linguistic Relativity. In: L. Nadel (Ed.) *Encyclopedia of Cognitive Science*, pp. 917–921. London: MacMillan Press.

Foulkes, S.H. (1964). *Therapeutic Group Analysis*. London: Karnac.

Foulkes, S.H. (1975). The leader in the group. In E. Foulkes (Ed.) *Selected Papers of S.H. Foulkes: Psychoanalysis and Group Analysis*. London: Karnac.

Friedman, R. (2015). A soldier's matrix: A group analytic view of societies in war. *Group Analysis*, 48(3), 239–257.

Goren, N (2016). "Immune system" in an analytical therapeutic group. In: R. Friedman and Y. Doron (Eds) *Group Analysis in the Land of Milk and Honey*. London: Karnac.

Grossmark R. (2007). The Edge of Chaos: Enactment, Disruption, and Emergence in Group Psychotherapy. *Psychoanalytic Dialogue*, 17(4): 479–499.

Harban, A. (2003). *The State of Human Dignity*. The Israel Democracy Institute.

Hopper, E. (2003). *The Social Unconscious*. London: Jessica Kingsley Publishers.

Simington, N. (1983). The analyst's act of freedom as agent of therapeutic change. *The International Journal of Psychoanalysis*, 10(3), 283–291.

Chapter 10

From Dead Ends to Live Exchanges

"Social Tolerance" in the Analytic Group

Liat Warhaftig Aran

Introduction

In this chapter, I will discuss the development of "social tolerance" in analytic groups. Social tolerance is an intersubjective achievement that develops between members of a group, including the conductor, but has an intrapsychic aspect as well. Analytic groups enable a meeting of various needs and experiences, and sometimes contradicting voices. I hold that emotional openness of a mature analytic group will support the evolvement of tolerance to social and political "otherness". The democratic spirit of the analytic group, which entails discussing of its norms, supports the practicing of "social tolerance". I propose that taking in social otherness as represented by other members of the group requires rebelling against one's old unconscious social identifications. I suggest that the conductor's unconscious intolerance and conscious social attitudes influence the group's "social tolerance" and should be reflected upon. I will demonstrate my personal journey to "social tolerance" and its effect on my group.

"Social Tolerance"

"Social tolerance" involves readiness to be open to contrasting attitudes and conflictual opinions of others, willingness to influence, be influenced and to compromise. Tolerance is close to the concepts of the depressive position (Klein, 1940), because it leads to increased capacity for compromise. Tolerance has common ground with the idea of "mutual recognition" (Benjamin, 1990), as relationships with the other offer the possibility to enjoy sharing and otherness without submission or control. However, I propose that the idea of "social tolerance" is focused on our social attitudes and identifications and emphasizes solidarity, which is readiness to express empathy and acts of care for members of one's social group, but also for groups with contradicting interests. "Social tolerance" is a sign of advanced societies, which requires not only freedom and equality, but also enough space for one to be able to care for others. When this quality of societies develops, it can deepen one's sense of belonging to society.

DOI: 10.4324/9781003200253-14

"Social tolerance" is a challenging achievement because it requires overcoming self-centeredness and since intolerance is embedded in societies, including in democratic societies. Discussion of the sources of intolerance is beyond the scope of this paper, but it can be worthwhile to mention in this context Carl Popper's 1945 book, "The open society and its enemies". Popper claimed that "utopic societies" are usually connected by one strong leader. In "utopic societies", arguing opposing views risks the ideology, which leads to a closed and rigid society. He claims that despite its flaws, democracy is the preferrable regime because it allows various points of view and changing its leaders.

"Social Tolerance" in Group Analysis

The literature indicates that the struggle for tolerance is often held by minorities (Dalal, 2014). In contrast, my aim is to explore the development of "social tolerance", which refers to members' sense of responsibility and readiness to care for their own interests and for the needs of other group members.

Following Berger's (2017) discussion of democracy in Foulkes's writing, I propose that the idea of "social tolerance" is close to Foulkes's ideas, even though it is not mentioned specifically. For Foulkes, mutual emotional care in the small group is expressed by exchange that involves willingness to share one's successes and difficulties while also leaving room for others' successes and difficulties (Foulkes & Anthony, 1975, p. 82).

According to the "basic law of group dynamics" (Foulkes, 1948, p. 9), group members and conductor determine together the group norms that obligate the group, a process that constitutes the behavioral aspect of "social tolerance".

I would like to claim that the analytic group is a good space for the development of "social tolerance". The process involves, on the one hand, rebellion against one's identifications with significant others and against various, conflicted social groups one belongs to. On the other hand, it involves a peaceful process of meeting others who are "like enough subjects". Aron (2017) argues that for one to doubt one's perception, one needs to experience the other as part of his DNA and not as a strange object. Aron argues that the idea of a mother's mirroring to her baby represents a mirror that is both similar and different. This form of distance allows influence and openness to the other, who is an "enough like subject".

My Journey Towards "Social Tolerance"

Two relationships have affected my development of tolerance: my relationships with my parents and grandparents. I grew up in a religious family that lived in a mixed community of secular and religious Jews in a Jewish settlement beyond the Green Line. My parents arrived there due to rightist ideology and found themselves a part of a mixed community, which wasn't the original reason for their decision to live there, but gradually they came to identify with the idea and became involved in the community. I grew up feeling that tolerance has to do with dialogue and compromise, but when two of my siblings and I chose to leave religion, I faced my parents' disappointment, which had hurt me and surprised me in view of the tolerant attitude I have experienced at the settlement. Today, after many years, I feel that my parents came to accept me and my decision to leave religion. In retrospect, I experience my parents' struggle to be true to themselves and still accept the other as a live process, which involves disappointment, compromise, and acceptance, as a moving process of developing tolerance.

My grandfather, Dr. Zorach Warhaftig, a religious man and a jurist, who was one of the lawyers who signed the Scroll of Independence and was the minister of religions for many years, agreed to my request at adolescence to study Talmud together, but also to read poems by Yona Wolach, a provocative poet who certainly wasn't popular in the religious community. In 1947, when he served as minister of religions, he suggested the "status quo" principle that specifies legal guidelines for the complicated relationship between religion and state in a country that is torn between different nations and between secular and religious Jews. The "status quo" principle is identified with "consociational politics", according to which in countries that involve many nations, decisions about controversial issues are made by subgroups' leaders through negotiation and not by the majority's decision, in order to maintain stability and representation of diverse groups in the population. I was impressed by my grandfather's active, incessant efforts to engage in negotiation with rival political parties of the conflicted religious sector and outside it, and I experienced him as a leader whose actions demonstrated tolerance.

As opposed to this practice of tolerance regarding religion that I experienced in my childhood home, I experienced their attitudes regarding the Israeli Palestinian conflict as extremist and intolerant. As a result, I developed antagonism towards extremist attitudes and hating of the other and it was always difficult for me to hear the hatred expressed on both sides of the political map towards Arabs, ultra-orthodox Jews and seculars. My search for a tolerant home was expressed in the professional field as well. I have found in group analysis and relational psychoanalysis a tolerant home that allows multiplicity of professional languages. Still, in the political field, I have encountered an almost absolute hegemony of the political left and experienced some of its messages regarding settlers, religious Jews and ultra-orthodox Jews – who remain a part of my childhood and of myself – as extremist. I reacted to this by positioning myself in the center of the map, to avoid radicality and hatred.

The writing of this chapter allowed me to reflect on the complexity of the tolerance experience, which can exist regarding one issue but not another. I also reflected on my choosing of a centrist attitude as a tolerant attitude that objects to extremism, but in some cases, can also express avoidance of taking a stand, which decreased my ability to develop dialogue between positions – something that is also vital for developing tolerance. In the example that I present below, I show how I managed to step out of my centrist position and how this led to development of social tolerance in my group.

Example

An analytic group that has been meeting for a for few years included seven participants: six Jews and an Arab.

In previous years, we used to start the group 15 minutes late to allow an Arab participant who celebrated the Ramadan holiday to get a chance to eat after the fast before coming to the group, a change in the setting that I had initiated. This year, Independence Day was celebrated on the day of the group meeting and during the month of the Ramadan holiday. At the end of the session, I suggested to the group to reschedule the group meeting and to start, as usual, fifteen minutes later. I didn't leave time for discussion and the group quickly agreed to my suggestion. In the following session, the atmosphere was one of emotional detachment. Dana, an assertive participant, told of a conflict she had had with her aunt, which ended with a rift. Dana was pleased with her tough reaction since her aunt had hurt her badly in the past. The group reacted with polite appreciation of Dana's toughness, without relating to her aggression and refusal to engage in a dialogue with her aunt. Sari said that lately the group conversations feel shallow to her, like "small talk" on the bus, and that she is considering leaving the group. My association was to bus bombings, which were frequent in Israel at that time, but I kept it to myself since I was afraid of offending Amira, an Arab participant. Gal asked Dana about her experiences as a new immigrant, but Dana argued decisively that she has always felt special and not different. Although this question did not lead to exploration of the issue of being different, I suddenly recalled the changes in the setting that I initiated before this session and invited the group to relate to this. Amira said that for her, Independence Day is a day of mourning. Others argued that the thoughtfulness regarding Ramadan is acceptable and important to them but ignored her comment about Independence Day. It seemed to me that the group was protective of Amira because she was the only Arab in the group. The discussion of the setting was brief and led to a political discussion. Amira expressed anger at her experience of government's discrimination against Israeli Arabs, pain about the "Nakba" (the expelling and escaping of Israeli Arabs to Arab countries in 1948) that some Israeli Arabs commemorate on Israel's Independence Day, and general rage towards the state of Israel, which she compared to the Nazis. The atmosphere was cautious; some of the members stayed silent, while others expressed interest in Amira's experience. At the end of the session, Dana cried and said that she misses her dear aunt. Her sharing made the atmosphere a little more emotional and intimate and Sagit told of abuse she had experienced in elementary school. In retrospect, I realized that the group was able to share openly aggression-related events mainly from a victim's position, when aggression was attributed to external factors, since it was experienced as a risk for relationships and thus was not explored inside the group.

Only two group members attended the following session, one of them was Amira, a fact that I related to Amira's phrase that I, too, had trouble with: that "the state of Israel is treating Israeli Arabs just like the Nazis treated Jews". I understood the members' absence as their difficulty to be in a conflicted discourse in general, or in a complementary state in which otherness is experienced as elimination. I thought that my decision regarding the change in the setting expressed my desire for "social tolerance", but since I discussed it with the group only partially, perhaps the group experienced it as my desire to please everyone and avoid conflict.

In the following sessions, the group met online because of the coronavirus pandemic. The topic of the Israeli-Palestinian conflict was marginalized as the group was preoccupied with the pandemic and lockdown.

Towards the end of the lockdown, after a few weeks of working online, I announced that in the beginning of next week we would be able to meet in person. Sagit, who suffered from anxieties, expressed strong fear of contagion, and preferred to continue meeting online and so did Gal. She shared, shamefully, that it is a known fact that the Arab sector, as well as religious Jews sector, that suffered more from the virus. Since our group included Amira, an Arab, and Shimon, who is a religious Jew, she was even more anxious about meeting in person.

The other members preferred to meet face-to-face since they felt that they were unable to express themselves during the online sessions. At the same time, some of them were hesitant regarding the obligation to wear masks during the face-to-face sessions. Sagit was angry with me for not finding a solution that would allow meeting in the open-air without masks, while others were angry with Sagit for her intolerance for Amira and Shimon. I refused to meet without masks because it was against the guidelines, and I realized that I would not be able to please everyone. Hence, I suggested to the group to continue meeting online to maintain homogeneity in the group, or to meet in our room wearing masks. The group had a difficult time deciding, each position was experienced as intolerable by one of the subgroups and this resulted in continuous tension. I decided to keep meeting online for another two sessions to express consideration for those who fear meeting face-to-face and then to resume face-to-face sessions wearing masks, when members who fear contagion would join us online. I felt insecure about the unstable setting and was worried of losing participants. I hoped that the group would experience my adherence to the health guidelines as beneficent holding and my "changing preference" of the subgroups' contradicting needs as fair.

Finally, we resumed face-to-face sessions while Sagit and Gal joined us online. The group discussed various matters in a relatively open spirit and intimacy. During these meetings, some of the participants expressed criticism of Sagit, who they experienced as passive during the online meetings, while they made efforts to include her. They interpreted this as Sagit's ambivalence about the group.

When the national vaccination program started, Sagit and Gal returned to the face-to-face meetings. The group welcomed them but insisted on exploring their decision to stick with the online format: they wanted to know whether it resulted only from their fear of contagion or also from ambivalence about the group. Sagit admitted that she has been disappointed with the group, since she expected her life to change already in ways that it did not. Oded was especially angry about Sagit's refusal to come to face-to-face meetings. When he was invited to explore his powerful resonance, he shared his fear of authority figures as someone who grew up in a post-communist country, and his envy of Sagit who could challenge my authority.

However, other members were happy that Sagit was able to come and speak of her disappointment. I proposed that Sagit's attitude towards the group resembled her relationships with partners, when after enthusiastic beginnings she experienced disappointment, withdrew, and remained lonely. I complimented her for her insistence to stay in the conversation about her disappointment and complimented the group for their willingness to "pull her back" to the group. Sagit was surprised by the warm acceptance of the group and was curious about my interpretation.

The political conflict we had was left untouched for a few weeks, along with Sagit's comment about religious Jews and Arabs as "bringing" Covid to the group. It seemed that the group needed to practice tolerating conflict regarding safer topics such as the pandemic before returning to explosive matters. In the subsequent session, I decided to reraise for discussion the time of the session during the Ramadan, which had not yet end. The group expressed various opinions, few were ready to start later, but Dana said that she will not be able to finish later.

Since the group did not agree unanimously on the change, I decided to leave the regular time of the meetings as it was. This discussion led back to Amira's comparison of the Israeli government to the Nazis. Dana said that her grandparents were saviors of the holocaust and that Amira's comparison of the Israeli government to the Nazis was unbearable for her. She continued and said that if she hadn't known Amira from the group and liked her, she would have cut off their relationship. Amira said her only option was to choose to avoid this subject, but that she cannot change her experience. Others said that they want to listen to them both. The group continued to explore Sagit's comment about Arab and Jewish religious societies as bringing Covid to the group. Shimon and Amira expressed their painful experiences as minorities, but Amira shared also her feeling of strangeness among Arab Israelis whom she finds as violent. I felt that we were in a space of verbal live exchange rather than enactments and that mutual understanding grew along with areas of "dead" (stopped) communication.

Analysis of the Case

I suggest that my group experienced the development of "social tolerance".

In retrospect, I realized that my decision to change the day of the sessions (because of Independence Day) and to start the sessions later (because of the Ramadan) were unconscious aspects related to my personal history. This may have affected the group's ability to discuss these issues. Perhaps, I tried to "stay centrist", in accordance with the position I have adopted in my personal life regarding political issues, and avoided taking a position that would put me at risk of being identified with "extremists". Hopper (2003) suggests that the social unconscious restricts our memory and awareness of social traumas, which can explain my forgetfulness in the session. It is possible that my individual history and the social unconscious defended the group against being in touch with rage and helplessness.

By my decision to change the setting, I communicated to the group that it was important to me to be thoughtful of Muslim Amira and of Jews, but since I did not open the matter for discussion, perhaps the group experienced me as "dictating", or felt that dialogue or conflict regarding "otherness" is too dangerous. Eventually, my decision probably decreased the group's ability to develop a tolerant political discourse. In that session, Amira spoke of Arabs' expelling from their homes during the Nakba, but perhaps she identified me with the controlling conqueror who forces her to be considerate regarding Independence Day for the sake of the group session. The Jewish group members reacted politely and cautiously.

In terms of the developmental stages of group "social tolerance" that I propose, the group was then in the first stage that is characterized by enactment of the social unconscious. Experiences of victim and perpetrator were acted upon the group stage, the absences expressed difficulty containing the social-political trauma in the discourse, words served as actions, and no one was able to listen to the pain without collapsing to a position of guilt and blame (Benjamin, 1990).

In the next sessions, the group managed to contain more conflict in its discourse about the setting in the context of the pandemic. In view of my realization that I may have unconsciously delayed open discussion in the group and thus also the development of "social tolerance" in the group, I raised again the Ramadan issue and opened it for discussion. Vice & Gildenhuys (2016) describe a group with interracial tension and argue that when meeting powerful intergroup conflict, a respectful and ethical conduct on the conductor's part is not enough. The conductor must be ready to meet anger and hatred. By raising the setting issue again in the context of face-to-face or online settings and regarding the Ramadan, I communicated to the group that I have left the "status quo" area, that I was willing to face anger towards me as a conductor and a Jew. I hoped that they would feel that I and the group can tolerate disagreements and aggression without "eliminating" each other and will be inspired to rebel against some of their own historic social identifications. I felt that my position as an authority that is ready to express my subjectivity (my political opinion as to readiness to include minorities and adherence to the Ministry of Health guidelines) along with an open discussion about the changes in the setting promoted social tolerance in the group. I also believe that I modeled "social tolerance" by conducting "changing preferences" to the opposing subgroups, meaning my decision about meeting online for a few more sessions and then resuming face-to-face meetings. However, the conductor's modelling was not the only factor that contributed to the development of "social tolerance" in the group.

I believe that via the natural ongoing process of the analytic group, through mirroring and resonance processes (Foulkes, 1948; Foulkes and Anthony, 1975), participants were able to contain more intolerable psychological experiences without turning to actions or anger. Sagit developed her tolerance for the psychological processes and neediness of others and Oded learned how to tolerate differences.

I suggest that the development of social tolerance involves rebelling against previous social identifications, such as mine (leaving the centrist position and the right winged position) which often involves powerful enactments. Nevertheless, "social tolerance" also involves an encounter with "enough like subjects, through the group's working through of mirror reactions, which involve similarity and exchange that refers to difference (Foulkes, 1964).

Not everyone in the group was satisfied with the results of the discussions about the setting, but I believe that the open discourse that included attending to the participants' contradicting needs promoted "social tolerance" in the group.

The Conductor

A conductor's awareness, even if only in retrospect, of his unconscious attitudes regarding tolerance is vital to his work. A conductor who wishes to remain neutral and objective regarding social and political issues puts the group at risk of silencing conflicts and delaying the development of "social tolerance" in the group. This does not mean that the conductor must always reveal his political views, but sometimes his behavior reveals them, and in such cases, it is better to stand behind his views openly to communicate to the group that open discourse of contradicting views is safe. As I have shown, a conductor's decisions regarding the setting can disclose his unconscious attitudes regarding tolerance and require self-reflection. My decision to change the day and time of the group sessions because of Independence Day and the Ramadan, without taking responsibility for this decision and discussing it with the group delayed the development of "social tolerance", whereas my taking of responsibility encouraged open discourse of the political issue.

Berman (2019) holds that members' psychological development increases via meeting with otherness in a group. I suggest that only if the conductor meets and recognizes his internal otherness in the context of social conflicts can the members of the group meet otherness inside them and between them and develop "social tolerance".

Even though accepting majority's opinion is a democratic idea, it could often lead to neglect of the needs of minorities. Dalal (2014) called it the obedience of minorities and was doubtful about its value to the development of tolerance. Therefore, the "changing preferences" that I conducted regarding the Covid situation represents an attempt to avoid majority's taking over and a modelling of "social tolerance".

Studies on societies that cope with difficult living conditions point at their tendency to develop rigid ideologies and victim-perpetrator roles that justify these ideologies (Staub, 1999), while denial of these processes leads to their enactment on the group stage (Hopper, 2003).

Therefore, I propose that in cases of lively political conflicts, the conductor should expect intense conflict situations in which the group experiences split victim and perpetrator self-states. The conductor could find himself in an enactment and he should be willing to also become an object of hatred for the group members (Vice & Gildenhuys, 2016).

In regards of the issue of social subgroups, which are usually perceived in group analysis as expressing intolerance. Morray & Liang (2005) suggest that conductor's perception of grouping into social subgroups as a legitimate need for protection in a violent reality and eventually may encourage more "connection" between different subgroups.

Discussion

In this chapter, I have suggested that the analytic group promotes an experience of "social tolerance", which refers to one's capacity to meet an "other" – whose otherness is sometimes threatening – to allow him inside and let him leave an impact. I propose that a significant part of the development of "social tolerance" in the analytic group is related to holding the setting. The conductor makes decisions regarding the setting, but I believe that the democratic atmosphere of the conductor's discourse with the participants about the setting, too, enables a practicing of "social tolerance".

I would like to suggest that tolerance is a complicated concept and that most of us feel "social tolerance" for certain issues but not to others. My argument is that "social tolerance" is an intersubjective achievement that develops through relationships. It relates to one's family and social identifications, when interpersonal conflict in the group can represent conflict regarding internal identifications with significant others from one's past, which represent social experiences and values. My contention is that in societies that are characterized by intense social and political tension, encounter with otherness is experienced as threatening one's identity and sometimes physical safety. Therefore, for one to be open to a meaningful encounter with social otherness in the group, one needs to "rebel" against one's primary social identifications. Group conflict can represent one's internal conflict between loyalty to one's primary identification and letting oneself be influenced by the other. In the context of social-political identity, the conflict could be intense, as was demonstrated regarding the Israeli-Palestinian conflict. In addition to rebellion, "social tolerance" develops through encounter with an "other" who is an "enough like subject" (Aron,2017), that is, encounter with otherness in the context of much similarity, through a gradual process of mirroring and exchange. I believe that it is a complicated process that does not involve all identifications at the same time and thus leaves "islands of intolerance" in one's mind.

In addition, it is important to note here the democratic culture that is unique to the analytic group, in which the discussion of the setting takes place. This discussion obligates all participants and conductor to take into consideration the interests of all participants, thus offering them an opportunity to practice "social tolerance".

Vice Gildenhuys (2016) described changes in social identity in a closed group in South Africa. They described the enactment of social traumas in their group via a binary division to subgroups of victim and perpetrator that gradually developed into mutual listening and understanding, with more sadness than aggression and a growing sense of belonging. In the third phase, intragroup differentiation had developed, along with mature hope and readiness for compromises. However, I propose that groups that experience ongoing intragroup conflict should expect enactments even after reaching the third phase.

Concluding Remarks

In conclusion, I find myself torn between a realistic perspective regarding the limited prospect of promoting "social tolerance" and the aspiration to "social tolerance". Intolerance is embedded in society, including group analytic societies. It is also important to note that the analytic group is limited in its capacity to develop "social tolerance", since it is not its main goal and because the social composition of a Jewish majority and Arab minority, which is characteristic of most analytic groups in Israel, constitutes a limitation for the generalization potential of tolerance (Zigenlaub, 2020).

Still, as group analysts we aim for "social tolerance" and in the analytic group there are precious moments of "social tolerance", of experiences of personal freedom, which are related to rebellion against previous binding social identifications and restraints (Hopper, 2003) and to a deepening of one's sense of belonging to humanity and responsibility for the other and for society.

References

Aron, L. (2017). Beyond tolerance in psychoanalytic communities: Reflexive skepticism and critical pluralism. *Psychoanalytic Perspectives*, 14(3): 271–282.

Benjamin, J. (1990). An outline of intersubjectivity: The development of recognition. *Psychoanalytic Psychology*, 7: 33–46.

Berger, M. (2017). The ethical envelope of the analytic group: some thoughts about democratic values implicit in group analysis. In Friedman, R. & Doron, Y. (eds) *Group Analysis in the Land of Milk and Honey*, pp. 3–18. London: Karnac.

Berman, A. (2019). Therapeutic semi-safe space in group analysis. *Group Analysis*, 52(2): 190–203.

Dalal, F. (2014). The struggle to live and let live: The psychology, ethics and politics of tolerance, or, why discrimination is preferable to tolerance. *Journal of Psychotherapy Aotearoa New Zealand*, 17(2): 159–172.

Foulkes, S. (1948). *Introduction to Group Analytic Psychotherapy*. London: William Heinemann Medical Books.

Foulkes, S. & Anthony, E. (1975). *Group Psychotherapy: The Psychoanalytic Approach*. London: Penguin Books.

Foulkes, S. (1964). *Therapeutic Group Analysis*. London: Allen & Unwin.

Hopper, E. (2003). *The Social Unconscious*. London: Jessica Kingsley Publishers.

Klein, M. (1940). Mourning and its relation to manic-depressive states. *International Journal of Psychoanalysis* 21: 125–153.

Morray, E. B. and Liang, B. (2005). Peace talk: A relational approach to group negotiation among Arab and Israeli youths. *International Journal of Group Psychotherapy*, 55(4): 481–506.

Staub, E. (1999). The origin and prevention of genocide, mass killing and other collective violence. *Peace and Conflict: Journal of Peace Psychology*, 5(4): 303–336.

Vice, H. & Gildenhuys, A. (2016). reshaping social identity: a qualitative report on experiences in an interracial median group. *Group Analysis*, 49(2): 101–123.

Zigenlaub, E. (2020). Acknowledging the collective narrative of the "Other" in dialogue groups: The case of Israeli Jews and Arabs. *Group*, 44(1): 7–26.

Part 4

Tolerance and the Socio-Political

Chapter 11

Polarization on Social Media

A Psychoanalytic and Group-Analytic
Reflection on the Failure of Tolerance

Avi Berman

One of the most dramatic aspects of the digital revolution is the establishment of ubiquitous cyber communication. Not only has it facilitated interpersonal communication, rendering it both simple and immediate, it has also created a virtually unlimited distribution mechanism. Online, one can speak one's mind to a vast circle of people, far exceeding one's previous capacity to find an audience. Complete strangers have become infinitely accessible. This process also saw the emergence of groups of interlocutors, who congregate around certain issues, ideas or views. All kinds of materials are spreading about willy-nilly in cyberspace; people go shopping, deals are signed and delivered. At first glance, all that has been happening over the past few decades looks like a universal breakthrough; but this revolution is happening so fast that attempts to fathom its meaning are falling behind the manifold changes that keep unfolding before our very eyes.

The discourse on the online communication revolution often centers on harm versus benefit. Those who highlight its benefits stress that communication has been made available to everyone, in a way that eliminates class difference and breaches the walls of exclusive social groups. Therefore, some claim that digital technology has a democratizing effect (Law, 2016). People's potential for belonging to a virtual group has grown significantly, thereby alleviating altogether experiences of loneliness, social isolation and depression (Bacon, 2018; Bainbridge, 2019). Many people who first meet on the internet form full relations later. Many get married. During Covid-era lockdowns, social networks have proven that they can serve as a source of belonging, relieve anxiety and provide sources of relevant knowledge. Indeed, in many cases, social networks ignore the interests of regimes of privileged groups, allowing the sharing of information which had so far been kept secret. A case in point is Russia's decision to shut down certain social media companies after invading Ukraine to keep destabilizing information about the war and its costs away from the Russian public. One can say that, in any field where many people share a broad common denominator – such as common identities, shared emotions, shared dangers or shared joys – social networks have proven their merit in bringing

DOI: 10.4324/9781003200253-16

people together. It is a well-known fact that powerful and influential social protest movements have spread through social network communication, movements who's exponentially growing reach had affected (and still does) the entire world. The #MeToo and Black Lives Matter movements are examples of this.

However, in recent years, we have become increasingly aware that social networks might increase and even create polarization, when it comes to the views of individuals, groups and different parts of society. Such polarization might, in turn, increase feelings of antagonism and lead to acts of mutual hostility. Indeed, content posted on social media often seems to be inciting against anyone holding a different view, delegitimizing them and even promoting violence against them. In this chapter, we will discuss the potential (and realized) impact of social media polarization on the emergence of a cultural climate of intolerance to difference and a plurality of perspectives, thus hindering the potential for tolerance.

I do not intend to claim that cyber networks have invented something new about tolerance that did not exist before. Xenophobia, incitement, the formation of opposing groups, the dictation of beliefs and feelings by vested interests – all of these have existed throughout history. It seems that the unique significance of cyber networks in terms of tolerance and intolerance lies in their massive distribution, now a World-Wide-System, and in humanity's increasing dependence on hand-held electronic devices, that are gradually almost becoming a part of the human body. It has never been easier for interested parties to influence people remotely and the techniques for achieving this influence are constantly being upgraded. Election campaign headquarters or network companies are able to create closed societies and use these to dictate their contents to millions of people at the touch of a key. The combination of these factors might increase the threat to tolerance.

I will begin by demonstrating polarization on social media, through a talkback-based discourse on Covid vaccination in one of Israel's digital newspapers.

***

A polarized and hostile debate between those supporting the Covid-19 vaccine and those opposing it broke out after a discussion in the Israeli parliament that was held on Zoom and open to public participation. In this discussion, as Sharon Alroy-Preis, head of public health services at the Israeli Health Ministry, was talking, a woman who attended the discussion on zoom interrupted her, blaming Dr. Alroy-Preis for was being paid by Pfizer, the company that manufactured Covid-19 vaccines, and was therefore biased and even downright deceptive. The immediate official response officially denied these claims, but the polarized discourse had already outburst on the internet networks.

The following excerpts include samples of the arguments made by those opposing vaccination and those supporting it:

- The "Green Pass" [Israel's official 'Covid-pass'] is a terrible thing – creating discrimination and turning our society into a society of privilege versus second class citizens. I'm asking everyone to try their best not to discriminate anyone on any grounds. We need a healthy society, not a society of control freaks.
- Get out of our veins, we're not getting vaccinated and there is no way we are handing our children over to dubious science, four million people vaccinated out of nine million, you're out of your minds, it's only going to get worse, you should quit, you have failed, goddamned villains!
- Pay no attention to all the trolls, like those who manipulate your mind. these people are promoting forced vaccines they are getting paid for it like all the media channels! All the doctors are being shut up and they're losing their jobs for speaking out about the poison vaccines, there isn't a single one who dares talking about the agenda 21 !!!!!!!!!!!!
- Yes!!! Finally!!! Vaccines kill! There's only 7 million people left in the country, 2 million died from the vaccines but it's all covered up…
- Pay respect for that woman who attacked Alroy-Preis! She's on the right side of history.
- So tired of that Preis lady, as long as she keeps threatening, she's gonna get threatened and the truth about her needs to be heard except but usual the ministry of sickness keeps shutting up anything that doesn't suit their agenda, just as they're hiding the comments of people hurt by the vaccine.
- Yeah go kill off your healthy children, don't cry, at best they'll turn out sterile!!!!

And on the other side:

- What triggered the analysis was a publication in the New England Journal of Medicine, on September 15th 2021, of the findings of a study on the efficacy of the booster shot, done by a group of researchers along with Dr. Sharon Alroy-Preis, head of public health services at the Israeli Health Ministry, according to which the booster shot makes you 11.3 times less likely to get infected by Covid-19 and 19.5 times less likely to develop serious illness.
- Why are you cursing and why wish such terrible things to people? Where is all this nastiness coming from? Didn't get enough hugs as a child? Someone holds a different opinion than you and you instantly become a keyboard superhero … wow …
- Nice cursing. you are pathetic, when are you going to send me off to Syria you weed and cocaine snorter??? Just five million left in Israel, 4 killed by the vaccine … go curse some more you low-life miserable creature…

- I'm doing myself a favor by taking this vaccination. Go inject yourself cyanide I don't mind. People are dying without the vaccine but you are an ostrich sticking its head in the sand, not seeing what's going on around you, it's because of people like you that the holocaust happened, shame on you
- As time goes by and proof of how efficient and vital vaccination is becomes more available, the wackos in the anti-vaxxer cult only cry out louder, it's going to end in murder. We have to put a stop to this cult, to their website, declare them a dangerous cult and state that the materials they are spreading online are seditious. It should be an international effort. Biden, the US president, already declared that they are murderers.
- Totally, the incitement and the lies are getting to people and one of these loonies in going to end up pulling the trigger like Yigal Amir [the man who assassinated prime minister Yitzhak Rabin]. Read the comments here and tell me I'm wrong.
- A piece of advice for the anti-vaxxer who interrupted the discussion – turn on your vibrator on medium or higher and chill the fuck out – moron.
- I couldn't give a shit about you, you're not even on my radar, I need to keep making a living because I love my job and my paycheck and you anti-vaxxers cult can keep on howling. I don't give a damn about you and your fucked up kids, worst case scenario one of them dies and then you'll have some more you keep spewing out babies non-stop anyway so no big deal if one of them dies from the vaccine!

We are witnessing the formation of two opposing and polarized sides, that are aggregating around the total justification of their position and the absolute rejection of and intolerance towards that of the other side. At the beginning of this conflictual argument a moderate question is presented to the other side; it is either ignored or met with expressions of anger and accusation ("goddamned villains" versus "it's because of people like you that the holocaust happened"), or with mockery, scorn and dismissal ("a society of control freaks" and "cocaine snorter" versus "you keep spewing out babies non-stop"). Some of these messages are highly aggressive, including wishes of harm on members of the other side to the extent of wishing illness and death on them ("get the fourth shot and go kill off your healthy children" versus "inject yourself with cyanide for all I care"). Other messages highlight paranoid messages ("[they're trying] to manipulate your mind" versus "one of these loonies is going to end up pulling some Yigal Amir stunt [...] it's going to end in murder"). It can be seen that on both sides there is a steady gradual escalation of expressions of aggression and hatred. Finally, the messages of this argument between proponents and opponents of the vaccine seem to resonate collective traumas involving the holocaust, class differences and social oppression.

The messages entail seemingly fact-based arguments, which are presented as if there is no need to offer any evidence or proof supporting them. They are also utterly ignored by the other side. Anything that seems like an attempt to refute the opponent's claims gets no response and the entire discourse has the quality of utterly giving up on any attempt to discuss actual facts. Moreover, it appears that any alternative viewpoints are dismissed in advance, due to the absolute resoluteness of the speakers on either side. Within each side, attention outwards seems limited and even diminishing. Otherness is not invited into dialogue and even experienced as hated in advance.

The separatism and entrenchment of these two groups is absolute. No mutual consent is created, no expression of any shared 'togetherness' or cooperation. It is a kind of digital war, in which people shoot at the other side from their trenches, behind made-up names, free of any accountability or concern. What used to be a face-to-face encounter with flesh and blood people (even in a crowd or a mass) is changing, before our very eyes, into mutual anonymous attacks written in a closed room and sent out to multitudes of people at the push of a button.

The fact is that within each side there is not a single message of calming things down or restraint of his comrades. Not only is aggression within each side allowed to roam free, it is even silently accepted by a mass of readers who refrain from expressing their opinion. Paradoxically, it seems that tolerance is extended to those espousing the same view as oneself and completely withheld from those holding the different views. Tolerance, defined by the Oxford Dictionary as the ability or willingness to tolerate the existence of opinions or behavior that one dislikes or disagrees with, does not prevail between the two sides. There is no indication of any willingness or intention to facilitate the co-existence of opposing views or contain disagreement. Moreover, one can assume that the overt aggression repels those who feel uncomfortable about it form intervening. They may wish to avoid expressing their reservations about the menacing speakers in their own side, after having encountered the venom these speakers have directed at others. Their silence leaves the conflict to the most aggressive as they themselves gradually become silent bystanders.

'Show Me the Money:' Putting Profit Before People

I will expand on the social and interpersonal mechanisms that may explain this in the next section, offering psychoanalytic and group-analytic interpretations thereof. However, beyond the interpersonal and intergroup processes, it seems that the very business model of many social networks leads them to take advantage of polarization to make a profit.

Social networks essentially function like huge e-commerce markets, where products and services are offered to hundreds of millions of people (who are now about two thirds of the world's population). While declaring that their intentions are to help bring people together, the companies who own and run these networks earn huge sums of money by advertising products and services. Consider the following statement of intent by one of Facebook's spokespeople:

> The goal of the Meaningful Social Interactions ranking change is in the name: improve people's experience by prioritizing posts that inspire interactions, particularly conversations, between family and friends [...] We're continuing to make changes consistent with this goal, like new tests to reduce political content on Facebook based on research and feedback.
>
> (Washington Post)

Despite such declarations, Facebook's business-social policy has been severely criticized recently, following former employee Francis Haugen's disclosure of internal company documents that indicate that Facebook's management knowingly exploited polarization for profit.

> Haugen told British and American lawmakers last month that Facebook would fuel more violent unrest worldwide unless it curbed its algorithms which push extreme, divisive content and prey on vulnerable demographics to keep them scrolling.
>
> (Reuters)

The controversy surrounding Facebook's business policy is just one example of a global-scale social occurrence in which the business policies of social networks preserve and maintain polarization while eroding tolerance. Looking into the relationship between social polarization and financial gain reveals that the business model of these companies is to ensure that each user is exposed to network content for as long as possible, while being as actively engaged as possible. The more time a user spends in front of the screen and the more engagements they are involved in (likes, comments, shares, etc.), the greater their exposure to ads for products and services and the more likely they are to spend money.

It turns out that content that is controversial, divisive or anger-provoking is more likely to pique users' interest and increase their number of engagements. This means that, as the documents leaked by Haugen suggest, network companies may create a built-in preference for controversial and angering content in order to increase their profits by exposing users to buying opportunities.

> Engagement-based ranking does two things: one, it prioritizes and amplifies divisive and polarizing extreme content and two it concentrates it," Haugen said. "Insofar as problematic content is often more engaging than unproblematic content, ranking-by-engagement runs the risk of favoring the problematic. [...] The posts that sparked the most comments tended to be the ones that made people angry or offended them.
>
> (Reuters)

The choice of which content is presented to network users is determined by an algorithm created by a team of programmers, in line with company policy. The algorithm aims to study the consumption habits, preferences and inclinations of each individual user as well as the overall content and expressions that thrive across the network. In accordance with this information, the algorithm presents each individual user with a personalized feed that reflects their expressed interests. This creates a feedback loop by which the algorithm keeps reinforcing each user's existing viewing habits by flooding them with familiar content that supports their present outlook, while *de facto* preventing them from encountering new and different points of view.

However, when social networks stream content that reinforces existing polarized attitudes and reduce dialogue with others and otherness per se, the basic conditions for the development of tolerance cannot be met. Moreover, a business model that favors the kind of divisive content that provokes anger and increases engagements makes the encounter with otherness inherently more aggressive and intimidating. Through the selective prism of the social network's algorithm, the other becomes more threatening and more likely to evoke repulsion than curiosity.

Consider, in this context, Žižek's analysis of how capitalistic dictates penetrate our lives, transforming the super-ego through the invasion of consumerist social law:

> The superego is, therefore, the obscene and despicable inversion of the permissive "You can", into the prescriptive rule "You must". At this point the permitted pleasure becomes an ordered pleasure. You need. You must because you can [...] we have here the opposite paradox of the pleasure itself, that chasing after it becomes a duty. In a permissive society the subjects experience, as a kind of duty, the need "to have fun", to really enjoy themselves, and as a result they feel guilty because of their failure to be happy.
>
> (Žižek, 2000, p. 21)

To this formula we can add the missing part: the imperative to enjoy can be transformed into the duty to buy; shame about what you do not have is how external power becomes internal motivation. The collective mind, when overwhelmed with capitalistic oedipal messages, property even when one has no money. Insidiously, one does not feel like property: what you do feel is the belief that following the dictates of capitalism is tantamount to self-fulfillment – you will be happy this way, if not today, then surely tomorrow.

A Psychoanalytic and Group-Analytic Perspective

Thus far, our accumulated knowledge about the impact of technological changes on individuals, groups, organizations and societies has not been cohesive. It is difficult for research efforts to keep up with the pace, diversity, impact and ubiquity of these changes in a way that would allow us to fully comprehend their implications (Ofer, 2021). However, certain aspects of psychoanalytic and group-analytic thinking can be utilized to fathom these consequences.

Despite the proven contribution of cyber networks mentioned above, there is growing fear and concern in contemporary psychoanalytic thinking about their potential to alter or harm people's personalities and distort the deep meanings of interpersonal relationships. Several authors have argued that this is indeed the case and that social network use might inhibit the normal development of users' personality, especially for younger users.

It should be noted that the emotional worlds of children who grew up in the previous century involved a more or less conventional constellation of two parents, their children and their biological family environment. This structure is now changing through the addition of new configurations, some of which rely on fertility technologies that challenge even the basic conceptualization of the Oedipal constellation. In addition, as Lemma (2017) argues, children's interface with screens plays an increasingly significant role in their physical/psychic/sexual experience. According to Lemma, such stimuli do not require intricate psychic work and create a culture of instant gratification, enhanced consumerism, voyeurism and the idealization of exhibitionism. The gratification of primary needs is also mentioned by other authors, with Bainbridge (2019) adding that "the term 'binge watching' connotes both gluttony and addiction" (p. 65).

The digital possibilities available at the touch on a keyboard might be experienced as the realization of one's archaic wishes for effortless rewards. This is not just about sexual gratification through porn or the ease of online shopping. Relationships may also come to be experienced as consumer commodities, as more and more people look for and find their partners through simple online applications, which allow one to change their choices like choosing a movie on a streaming service: the next will surely be better, more fun. In psychoanalytic terms, the increasing availability of instant gratification online might revert the hard-won achievements of sublimation, working through and resorting to one's inner resources, which are grounded in the crucial human experience of absence and lack (Bion, 1962).

Some authors (Knafo & Lo Bosco, 2017) mention the emergence of perversions of interpersonal relationships, the extreme version of which is addiction to social networks (Turkle, 2015; Muchnick & Buirski, 2016). Bainbridge (2019) argues that, in cyber culture, interpersonal relationships may become more imaginary than real: "Relatedness is now imagined in the ether rather than lived in reality for many people, conjuring up what Sherry Turkle terms as being 'alone together'" (2011).

Some claim that the use of cyber technology also has a negative impact on overall human cognitive function, in ways that might harm our functioning as human species. Social networks strive to take over the human attention span, creating constant and unrelenting distractions which impair their users' ability to concentrate. Hari (2022) argues that the use of such technology disrupts sleep and reinforces the hold of screen culture on human leisure, supplanting activities such as reading books and acquiring information from diverse sources. According to Hari, our attention is being stolen from us unawares. 'Stolen focus' might come at the expense of one's free-floating, associative attention, in which distractedness and curiosity about newness and otherness offer an opportunity for personal and interpersonal development. The latter kind, which Bar (2022) calls 'mindwandering,' represents open, associative and gradually expanding attention, a kind of potential space (Winnicott, 1953/2003) that can contain opposites and even contradictions. Such open attention represents an inclusive creative space, from which all manner of innovations may arise. It facilitates tolerance and may even enhance it. Optimally, the two poles of closed, focused attention and open, floating attention should be part of a dynamically balanced system, which allows mutual enrichment and back-and-forth movement. The impact of contemporary cyber technology risks making closed attention excessively dominant, in a way that pushes this system out of balance, reducing the impact and contribution of open attention.

Considerable psychoanalytic and group-analytic attention is devoted to observing social phenomena taking place on social networks or as a result of their impact. Many authors note the dangers of disinformation on social media, which can distribute lies to the masses as easily as the truth. The dominance of cyber culture involves a certain decline in reliance on mainstream information outlets, such as television news programs, and an increasing tendency to rely on social networks, which are especially vulnerable to lies and disinformation (Beland et al., 2020). The 'stolen focus' may stem from the intervening of capitalism in our lives (Hari, 2022), as users are constantly seduced into and rewarded for directing their attention to commercial needs. This seduction-reward dynamic may overtake users' free will, while intentionally obfuscating their ability to notice what is actually going on and make different choices (Williams, 2018).

Such reliance on cyber networks for information might lend itself to abuse and exploitation by interest groups. Today, political campaigns often spread information and disinformation in order to defeat opponents. Trump's years in office are harshly criticized for his deceptive use of social media, with some authors arguing that he and his staff spread vast amounts of distortions, disinformation and outright lies in a way that profoundly undermined social trust. Brenner (2021) views Trump's presidency as combining two plagues – "a highly contagious virus and a disinformation campaign gone viral" – attributing Trump with intentional and witting use of social networks to incite the public against his opponents and remain in power. Rudden (2021) views the 'January 6th insurrection' as resulting from deliberate incitement by Trump and his supporters on social networks.

Thus, incitement can also be promoted by online communication. Xenophobia is a ubiquitous component of the contents spread online, contributing to the growth and severity of social polarization in recent years. Gadotti and Valente (2021) have found that, during the Covid-19 pandemic, social polarization in Brazil grew on social networks, exacerbating disagreements and increasing intolerance. Also exploring the role played by social media during the pandemic, Kalsched (2021) notes that "collective imagination can be hijacked by social media" and replaced by conspiracy theories which are haphazardly dictated and distributed. Some authors view this as an invasive "virtual impingement" (Balick, 2012).

Regression to a Cyber-Womb

Beside the possibility of easy, fast and simple interpersonal communication, social networks also offer a sense of belonging to a group, empowering the self-worth of its members. In group analysis, the need to belong is considered innate as well as a component of mental health (Foulkes and Anthoney, 1957, p. 21). In some theoretical approaches, the need for positive self-worth is considered as vital as physical nourishment (Kohut, 1971). The social network seems to be working well in this area. It creates a "hall of mirrors" (Foulkes and Anthoney, 1957, p. 150) where everyone who belongs to the group is reflected through the "likes culture" of everyone else and reciprocates by being a positive mirror for others. Moreover, the essence of inner group relations is conceptualized in group analysis by the term "Matrix." Both main meanings of this concept are relevant to us in this chapter: first, as "the common pool of meaning, the total network of communication, the matrix of the group" (Foulkes and Anthoney, 1975, p. 122); second, as a *womb*, a platform for life and growth (Webster dictionary, 1981).

Being included in these groups addresses an important personal need to belong and to mutually maintain positive self-esteem. Indeed, social networks are home to various support groups, whose members engage in open, profound personal conversations, which are personally valuable and even therapeutically significant. There are several mass platforms – including Facebook, Instagram, WhatsApp, etc. – where any user can create their own online groups and join others as a member. However, the effort to belong requires constant maintenance in the form of sharing one's opinions, reporting on one's personal life, uploading pictures and videos documenting events from the user's life as well as commenting on all of the above. In each of these groups, the unspoken expectation is that members should express support and admiration towards the contents uploaded and comments shared by other members. This expression is often performed through the like/dislike indicator, which has become ubiquitously accessible throughout all platforms, with a high number of likes raising, or at least preserving, one's positive self-worth.

Thus, the cyber group pushes its members to become increasingly similar, according to its implicit norms and rules. Anyone perceived as different, disagreeable or irritating might end up ignored, marginalized, devalued, and eventually excluded. Differences might be perceived as negative and attributed to those outside the group or to members of other groups. It seems that such rules, as well as the price they exact, are silently accepted by members or even pushed to their pre-conscious.

Being part of a cyber group inevitably entails the exclusion of the unfit. There are mechanisms for removing people from the group (such as 'unfriend-ing' or 'blocking' someone on Facebook). Belonging to a social network group may subconsciously entail built-in indifference to the exclusion of others, as those excluded become literally transparent to group members. Each user unwittingly becomes a bystander to the exclusion of others, while they them-selves are preoccupied with maintaining their own inclusion. This introduces intolerance into the interpersonal reality of social networks. While the ambi-ence of the group looks and feels welcoming, it might be intolerant to those it finds unfit according to its unwritten norms of belonging and affiliation.

Unlike cyber groups' communication, the full interpersonal encounter may assure discreetness and enables the expression of difference, insecurity and per-sonal distress, thus potentially serving as a containing and tolerant space. It seems that virtual communication offers easy and imaginary relations, which do not require responsibility and concern and free us – at least to some extent – from getting to know the other in a true and profound manner, with all the similarities and differences they hold. Substituting the former for the latter may leave people increasingly devoid of experiencing the challenges involved in tol-erance. Moreover, the increasing preference for imaginary relations over actual ones may turn the other into a stranger and even make knowing them obsolete.

Knafo (2015) describes cases in which men prefer living with full-sized fem-inine dolls (with functioning 'genitalia') to struggling with real relations with women. "There is no stress," says one of these men. "I won't lose half of my assets to a bitch," says another. "I want to enjoy all the carnal satisfaction with none of the real-world difficulties of honoring another person in a relation-ship," adds a third (p. 488). Note the total rejection of otherness expressed in their preference of dolls to women. I suggest that the imaginary perfect, flaw-less doll is a metaphor for the omnipotent archaic wish for total compliance and boundless acceptance that is promised in the social networks' sub-grouping, provided that one respects the rules of similarity.

I suggest seeing this withdrawal as a regression to a sort of common womb-like primordial matrix, where members can lead a hybrid life, split off from complicated and frustrating external reality. Within this hybrid life, while rela-tionships between people do exist, including active group matrix communica-tion, the regression to the primordial matrix encloses these relations within a commonly imagined cyber womb.

I propose the terms *Primordial Matrix* and *Cyber Womb* to conceptualize a collective illusion of a cyber space where all needs are met. When individuals collectively agree to allow group norms to define their emotional needs, they may indeed feel that they belong to an embracing group and live in a sense of relationships' plentitude. Their needs for recognition and positive self-esteem are also abundantly satisfied, provided that they rein in individual differences to conform to the domain of similarities. Their epistemological needs seem to be taken care of, too. The cyber womb can provide its participants with an illusionary sense that they know all they need to know about the reality they live in, while remaining totally ignorant of the extent to which they are following someone else's dictates. Indeed, it appears that most users might be kept utterly dissociated from recognizing that their experience of affluence and freedom of choice is underpinned by the dictates of business or political interests, which aim to prevent access to information to/from fields of content that fail to coincide with their agendas.

A new expertise is being created. Mind engineering experts turn network participants into people whose feeling and beliefs are dictated outside of their (stolen) consciousness. It is therefore possible that we are witnessing the emergence of a cyber culture in which consumption habits are formed alongside the hidden agendas that support them: easy communication, accessible information and instant gratification at the price of relinquishing one's freedom of thought and opinion, diminishing the human capacity for tolerance. Moreover, locking people in what is familiar to them, causing them to see the other and their otherness as disruptive, reinforces paranoid-schizoid psychic states.

Following Steiner's (1990, p. 226; 1993) notion of psychic retreat, turning a blind eye to reality might emerge as a defense mechanism fending off painful truths. This might involve denying and dismissing feelings of guilt and responsibility and a retreat from truth to illusionary omnipotence. I suggest that cyber-womb groups may form a privileged interpersonal environment that maintains a shared experience of entitlement. A self-perception of omnipotence may arise from a sense of belonging to an enormous cyber group. Indeed, in many cases, this experience does satisfy omnipotent wishes and enables a reduction of responsibility and guilt towards others as well as a rejection of complexity. This combination of entitlement and exemption from guilt can result in shameless cruelty toward excluded people.

As concern for the other is disavowed, violent behavior, shaming and sexual perversion may be more common in the emerging cyber culture. Because device use is often unsupervised by parents or even unknown to them – as some parents are far less digitally savvy than their children – the age of both perpetrators and victims may become younger and younger (Knafo & Lo Bosco, 2017). In these cases, it seems that the combination of easy access to other people on social networks and the emotional compartmentalization these networks create, hinders the user's experience of acceptance and concern. Tolerance might be reduced in the user's world of interpersonal relating or replaced with objectification.

As mentioned, the increasing use of social networks impacts human attention, with users' 'closed attention' becoming excessively dominant at the expense of 'open attention.' This may entail serious consequences for interpersonal relations in general and the level of human tolerance in particular. Open attention is what allows us to be curious when encountering otherness and difference; it is what enables us to learn from what is unfamiliar to us and thereby engage in an exchange of ideas. Tolerance is also severely impaired by tense, even outright hostile, inter-group relations. By zooming out to the state of society at large, we see how, just like the pro- and anti-vaccination proponents with whom we opened this chapter, online groups can enter confrontation with one another. Just as attention can be stolen to promote the interests of various parties, personal identities might be hijacked in favor of collective identities. Perhaps belonging to a group dictates that one must proclaim that they unreservedly embrace the group's identity. Users might avoid opposing their group's prevailing sentiment for fear of being excluded, as it seems that hostility can terrorize even those who are seemingly on its side, keeping them in check.

Polarization between groups is not a new phenomenon and has existed as part of human nature, independently of cyber culture. The split of the social domain into opposing groups of "us" and "them" is a basic structure in the social organization of human beings; it is almost a given of human nature. Within this split the "them" group may be transformed into an enemy, imbued with projections and other negative attributions, through an ideology that tends to resist dialogue and exchange. This process might be impulsive, unavoidable, and unconscious (Berman, Berger & Gutmann, 2000).

Hopper (2003) argues that, in response to existential and annihilation anxieties, society as a whole mobilizes the social defense mechanism of aggregation/massification. Within cyber networks, groups of "us" and "them" are formed, maintaining a hostile split between them that results from the aggregation defense mechanism. Within each group, the need for belonging translates into common attitudes of averseness and hatred towards other groups, thereby turning intolerance into a prominent social glue. It grows even more acute in cases where in-group messages attribute danger and threat to the opposing group (even when this is the result of projection). Intentional incitement, accompanied by disinformation and accusations of 'fake contents,' might intensify and reinforce the paranoid-schizoid character of this social unconscious organization. When this state becomes extreme, we believe it might result in a vicious circle in which aggregation becomes the key defense mechanism, intensifying the very anxieties from which it is supposed to protect.

It seems, then, that the fate of tolerance in social networks is related to the degree to which the cyber womb is closed and shut off from diverse and difference-laden external reality. There is still a possibility that the internet womb will be a space where self-confidence and mutual-recognition grow, where people are encouraged to follow their curiosity about others and otherness. In these cases, the womb can give birth to people ripe for tolerance, just as online dating can eventually materialize in marriage. The opposite possibility is that this womb will remain the permanent home of those who shy away from an encounter with any reality not mediated by their cyber-belonging. Now, we come to the possible contribution of psychotherapy.

Psychotherapy

In recent psychoanalytic literature, it has been argued that cyber culture "hijacks" the unconscious (Knafo, 2015) or "colonizes" it (Evzonas, 2020) for its own needs. Indeed, it is conceivable that the current intensity of screen-use and the growing duration of online social interactions may come to shrink our inner world. The intrapersonal space in which fantasies are created, wishes and fears resonate and experiences are processed may be diminished and impaired. It is possible, then, that cyber culture hinders the birth of subjectivity in young people and its preservation in older people. People who are affected by this are likely to turn to psychotherapy out of the feeling that their personal identity is dissolving, out of loneliness, social fears and the resulting depression. As therapists, we should expect that our patients' personal encounter with cyber culture will be brought into therapy. It is to be expected, then, that we will meet patients for whom cyberspace is an important part of their lives. Among them, we might encounter a new kind of secluded lifestyle.

Moreover, the exposure to cyber society might cause people to internalize its characteristic social processes and assimilate its inner relations and values. What happens to young people who identify with the need to belong at the cost of impoverishing their personality? What happens to their psyche when they routinely avoid exclusion by participating in the exchange of support and admiration? What happens to people who are constantly distanced from the other, otherness and the challenge of tolerance inherent in interpersonal differences?

Noa

Noa is a pretty, energetic, witty and up-to-date 29-year-old woman. She works as a human resources manager at a hi-tech company. However, she came to therapy because of difficulties in steadily belonging to a group of friends and finding a partner. When in the company of potential friends or partners, she felt various anxieties that thwart the growth of these relationships, even though they began in an atmosphere of pleasantness, passion and hope. She said that she was easily hurt and often reacted with anger and offence. During the period from which the following description is taken, she was in twice-weekly psychotherapy.

Noa's father is a medical doctor and her mother is a teacher. During her early childhood – she had realized this later – her father had been busy as a fresh medical intern: apart from isolated, unexpected and momentary expressions of love, he was present-absent, nervous and preoccupied – a still-faced father. The worst was his angry, cold scolding. Unable to decipher these enigmatic alternations no matter how desperately she tried, Noa became anxious and agitated. When he reprimanded her, Noa shrank in pain, feeling rejected and humiliated. In those moments, her mother rushed in to relieve her pain, hug her and comfort her. Noa and her mother created a protective bubble of softness and comfort, which was probably necessary for them both. The comforting bubble they co-created remained at Noa's disposal throughout her life, allowing her to retreat there when facing stressful and painful situations. However, this protective dyadic bubble prevented her from coming to terms with her father's otherness. There was no dialogue with her father's strangeness, which left her scared and rejected as well as prevented the development of an age-appropriate Oedipal romance with him. Over the years, her relationship with her father softened and improved, but the sealed-off shelter of her relationship with her mother remained active and she regularly resorted to hiding there in response to interpersonal distress in the following years as well.

In elementary school, Noa was socially excluded. Looking back, she now sees those experiences as traumatic. They were four friends. As they walked together, she found herself pushed onto the sidewalk to be included. She was hurt. She complained to them while hoping to copy-paste her mother's pattern of responding with an enveloping hug, into their relationship. It did not work. Her friends continued to drift apart until, one day, they stopped including her altogether. Noa felt banished, humiliated and helpless, lonely and lost. The bubble of her relationship with her mother comforted Noa during this period as well: she shared her insult with her mother and her mother resolved the issue with a hug.

In our meetings, she told me that she belonged to a small group of dance enthusiasts (she herself hardly danced), who met to watch dance shows, their relationship following the performance schedule. Moreover, she was active in various WhatsApp groups, which occasionally led to real-life social gatherings. While talking at length about her disappointment with the insufficiently welcoming attitude of her friends, she barely made eye contact with me. In time, she felt more relaxed in the therapeutic setting and began experiencing me as a listening ear and an understanding heart. Beyond that, I did not feel the development of any personal transference towards me. As I tried to understand the meaning of her transference to me she once said: "For me you are the world outside". It seemed that both the therapy room and the WhatsApp groups to which she belonged acted as derivatives of the bubble she and her mother had created together.

Repeated Covid lockdowns created the perfect justification for her to delve even deeper into her online groups. Relieved, she exclaimed: "Covid killed the FOMO." Indeed, the lockdown – which kept everyone from leaving their homes – solved her problem: it eased her envy of people who engage in real relationships, freeing her from this challenge. In therapy, we were empathically exploring her fears of going out, meeting people for the first time and taking the risk of being rejected again. I understood the relief she felt in response to the pandemic restrictions.

When the lockdowns ended, she gradually began to feel that her bubble-bound life was becoming a barrier that constricted her life and her vitality. I drew attention to her internal barrier, hypothesizing that going out involved an experience of personal risk and that she may be aware that there are situations and moments when no one can accompany her or go out in her place. Noa felt hurt by me. She felt that I was abandoning her and experienced me, with anger and pain, as she did the father who had turned his back on her when she was a child. The experience of protection, which up until that point was growing and becoming more established in our relationship, disappeared in an instant.

The next period in therapy saw Noa oscillating between the comfort and trust she came to feel with me and feelings of tension and threat that arose when she experienced me as 'pushing her out into the wilderness.' Anything short of absolute comforting support felt jarring and painful to her. Like the gradual construction of a depressive position, Noa slowly assimilated our relationship as protective and challenging, similar but different. Her willingness to remain with the ambivalence and partiality of her experience of safety gradually helped her leave her bubble.

She started meeting people. She even entered a relationship with one of them, Jonah, whom she described as a 50-year-old bachelor, who had ended every relationship in his life within several months. As the therapy progressed, she realized that she chose to get close to him both because she hoped that he will stay with her and because if, God forbid, they should break up, the inevitable fate of her predecessors will help her avoid overly harsh self-recriminations. He invited her to his elegant apartment and made her dinner. Noa was fascinated and excited by her encounter with these new smells, tastes and touch. The bubble was replaced by real relations.

Soon enough, Jonah did something that hurt her and Noa wanted to end the relationship, hoping to avoid further pain. To her surprise, he was angry with her; he expected her to stay and talk and stop threatening to break up. For the first time, she found herself face to face with a living, mutual interpersonal reality in which she was both hurt and hurtful. The relationship indeed ended several months later but, with the help of the therapy, Noa was now well outside the enclosed bubble that both protected her and shut her away.

* * *

It seems to me that contemporary psychoanalytic psychotherapy should get to know the cyber life of the patients with the assumption that this life exists simultaneously, and sometimes in a dissociative and partially inaccessible to the therapeutic discourse. There may be new forms of transference towards the therapist (like the hostile external reality outside the cyber bubble).

I wish to propose that psychotherapy can play an additional and unique role vis-à-vis the threat posed by the flaws of cyber culture, as these are manifest in social networks. Psychotherapy can contribute to preserving one's subjectivity when it is threatened by the dictates of belonging on social networks. Both individual and group therapy can facilitate recognition of what is different and unique in each person, fueling the hope that such difference can also be accepted by others. Psychotherapy can help extricate people from begin manipulated by the dictates of special interest groups. Sometimes, this involves empowering the person's ability to tolerate a certain extent of fear of exclusion, so that they could risk making their personal voice heard. It seems that the same things that help patients become subjects, owning their personal opinions and tastes and their right to deepen and broaden their experience and knowledge, also promote tolerance. Whatever helps the patient withstand the temptation of instant gratification in pre-designated areas allows them to encounter otherness and benefit from it. Whatever helps the patient embrace their own difference and expect that others accept it as well, may help them contain the other's difference without resorting to exclusion.

References

Bainbridge, C. (2019). Box-set mind-set: Psycho-cultural approaches to binge watching, gender, and digital experience. *Free Associations*, 75: 65–83.

Bacon, R. (2021). Review of Psychotherapy, Ethics, and Society: Another Kind of Conversation: Michael Briant. *Contemporary Psychoanalysis*, 57: 373–388.

Balick, Aaron. (2012). TMI in the transference LOL: Psychoanalytic reflections on Google, social networking, and 'virtual impingement'. *Psychoanalysis, Culture & Society*, 17(2): 120–136.

Bar, M. (2022). *Mindwandering: How It Can Improve Your Mood and Boost Your Creativity*. Bloomsbury Publishing. London.

Beland, U., Stuart, R. & Vonofakos, D. (2020). International Listening Post Report Summary: The World at the Dawn of 2020. *Organizational and Social Dynamics*, 20: 118–122.

Evzonas, N. (2020). Gender and "Race" Enigmatic Signifiers: How the Social Colonizes the Unconscious. *Psychoanalytic Inquiry*, 40: 636–656.

Foulkes, S. H. (1948). *Introduction to Group Analytic Psychotherapy*. London, Karnac Books.

Foulkes, S. H. & Anthoney, E. J. (1957 (2003)). *Group Psychotherapy: The Psychoanalytic Approach*. London & New York: Karnac.

Gadotti, C. M. & Valente, V. L. (2021). Brazil: Hate and intolerance in times of pandemic in a mixed-race country. *Journal of Analytical Psychology*, 66: 719–728.

Hari, J. (2022). *Stolen Focus: Why You Can't Pay Attention?* London: Bloomsbury Publishing.

Kalsched, D. (2021). Intersections of personal vs. collective trauma during the COVID-19 pandemic: the hijacking of the human imagination. *Journal of Analytical Psychology*, 66: 443–462.

Knafo, D. (2015). Guys and dolls: Relational life in the technological era. *Psychoanalytic Dialogues*, 25: 481–502.

Knafo, D. & Lo Bosco, R. (2017). *The Age of Perversion: Desire and Technology in Psychoanalysis and Culture*. New York: Routledge/Taylor & Francis Group.

Kohut, H. (1971). *The Analysis of the Self*. International University Press.

Lemma, A. (2017). *The Digital Age on the Couch*. London: Routledge.

Muchnick, R. & Buirski, P. (2016). Social media as organizing but not transforming self-experience. *International Journal of Psychoanalytic Self Psychology*, 11: 142–151.

Rudden, M. G. (2021). Insurrection in the U.S. Capitol: Understanding psychotic, projective and introjective group processes. *International Journal of Applied Psychoanalytic Studies*, 18: 372–384.

Steiner, J. (1987). The interplay between pathological organizations and the paranoid-schizoid and depressive positions. *International Journal of Psychoanalysis*, 68: 69–80.

Turkle, S. (2015). *Reclaiming Conversation: The Power of Talk in a Digital Age*. New York, NY: Penguin Press.

Williams, J. (2018). *Stand Out of our Light: Freedom and Resistance in the Attention Economy*. New York: Cambridge University Press.

Žižek, S. (2000). *On Super Ego and Other Ghosts*. Tel Aviv: Resling Publishing.

Chapter 12

Tolerance and the Crowd

An Improbable Duet

Rina Dudai

At the very beginning of his paper, "Group Psychology and the Analysis of the Ego," Freud argues that the distinction between the psychology of the individual and that of the group or crowd is unjustified. He thereby seeks to pave the way for a psychoanalytic exploration of broader social contexts (1921, p. 69). Thus, he views crowd psychology as concerning the organization of the individual into a certain group, at a certain time and for a certain purpose. In this context, Moscovvici (1981) argues that "Freud's interest in crowd psychology was a radical turning point and a real revolution in his research and hence in psychoanalysis" (p. 227), adding that "the unconscious made incarnate in crowds terrified him [Freud]" (p. 222).

Adorno (1951) claims that, in his paper, Freud was using psychological categories to anticipate the rising dominance of the fascistic essence of the crowd long before the rise of fascism and Hitler's political ascent (p. 120). According to Adorno, Freud was looking for the missing link that turned the crowd into a crowd and singled out the *bonding* power that stemmed from the *libidinal nature* of the collective mind. According to Freud, the individual in the crowd operates under conditions that allow them to eschew the repressions of the unconscious. Further developing Freud's ideas, Adorno understands the workings of the crowd as an *archaic regression* to a primordial, pre-Oedipal state, that lies beyond representation and language (pp. 122, 125, 132). He calls this a society at its "zero-degree" or a "raw" mental state (in Jonsson, 2013).

Freud opens his paper with an entire section devoted to the observations of French psychologist and sociologist Gustave Le Bon, quoting from his 1895 book, *The Crowd: A Study of the Popular Mind.* In this book, Le Bon argues that the individual who is assimilated into the crowd tends towards conformism, in a way which hinders the force of reason. Le Bon argues that

> The most striking peculiarity presented by a psychological crowd is the following: Whoever be the individuals that compose it, however like or unlike be their mode of life, their occupations, their character, or their intelligence, the fact that they have been transformed into a crowd puts them in

DOI: 10.4324/9781003200253-17

possession of a sort of *collective mind* which makes them feel, think, and act in a manner quite different from that in which each individual of them would feel, think and act were he in a state of isolation. There are certain ideas and feelings which do not come into being, or do not transform themselves into acts except in the case of individuals forming a crowd. The psychological crowd is a provisional being formed of heterogeneous elements, which for a moment are combined, exactly as the cells which constitute a living body form by their reunion a new being which displays characteristics very different from those possessed by each of the cell singly.

(1895, p. 4)

Le Bon further contends that

Different causes determine the appearance of those characteristics peculiar to crowds:
1. The sentiment of responsibility which always controls individuals disappears entirely.
2. Phenomena of a hypnotic order. In a crowd every sentiment and act are *contagious*. And contagious to such a degree that an individual readily sacrifices his personal interest to the collective interest.
3. A crowd in action soon finds himself – either in consequence of the magnetic influence given out by the crowd, or from some other cause ... which much resembles the state of fascination in which the hypnotized individual finds himself in the hands of the hypnotizer. The activity of the brain being paralyzed in the case of the hypnotized subject, the latter becomes the slave of all the unconscious activities of his spinal cord, which the hypnotizer directs at will. The conscious personality has entirely vanished; will and discernment are lost. All feelings and thoughts are bent in the direction determined by the hypnotizer.

(pp. 6–7)

For Le Bon, the subject "is no longer himself, but has become an *automaton* who has ceased to be guided by his will. The crowd is also always intellectually inferior to the isolated individual" (pp. 8–9). An individual, according to Le Bon, "may accept contradiction and discussions; a crowd will never do so. Dictatorialness and intolerance are common to all categories of crowds" (pp. 24–25). He also adds that

Authoritativeness and *intolerance* are sentiments of which crowds have a very clear notion, which they easily conceive and which they entertain as readily as they put them in practice. Crowds exhibit a docile respect for force, and are but slightly impressed by kindness, which for them is scarcely other than a form of weakness.

A crowd is always ready to revolt against a feeble, and to bow down servilely before a strong authority. The crowd always obedient to its extreme sentiments, passes alternately from anarchy to servitude and from servitude to anarchy.

(p. 25)

Following Le Bon, Freud (1921) contends that

A group is impulsive, changeable and irritable. It is led almost exclusively by the unconscious. The impulses which a group obeys may according to circumstances be generous or cruel, heroic or cowardly, but they are always so imperious that no personal interest, not even that of self-preservation, can make itself felt. *Nothing about it is premeditated.* Though it may desire things passionately, yet this is never so for long, for it is incapable of perseverance. *It cannot tolerate any delay between its desire and the fulfilment of what it desires.* It has a sense of omnipotence; the notion of impossibility disappears for the individual in a group.

(p. 77)

Freud is grounding his argument in two elements that contain Le Bon's most important observations: first, the collective inhibition of cognitive capacity; second, the crowd's elevated levels of emotionality.

I have chosen to discuss these qualities through Fritz Lang's *M*: an expressionist film produced in Germany in 1931, shortly before Hitler's rise to power. The film portrays the behavior of individuals as part of a crowd in a crisis state. Lang (1931) explores the crowd's behavior as it operates without following any singled out leader, but 'the rules of the street.'

Discussion of Fritz Lang's M

The film *M* is a milestone in the history of *talkies* (non-silent films), which first came out in 1927. In this 1931 production, Lang presents a piece that oscillates between a realistic, documentary-like portrayal of external reality – featuring German society on the eve of Hitler's political ascent – and a depiction of the uninhibited frenzy of internal psychic reality. This hybrid quality has made the film a unique combination of the *film noir* genre, which expresses the zeitgeist and actual historical events, and the expressionist genre, prominent in contemporary German cinema, which highlighted inner realities, psychic processes and hallucinations. This oxymoronic combination created a singular juxtaposition of external reality and inner psychic worlds.

The Film's Expressionist Elements

Expressionist art – and especially German expressionism – emerged at a time of social unrest and upheaval: the years of economic strife following the first world war, which saw the deterioration of social institutions. Expressionist German cinema developed in the wake of the first world war and remained dominant until the early 1930's (January, 1933). Many scholars of German expressionism in film, including Kracauer (1947, pp. 215–222) – author of *From Caligari to Hitler* – have argued that expressionist films are social documents that explain the rise of Nazism.

As an artistic movement, expressionism highlights the artistic expression of emotions, mainly negative: angst of everyday people, expressing their fear and malaise. Expressionistic portrayal breaks and distorts the external façade of realism, contrasting with artistic approaches that emphasize harmony, order, balance and symmetry. Expressionism focuses on the presentation of distress, anxiety and fear and is preoccupied with death or the powers of darkness – ghosts, demons, witches and Satan's minions – and their pull towards the other world. These conventions imply that the everyday world is merely a point of departure, from which one travels into other worlds – domains of dark, evil urges and realms of the irrational. Expressionism thus situates itself on the boundary between familiar, routine realistic reality and the dark world, serving as a no-man's-land which transports us from the ordinary into the bizarre and frightening.

This liminal quality of expressionist art is manifest in a preoccupation with mirrors, reflections and mirror-images. In this vein, its portrayal of the human figure always shows it a split figure inhabiting a dual world. This duality is ubiquitous: behind the normal façade, lurks the other half, the dark, demonic, instinctual half, which does not abide by the laws of order, which is controlled by drives and drawn to anything taboo or forbidden. This duality is often expressed through representations of shadows or mirrors: the figure's reflection in the mirror always reveals another aspect; the shadow is present as a black figure which – through unreal and elusive – is menacingly tethered to the actual person.

Fritz Lang's *M* highlights the dual nature of its protagonist: the external guise of an everyday man conceals unstoppable instinctual forces. The killer is a plump little man who is dressed just like everyone else and rents a small room from a respectable landlady. Throughout the entire film, the struggle is internal and only at its end is the protagonist granted the right to verbally express his urges with a scream. Lang chose the leading actor, Peter Lorre, because his 'everyman' appearance allowed him to portray a bourgeois man who could not possibly be suspected of being a serial killer (Kracauer, 1947, p. 220). Through his dual presence – run-of-the-mill person and serial killer – the protagonist represents the potential for evil that lurks in all of us. While his landlady describes him as a quiet, proper and upright person, when we see him walking down the street and looking at his reflection in a store window, we see his figure surrounded by the knives on display inside the store. At the end of the film, after he has been trapped by the blood-thirsty crowd, he looks like a hunted animal. When he cries out to the crowd, begging for his life, he presents himself as a prisoner of his uncontrollable urges: "I am always forced to move along the streets, and always someone is behind me. It is I. I sometimes feel I am myself behind me, and yet I can't escape…" (Lang, 1931, 1:42:09–1:42:50).

The images show the killer's shadow cast on the poster promising a reward to anyone who finds the killer; and the figure of the next victim reflected in the mirror inside the store window, at which the killer is looking.

All these characteristically expressionist elements simmer throughout the film like a shadow or a mirror-image (in expressionist terms), acting as a slowly emerging foundation that enables the crowd's instinctual outburst at the end of the film. While the crowd depicted in the film seems to be mobilized for a good cause – catching a serial child murderer – once the killer has been caught, the blood-thirsty crowd would have lynched him, had the police and the court not intervened.

The Course of Events

The first part of the film presents a mystery: little girls are killed one after the other and the killer is still on the loose. The second and main part of the film features the attempt to track and find the killer, a process which leads to its third and final part – the discovery, the resolution. The film presents us with a city: with street ads, a school, houses and a human landscape that is organized into well-established hierarchical systems, such as the police (including the criminal secretary, the police chief and the police inspectors), the underworld (with the mafia boss and various safecrackers, pickpockets, thieves and prostitutes) and the social margins with its panhandlers. In between these milieus, we meet the normal, orderly society of everyday citizens.

The phenomenon Lang unveils in this film is the behavior of the everyday person when they become part of a crowd: the upstanding citizens may appear to be law-abiding, but inside each of them hides a hysteric. The scenes taking place out in the streets emphasize how everyone is a suspect, how the crowd condemns without a trial; how the crowd – in which the individual's identifying markers are effaced – is vengeful, hysterical, irrational, impulsive and intolerant.

I will now focus on two particular scenes – the opening and closing scenes – to illustrate the crowd's process of regression from external to internal reality, to the archaic realm of the collective psyche, as Freud and Adorno have described. Intolerance and the surge of the herd instinct lead the crowd to the brink of lynching a killer, who becomes a victim himself.

The Opening Scene

The film opens with a group of children standing in a circle and playing with a ball. The scene is shot from above, as if some unidentified eye, unrelated to any character, is watching things unfold, presumably foretelling what will happen later on. In fact, this scene presents the terror of something that had already happened, but had not been registered, a kind of "fear of breakdown," in Winnicott's (1974) terms. It is a seemingly innocent scene, in which traces of terror, which have been inscribed in archaic areas powerfully resurface when the collective unconscious threatens to break out.

But what is it that evokes terror in this ostensibly harmless scene? The scene is composed of empty images, which give rise to a sense of nameless dread, which paves the way for the future outbreak. The air of terror is created by means of several poetic devices that represent *absence*: synecdoche, fragmentation and repetition.

The use of *synecdoche* – describing a whole through one of its parts – places the whole out of sight, emphasizing its absence and leaving only the part as evidence of the whole's existence. This visual representation of emptiness, this enhancement of nothingness shows Lang's potent ability to use cinematic language to represent absence.

Consider, for example, the ball thrown at the notice board: the ball acts as a synecdoche, representing the absent girl. This scene became a cinematic classic by virtue of its ability to show so much with so little – with a single picture and without any words; it presents the entire horror story with one image: the girl throwing the ball is not in the frame; and so is the killer. The frame centers on a notice board, showing a notice concerning missing children who are presumed murdered. Visually, we see a shadow cast on the notice – that of the killer: the notice proclaiming the search for the killer becomes the meeting point for the shadow of the killer and the ball that belongs to the girl, the next victim. On the level of sound, we hear the killer's inviting voice asking 'what is your name' and the girl's innocent voice answering: 'Elsie Beckmann.' We see neither the killer's face nor that of the victim, but the entire scene is played out before our eyes as our mind fills in the deep gaps that our built into this horror scene.

Another synecdoche added to this array of signifiers is the voice of the killer. While the killer buys the girl a balloon, the soundtrack features a whistled version of Grieg's 'In the Hall of the mountain King,' referencing a scene in *Peer Gynt* where the protagonist is trying to escape *trolls* – demonic creatures that live in a dark and threatening underworld. Thus, in its very early stages, the film imbues innocent signifiers with grave, macabre references. In addition, the soundtrack plays a prominent role in resolving the hunt for the killer. The whistle, which becomes a kind of Ariadne's thread throughout the film, eventually leads to the killer being discovered and caught. It is the reason that the letter M, as a mark of Cain, is imprinted on the killer's coat, betraying his identity before he is able to commit another murder.

The use of *fragmentation* disrupts the narrative structure at crucial junctions, creating tension which intensifies the sense of horror. Instead of having one event lead to another, the film presents a web of fragmentary episodes, linked through analogy on grounds of resemblance. These events are reconnected not through the disrupted sequence but through the analogous element of absence and horror, which becomes increasingly imbued with negative emotions. The fragmentation itself emphasizes the analogous link of absence.

The opening sequence fragments into three different spaces, while the most prominent element governing the transitions between them is the absence they share:

- Elsie's second story apartment: Elsie's mother is making lunch as Elsie is supposed to come home from school. But Elsie is not there and the table that has been set for her intensifies her absence: the plate is empty and no one sits at the table.
- The stairwell, the window and the door mark the boundaries between different spaces, all of which are empty.
- The street is the place where disaster strikes – a little girl exits a school; concerned parents storm the school to pick up their children; a policeman stops traffic to allow a girl to cross the street; the innocent girl plays with her ball.
- The mother's cry – 'Elsie, Elsie' – goes unanswered. The empty plate, the empty chair, the utensils and the cooking pot, the stairwell and the empty yard, the empty lawn where we see the ball rolling without its owner, the balloon caught in the powerlines – all these seemingly unrelated images add up, through analogy, to create a dark narrative of absence and emptiness, signifying a sealed fate of loss.

The element of repetition in ever-widening circles. The film opens with girls standing in a circle, playing with a ball. The girl holding the ball stands inside the circle and sings a dreadful song: "The man in black will soon be here / With his cleaver's blade so true / He'll make mincemeat out of you!" (Lang, 1931, 0:00:53-0:01:12). When the song ends, whoever the girl is facing leaves the circle, as the last line echoes in everyone's ears, inscribing a sense of horror even in those not playing the game – as one neighbor cries out from a window: "The same cursed song over and over!" The neighbor continues, saying that she has asked the children to stop singing this awful song, as if hearing about the killer was not enough for them. This clearly explains to the viewers the source of the horror, which has remained unknown thus far: a serial killer is on the loose in the city, killing little girls. The same outwardly spiraling repetition is manifest in the police inspectors, who sit in a circle, and in the designated search areas, marked on a map with circles made by a pair of compasses. All these serve to heighten the sense of horror and dread.

Elsie vanishes and the street is thrown into turmoil. Any man walking with a young girl is suddenly suspected of being the serial child killer. The street becomes paranoid as the serial killer turns into everyone's common enemy. The circles of paranoia grow wider and wider: we see a circle of men in café, huddled around as one of them reads from the newspaper; the circles ripple outwards as do the circles of search areas on the police's map.

"Anxiety among the general public is heightened"

(Lang, 1931, 0:10:36)

"Anybody sitting next to you could be the murderer"

(Lang, 1931, 0:11:06)

"Any man on the street could be the murderer"

(Lang, 1931, 0:12:24)

The use of empty synecdoche; fragmentation and the attempt to link things together through the common denominator of emptiness; the repetition of widening circles – are poetic devices that create the condensed sense of horror that marks the film from its very beginning. The horror that builds throughout the film creates a negative bonding and cultivates a ready foundation for contagion, which by the end of the film, turns the crowd into a single mass, devoid of any individual characteristics.

The Closing Scene: The Trial

The trial scene sees the panhandlers, pimps, prostitutes and the rest of the underworld meet with the killer. It features a supposedly well-organized trial: we see a defense attorney holding books, a court of law, guards at the entrance. However, within this legal domain, Lang lets the emotional outbreak and the herd-reaction run rampant, demonstrating the duality of ostensible-order and chaos.

From this moment, the killer is hunted by the incited crowd that calls out for his blood. All the people who joined the search for the killer – the smalltime thieves and prostitutes on society's margins, the police bigwigs and the underworld all join forces in looking for the serial killer, now reduced to a hunted animal. Eventually the killer is caught and brought to justice in an underground hall of justice, in a basement.

While the setting is supposed to be that of a court, the scene is presented as a piece of theater. The crowd sits in a half circle and the trial is run according to the rules of a theatrical performance: the protagonist is the defendant, the serial killer, next to him stands the public defender and the viewers, as spectators, are located right in front of them. The crowd's level of tolerance is tested at this moment of truth, through the public quality of the trial. But while the legal realm is supposed to be governed by rational considerations, the court is overrun by the crowd's instinctual outbreak. The crowd decrees that the killer should be killed, erased from the face of the earth. The defense attorney asks for a doctor, claiming that the man is ill and deserves the protection of the state. The crowd, however, seeks revenge; it has nothing but contempt for the killer and the prostitutes proclaim: "go ask the mothers." Had the police not shown up at the very last minute, in a kind of *deus ex machina*, the killer would have certainly been lynched.

In words and phrases, this final scene collects the meanings presented throughout the film using spaces, objects and events. Questions of justice versus vengeance, rule of law versus vigilantism, free choice versus compulsion, rationality versus instincts and drives; normality versus illness; executioner versus victim and, above all, the sentence passed by the hysterical crowd, all converge into a situation bereft of all salvation, mercy or redemption. The crowd has the power to dissolve, one after the other, the ritual procedures of the trial and empty justice of its meaning. The underground court, the kangaroo court, renders the notion of a fair and just trial, which is guided by a position of tolerance, void of any meaning. Though the defense attorney tries to uphold and maintain the legal procedure, justice remains but an empty vessel and, had the police not arrived in time, a lynching would have taken place before our eyes.

This underground court scene turns the power relations on their head: the killer becomes the victim who pleads for his life; the crowd becomes the merciless assailant. As the killer is thrown about from side to side, as he protests that the crowd has no right to hold him, they answer:

> Right? There's only one thing right for a man like you – death!
> Right! Kill him!
> Kill the rabid dog!
> Kill him!
>
> (Lang, 1931, 1:38:05–1:38:15)

In a desperate attempt to defend himself, the killer pleads insanity:

> I can't help it
> I can't
> I really can't ... help it.
>
> (Lang, 1931, 1:40:34–1:40:49)

In response to the killer-victim's cries for help, the crowd grows even more blood-thirsty:

> Kill the monster! Kill him!
> Put the animal to death
> Rub him out!
> Get rid of him
> Annihilate the monster
> That's not a human being!
>
> (Lang, 1931, 1:47:35–1:47:42)

The defender's vain attempts to maintain a proper court setting come to nothing and the crowd eventually storms the killer to tear him limb from limb.

At this crucial moment, the police arrive on the scene and the incited crowd all raise their hands in the air to signal their submission to the higher authority of the law.

The film thus ends with the rule of law having the upper hand and, through a dissolve edit, the scene shifts to a proper court, with judges presiding over the proceedings and conducting a fair trial. The final scene shows a lamenting mother crying out that this justice will not bring the children back to life and that everyone must keep their children close.

Before our eyes, Lang shows how individuals come together to form an uninhibited crowd, how their sound rational thinking unravels and how they instantly become an incited mob, whose collective 'brakes' are diminished or even altogether removed, even when the goal they seek to attain – the catching of a serial killer – is a worthy one.

The Gradual Unraveling of Tolerance

Fritz Lang's *M* shows the unraveling of the collective mind and how a large group of people, who have come together to pursue a positive goal – stopping a serial killer who targets little girls – end up losing all capacity for inhibition and rational judgement and, by the end of the film, arrive at the brink of lynching the killer – who is himself a prisoner of his own urges. The process undergone by the crowd's collective mind is depicted as a regression which, despite the legal setting in which the film reaches its climax, leads the crowd to the 'zero degree' or 'raw state.'

Throughout this chapter, I have shown how the film uses the conventions of German expressionist art and the poetic devices of synecdoche, fragmentation and images of widening circles to manifest, before our eyes, a growing and intensifying air of horror. This air is responsible for creating the negative bonding which, through the mechanism of emotional contagion discussed by Le Bon, Freud and Adorno, impels the kind of regressive movement that Adorno calls 'archaic regression,' which connects to the psyche's crucible – its 'libidinal nature.' Once this process has been put into motion, it becomes compulsive and unstoppable. At that moment, all the conditions Le Bon described are in place and the crowd is primed for an uninhibited instinctual outburst.

Today, when crowds around the world are incited by extreme right-wing propaganda, one must be very alert to the initial stages of the poisoning of the collective mind. One must be aware of how such propaganda manipulates people on the level of what Adorno termed "archaic regressions." Through my analysis of *M*, I have attempted to highlight the air of horror, of a primal fear of breakdown, which Hitler-like leaders might use to incite crowds and undermine any attempt to maintain individual or collective tolerance.

References

Adorno, T. W. (1951). Freudian theory and the pattern of fascist propaganda. In *The Essential Frankfurt School Reader*, pp. 118–137.

Le Bon, G. (1895[2021]). *The Crowd. A Study of the Popular Mind*. New York: Dover Publications.

Freud, S. (1921). Group psychology and the analysis of the ego. *SE*, 18: 65–144.

Jonsson, S. (2013). After individuality: Freud's mass psychology and Weimar politics. *New German Critique*, 40(2(119)): 53–75.

Kracauer, S. (1947). *From Caligari to Hitler: A Psychological History of the German Film*. New Jersey, Princeton University Press, 1974.

Lang, F. (1931). *M*. [Film] Nero Film.

Moscovvici, S. (1981[1985]). *The Age of the Crowd. A History Treatise on Mass Psychology*. Tr. J.C. Whitehouse. Cambridge: Cambridge University Press.

Winnicott, D. W. (1974). Fear of breakdown. *International Review of Psycho-Analysis*, 1(1-2): 103–107.

Chapter 13

Intolerance and Processes of Fundamentalism in the Context of the Basic Assumption of Incohesion

Aggregation/Massification

Earl Hopper

Incohesion: Aggregation/Massification or (ba) I:A/M is the fourth basic assumption in the unconscious life of groups and group-like social systems, especially those which have been traumatised. Fundamentalism and scapegoating are the twin pillars of massification. Having discussed the dynamics of scapegoating elsewhere (Hopper, 2022a), I will focus here on the dynamics of fundamentalism, which is closely associated with intolerance as the opposite of tolerance. I will illustrate some of these ideas with data from my twice weekly clinical groups, the details of which have been changed in order to protect the confidentiality of the members of the groups.

A Brief Summary of the Theory of the Basic Assumption of Incohesion: Aggregation/Massification or (ba) I:A/M

My theory of the basic assumption of Incohesion: Aggregation/Massification or (ba) I:A/M (Hopper, 2023; Hopper, 2003b; Bion, 1961), can be summarised in terms of the following hypotheses:

1. Various events that cause the experience of inadequate containment and insufficient holding that can be characterised in terms of failed dependency;
2. The fear of annihilation characterized by intra-psychic fission and fragmentation and various psychotic anxieties associated with this, in oscillation with relational fusion and confusion with what is left of and with what can be found in the other, and various psychotic anxieties associated with this, based on seeking protection against the psychotic anxieties associated with each of the two polarized conditions;
3. The development of crustacean and amoeboid character structures, and of negative and positive encapsulations, encystment, and/or encrypment;
4. The propensity towards the enactment of aggressive feelings in aggression and violence based on traumatophilia, i.e. based on the sexualisation of aggressive feelings and on the use of sexuality as a defence against depressive

DOI: 10.4324/9781003200253-18

anxieties, as seen in the development of the trauma syndrome involving addiction, somatization, sadistic perversion, risk taking, delinquency, and criminality.

5. Incohesion is a manifestation and an expression of the intra-psychic phenomenology of the fear of annihilation and relational forms of defensive protection against the pain of this experience. This can be seen in the primary development of the socio-cultural state of aggregation and in the secondary development of the socio-cultural state of massification, and then in the defensive oscillations between them. These socio-cultural states are manifest in those patterns of relations, normation, communication, and styles of thinking and feeling, as well as in patterns of aggression, that are typical of them.

6. Incohesion is associated with the development of social psychic retreats such as ghettos and enclaves which are often based on sub-groupings and contra-groupings associated with social identities. The sub-groupings and contra-groupings within a contextual society characterized by Incohesion are likely themselves to become characterized by Incohesion and the dynamics of it.

7. Incohesion is characterised by the development of roles that are typical of aggregation and massification.

8. Traumatized people are especially vulnerable to the suction power of these roles, and, in turn, they are likely to personify them.

Massification and Fundamentalism

Massification is an overwhelming and "totalising" process. However, the core values of social systems which are in states of massification must be continuously re-cathected. The members of such social systems must continuously enhance their identification with them. Illusion, idealisation, and conformity must be maintained. These processes are closely associated with fundamentalism, both as causes and as consequences of it (Auestad, 2015).

1. Fundamentalism is based on the conviction that the knowledge given to us by those in authority is necessarily correct (Flemmen, 2014). "(F)undamentalism (is not and) cannot be based on experience" (Vogt, 1926 p. 280). Fundamentalism can be understood as a kind of "(m)ilitant piety" (which) emerges as a response "to a perceived 'crisis' ... involving a battle which goes beyond ... 'conventional political struggle' and ... which is experienced ... as a cosmic war between the forces of good and evil" (Armstrong, 2000, p. xi).

   Fundamentalism is manifest in each realm or sub-matrix of the tripartite matrix of a social system, i.e. the foundation matrix, the dynamic matrix, and the personal or interpersonal matrices of the participants in the system, and in each of dimension of the tripartite matrix, e.g. interpersonal relations, values, norms, and beliefs, patterns of communication, styles of thinking and feeling, etc. (Hopper, 2023a, 2023b). In the context of Incohesion, the defensive shift from aggregation to massification is a function of the increasing mutual intolerance of the members of various aggregated sub-groupings and contra-groupings other than their own, especially with respect to their conformity to core values and norms by which such groupings might be distinguished and denoted.

2. Such forces involve a set of personal and collective beliefs and practices which are prescriptive as well as proscriptive, and usually based on the Law of the Father, according to his original Word. The father figure controls his horde of children who might be a danger to him by grooming their hatred of enemy other-objects. However, the Law of the Mother (Mitchell, 1974, 2013) is also relevant. The mother figure demands that the sibling children control their feelings of competition and rivalry both with her and with one another. This can be realised through the displacement of these feelings onto people who are outside the family, be they individuals, families, and/or groupings of various kinds. Such "other-objects" become actual or potential enemies.

   The cohesion of the society depends on the regulation of these displacement processes, which mark the origins of all configurations that involve the development of "consciousness of kind" (Giddings, 1924) and subsequent identifications of "Us and Them" (Gutmann et al., 2009). Ironically, the origins of tolerance and intolerance can each be traced to the obedience to the Law of the Father and to the Law of the Mother: tolerance of those who are in the same moral community, and intolerance of those who are outside it (Durkheim, 1902-1903).

3. Fundamentalism is a comprehensive and distinguishing property of the "way of life" or the "habitus" of a particular social system (Dajani, 2017; Yair, 2017). The boundaries of membership are of vital importance, especially with respect to becoming a member of the social system and to relinquishing membership of it. Therefore, such processes are highly ritualised.

4. In the habitus of a social system characterised by fundamentalism, it is necessary to adhere very strictly to the core values and norms of the system. Norms of moral judgment are applied both stringently and absolutely (Ranulf, 1964). These norms are unconsciously manipulated in order to support the status quo (Hopper, 2003c). The application of sanctions against all forms of deviance and disobedience are organised and applied as a matter of duty. Conformity to the norms of gender roles, dietary practices, and the expression of feelings in general and of sexual and aggressive feelings in particular, is tightly regulated. For example, in the Jewish religion, even the many "little laws" known as *hallacha*, which are derived from the one big Law, must be followed precisely and literally. The quest for "law and order" dominates the political life of the habitus (Abella, 2018). Intolerance and its vicissitudes prevail.

5. Fundamentalism in societies is associated with the development of "nationalism". This is often associated with placing great value on military might, and on the authority of the major religion(s) of the society, or at least of their common beliefs. For example, in its "Pledge of Allegiance", the United States is identified as "One Nation under God". The control over borders and immigration becomes vitally important, and goes well beyond the rational assessment of economic needs. Pressures towards conformity and uniformity among geographical regions increase. Fundamentalism and nationalism tend to be associated with the emergence of fascism and totalitarianism (Arendt, 1951; Auestad, 2013; Pick, 2016).

Fundamentalism in organizations is associated with the development of fanaticism (Robles, 2013). The training Institutes and certifying organizations of traumatised professions function like cults in which loyalty to the "collective" becomes more important than the work itself (Hopper, 2012). Governance processes in such organisations tend to be supported by constant appeals to their Ethics Committees and their Codes of Ethics. Szonyi (2022) and Hopper (2022b) have argued that organisations characterised by fanaticism can also be described as "totalitarian".

Fundamentalism in smaller groupings such as committees is associated with the development of authoritarian leadership, submissive followership, and passive bystandership. These processes must be understood in terms of the dynamic matrix of the sponsoring organisation, whether this is a prison or a bankrupt corporation.

Fundamentalism in clinical groups presents particular problems. In part, clinical work must be understood in terms of the dynamic matrices of the professional organisations from which Group Analysts take their professional identities. The stratification of professional organisations can breed a kind of elitism associated with smugness and self-idealisation, which must be distinguished from authentic self-confidence and security in the development and maintenance of professional and clinical identities.

6. Those who personify the central roles of a social system characterised by massification and fundamentalism are likely to have, for example, an "authoritarian personality" (Adorno et al., 1950), a "fascist state of mind" (Bollas, 1992), and/or a "fundamentalist mindset" (Leo, 2017). Sebek (1996) has argued that the internal worlds of such people are likely to be dominated by a "totalitarian object".

Fundamentalism, Incohesion and Social Category Thinking and Feeling

Basic assumptions are each characterised by a distinctive form of thinking and feeling. The basic assumption of Incohesion is characterised by social category thinking and feeling. This style of thinking and feeling is based on the tendency to make binary classifications (Tajfel (1981).[1] Such "process reduction"

(Elias, 1978) is ubiquitous when the members of a social system feel that their leaders have both failed and betrayed them, and, therefore, when the cohesion of the social system is threatened, as seen in the un-integration of its patterns of relations, the in-solidarity of its patterns of values, norms and beliefs, and/ or in the incoherence of its patterns of communication.

Social category classifications are based on what is regarded in the culture as "natural". For example, first order classifications include age and sex and various manifestations of what are assumed to be breeding groups, such as skin colour, race, class, and even religious affiliations. For example, in the context of social category thinking and feeling, sex determines gender. Such classifications of people are often a matter of the religious beliefs that prevail in a particular culture. However, in modern post-Darwinian cultures, such beliefs are more often analogous to those associated with animal husbandry and plant cultivation.[2] Nonetheless, these biologically based social classifications are often regarded as "sacred". The relations among men in their familial roles as fathers, sons, and brothers, are closely connected with their relations within public roles within the power structures of the contextual society and its core institutions, which must also be understood in terms of the mirror images of these relations among women in their familial and public roles, and of course vice versa.

When processes of aggregation prevail, there is a continuous threat to the boundaries of each cultural category and social formation associated with it. The cultural category becomes a collection of the properties of the individual members of the social formation. Social formations are regressively transformed into social classifications. Individual identities are privileged over social identities, which are denied and disavowed. It is as though people have come to be known only by their "given" names. However, when massification prevails, the opposite occurs: all cultural categories and social formations are collapsed into one. Cultural attributes are privileged over personal qualities, and social identities are privileged over individual identities. Such phrases as "the one and the many" and "the many and the one" are likely to become politicised. In other words, socio-cultural classifications become the basis for the formation of identities in general (Appiah, 2018; Fukuyama, 2018; Murray, 2019; Volkan, 2006, 2020).

In the context of Incohesion, social category thinking and feeling is characterised by the following features (Hopper, 1981):

1. Continuous stereotyping of the individual members of a category. This involves an attempt to eradicate all individual nuance, and to refuse the freedom to interpret the key roles in the contextual social system.
2. Continuous comparisons and evaluations with respect to other categories and classifications. Matters of difference are transformed into matters of superiority, equality, and inferiority, which become the basis for the distribution of goods and rewards, including the entitlement to compassion and sympathy for the experience of social trauma and the right to victimhood.

3. Continuous attempts to clarify boundaries and to reduce any confusions in them, especially with respect to locations in multiple hierarchies of power, as seen in the incongruence of class and status rankings.

4. Continuous attempts to reduce and to regulate boundary crossings, for example, in immigration and emigration from one nation to another, in social mobility within any one nation, and in marriage between members of social categories. The offspring of mixed-race partnerships are especially important, because their offspring are not easily and readily classified, and their birth confirms that boundaries have been violated by their parents. For example, when one partner is "Black" and the other partner "White", their children are more likely to be "Brown". As a mixed hybrid colour, "Brown" necessitates the making of further classifications which threaten the existing binary classifications of "Black" or "White" (Penna, 2016).

5. Continuous attempts to privilege either the "cosmopolitan" basis of social classifications over the "local" basis of them, or vice versa (Merton, 1957). Local classifications tend to be "restricted" rather than "elaborate" (Bernstein, 1971), and "specialist" rather than "generalist". This is also seen in the appreciation of the concrete rather than the abstract, and the detailed rather than the patterned.

Illustrations of Fundamentalism in Clinical Group Analysis

It is difficult to provide clinical examples of the dynamics of fundamentalism from one's own clinical practice of group analysis. First of all, from a particular conductor's point of view: his rival has a fundamentalist mindset, his colleague has a firm frame of reference, and he himself has a secure clinical identity. Furthermore, people with a fundamentalist mindset tend to avoid psychotherapy, perhaps especially group analysis, which is characterised by the importance given to horizontal relations. They fear the experience of various psychotic anxieties associated with memories of traumatic experiences. In effect, they fear the experience of re-traumatisation, which is likely to involve the dissolution of defensive encapsulations of various kinds (Garwood, 2020). Nonetheless, if people with these personality characteristics do join a group, they are likely to become the focus of attention in the context of the roles that are generated by the basic assumption of Incohesion, i.e. they are likely to personify these roles. Although this can lead to favourable clinical outcomes, it often leads to their leaving therapy (Hopper, 2003b, 2005).

1. The problems presented by patients with a fundamentalist mindset can be illustrated by two cases of a "true believer" (Hoffer, 1951). In the first case, a woman who was a Group Relations "activist", and who had a senior position at the "Tavi", accused me of having "gone astray" in my identification with Foulkesian Group Analysis. She believed that all forms of group

therapy should be based on what she called a "Bionic orientation". She disagreed with another member of the group who insisted that she meant "Bionian". Although she knew that I was primarily a "Foulkesian", and although she remained in the group for over three years, she eventually withdrew in contempt of me and the group. She left the group after reporting that she had read my (Hopper, 1982) first article in *Group Analysis* in which I said that I could not decide whether Bion was banal or a genius. Ironically, she did not agree with my Kleinian interpretation that her contempt was a defence against her envy of my theoretical and clinical flexibility and freedom to be "myself". However, her decision to leave was precipitated by my observation that she had begun to feel that the group and I were not strong enough to "contain" her rage, which had led to her need to split the work of Bion from that of Foulkes, and to split her internal objects who represented these figures or who were represented by them.

I suggested that for her "Bion" and "Foulkes" were social categories. As she had begun to appreciate the value of the work of Foulkes and some of the limitations of the work of Bion, my style of thinking and feeling had become more difficult for her. She could not tolerate her own inability to categorise me as either Bionian or Foulkesian. I had become a hybrid of them.

Another example of a patient who had a fundamentalist mindset is a 55-year-old male who had become a Priest of a New Religion. He and his partner went to Thailand a couple of times a year both for recreation and for religious proselytising, attempting to recruit disciples for their Church in London, which also had branches in the United States. This man began to talk more and more about his sexual practices with his partner, including their search for threesomes involving sadomasochistic practices. They were also involved in the use of drugs, mainly weed and cocaine, often assuring the group that they did not use anything "stronger". They also had what they called a "special" relationship with their drug dealer, an older man who they called "Daddy". The patient insisted that his sexual activities were completely compatible with and integrated into the religious practices of his Church, and that they had found a way of being both at one with God and completely satisfied sexually through the mastery of pain, which they were able to "rise above".

After about a year in the group, the patient confessed that he and his partner had started a process which he hoped would lead to their successful adoption of a young boy from a Thai orphanage. The group and I began to focus on their wish to adopt the young Thai orphan in order to find a third partner who would be both compliant and completely dependent on them for their drug related sexual activities. He defended himself against his experience of shame and guilt by insisting that these practices were "religious rituals".

When this was not accepted by the group, his anxieties became overwhelming, and the patient gave notice that he would be terminating his membership of the group. Before terminating, however, he spent many sessions in which he accused the group and me of being "group analytical fundamentalists" who were driven by our theories rather than by our appreciation of his way of life, which he insisted would involve a much more comfortable and satisfactory existence for the proposed adoptee than was available for him in Thailand. Shortly before he left, I commented that he was provoking a kind of war between his form of religious fundamentalism and what he took to be my/our form of group analytical fundamentalism.

Eventually, I suggested that he was searching for a father in me in whom he could completely "believe", to whom he could submit, and before whom he could prostrate himself. Not being able to discover this kind of man in me, he sought a dependent and vulnerable Thai orphan boy to whom he could then become this kind of father.

In my opinion, this interpretation led to his decision to leave the group. However, the last straw was my suggestion, which was supported by other members of the group, that he might have been happier if the group and I provided him with a kind of group prison from which there could be no escape. This would involve both security and safety, as well as punishment. His response was that although I had read Sartre, I had got stuck on "No Exit", and that my interpretations were motivated by my need to maintain a full group.

Perhaps the problem was actually one of intolerance rather than tolerance, and of his having more respect for and appreciation of the former than of the latter. Whereas the group were intolerant of his beliefs and practices, they were tolerant of him. However, he was incapable of making this distinction (Berman, 2021). Nonetheless, it must be acknowledged that the group were deeply challenged by what they assumed to be his paedophilia. They were not entirely unhappy when he decided to leave.

2. Very early in my own career I experienced a conflict between what I took to be the development of fundamentalist mindsets on the part of several patients in one of my twice-weekly groups, and my own particular style of work and clinical identity. Three members of the group were training as group analysts, and another had announced her wish to become a group analyst. In other words, one half of the group had made a very strong identification with Foulkesian Group Analysis and had formed a shared very positive if not idealising Transference to me.[3] Thus, the dynamic matrix of the group was ripe for the development of fundamentalism in the practice of group analysis itself and the belief in its clinical efficacy.

Two of the candidates reported that many senior group analysts had let it be known that they were favourably impressed by "Hopper's work", and that "like Hopper" these candidates were doing "good work". One of the men began to wear waistcoats and to use colourful pocket handkerchiefs in his coat, which were, as Fashion Editors write, my "personal style signifiers". However, I felt that my flattering imitators were somewhat stunted in their emotional development, and that in the context of the newly created Institute, they had become "pseudo-mature". My interpretations of their "imitative identification" with me were to no avail.

I discussed this problem with two of my former supervisors who had different analytical styles. They agreed with each other that I was being a "perfectionist" and perhaps "therapeutically zealous", allowing the excellent to drive out the good, and the impossible to drive out the possible. I argued that they had themselves become fanatics, and that their point of view was influenced more by the dynamics of the Institute than by their concern for the welfare of the patients.

The two patients/students in question proceeded to qualify, and, as I anticipated, they immediately decided to leave the group. Within a couple of months or so, the remaining group of six "settled down". For almost a year they confessed to feeling that they should have told the two patients/students that in their opinion they were not really "ready". They were not "fully baked". However, they did not feel strong enough to confront them. In fact, it is very difficult to challenge people whose mindsets are supported by an organisation which has developed a fundamentalist habitus, which is hardly unusual in training organisations in our particular field, especially at particular phases of their development.

3. In recent years I have on several occasions been called a "psychoanalytical fundamentalist" and a "psychoanalytical cultist" who had no right to regard himself as either a scientist or a "real" Group Analyst. On each occasion, I had held onto my view that in clinical group analysis personal and interpersonal matrices are of primary importance. It is essential to analyse transference and countertransference processes both vertically and horizontally, not withstanding the fact that each of us is permeated through and through by socio-cultural facts and forces. For example, gender identity and choice of partner(s) are not merely a matter of "free choice", but also involve anxieties and fantasies rooted in early experience with mother and father.

In one case I insisted that a middle-aged man who was frequently caught up in violent fights with other men in strange pubs was both enacting and avoiding his anxieties associated with his unconscious struggles around having gay fantasies, and that although his being from Jamaica might have had quite a lot to do with this in an "intersectionalist" way, even if he had been a White Englishman, he was likely to have similar struggles. I insisted that he was using an ideologically based defence in order to protect himself from the anxieties that would arise if he looked more deeply at an important aspect of his personality and functioning.

The central patient in this clinical vignette was convinced that I was unconsciously biased and had extremely old-fashioned beliefs and attitudes about the aetiology of sexual orientation and sexual behaviour. It was felt that I did not really want to explore these matters from the points of view of the patient, but to impose my own point of view, which stems from my being a White middle-class hetero-normative patriarchal psychoanalyst. We tried to work with the idea that at the present time social category thinking and feeling in the wider contextual society was being recapitulated in our group, and that these patterns of equivalence were used to support the defences of the patients.

Although from my point of view the politics of social identity threatened to overwhelm the project of clinical work, from the point of view of the two patients, I was an intolerant psychoanalytical fundamentalist. This is not without irony, given my involvement in the study of the restraints and constraints of the foundation matrix and of socially unconscious processes in general.

Summary and Conclusion

In this chapter I have considered various aspects of intolerance in terms of the basic assumption of Incohesion, in which massification as a defence against aggregation following traumatogenic processes is supported by fundamentalism. Following a discussion of several aspects of fundamentalism, especially social category thinking and feeling, I have illustrated the emergence of fundamentalism through several vignettes of clinical group analysis. I have described the difficulties presented by patients who have fundamentalist mindsets, including two student group analysts. I have also described my being accused of having a fundamentalist mindset rooted in my social, professional and personal identity. These data indicated the importance of the dynamics of gender roles, relations to fathers and father figures, and even particular theoretical and clinical orientations in social category thinking and feeling as a central element in the development and maintenance of fundamentalism, as seen in social category thinking and feeling as a central element in the development and maintenance of fundamentalism in our profession.

Notes

1 This is typical of the paranoid/schizoid position of persons who perceive that they are in danger, which reflects a progression from the psychic fission and fragmentation associated with the autistic position. Although regressive shifts to the autistic position can and do occur, survival depends on the ability to think and feel in terms of "either/or".
2 Talking about human beings and their groupings in terms of what is not-human might be the basis of the so-called "humour" associated with social identities and social hubris (Rappoport, 2005).
3 Ordinarily, I would have not allowed this composition to have developed, because the guidelines for twice-weekly groups which were deemed suitable for candidates in training at the Institute of Group Analysis stated that such groups should not have more than two candidates in training at any one time. However, as often happens, the qualification process for one of the members was delayed, and the fourth person had entered the group without consciously intending to train in group analysis.

References

Abella, A. (2018). Can psychoanalysis contribute to the understanding of fundamentalism? An introduction of a vast question. *International Journal of Psychoanalysis*, 99(3): 642–664.

Adorno, T., Frenkel-Brunswik, E. Levinson, D. & Sanford, N. (1950). *The Authoritarian Personality*. New York: Harper & Brothers.

Appiah, K. A. (2018). *The Lies that Bind: Rethinking Identity: Creed, Country, Color, Class, Culture*. New York: Liveright Publishing.

Arendt, H. (1951). *The Origins of Totalitarianism*. Berlin: Schocken Books.

Armstrong, K. (2000). *The Battle for God: Fundamentalism in Judaism, Christianity and Islam*. London: Harper Collins.

Ashuach, S. & Berman, A. (Eds) In Press. *Sibling Relationships and the Horizontal Axis in Group Analysis*. London: Routledge.

Auestad, L. (2013). *Nationalism and the Body Politic*. London: Karnac.

Auestad, L. (2015). *Respect, Plurality and Prejudice*. London: Karnac.

Berman, A. (2021). Personal communication.

Bernstein, B. (1971). *Class, Codes and Control: Theoretical Studies Towards Sociology of Language*. London: Routledge.

Bion, W. R. (1961). *Experiences in Groups and Other Papers*. London: Tavistock.

Bollas, C. (1992). The fascist state of mind. In *Being a Character*. London: Routledge.

Dajani, K. (2017). The ego's habitus: An examination of the role culture plays in structuring ego. *International Journal of Applied Psychoanalytic Studies*, 14(4): 273–281.

Durkheim, E. (1902–1903). *Moral Education*. New York: Free Press.

Elias, N. (1978). *What is Sociology?* Colombia: University Press.

Flemmen, H. (2014). Fundamentalism, Nazism and Inferiority. In L. Auestad (Ed), *Nationalism and the Body Politic: Psychoanalysis and the Rise of Ethnocentrism and Xenophobia*. London: Karnac.

Fukuyama, F. (2018). *Identity: The Demand for Dignity and the Politics of Resentment*. New York: Farrar, Straus & Giroux.

Garwood, A. (2020). *Holocaust Trauma and Psychic Deformation*. London: Routledge.

Giddings, F. (1924). *The Scientific Study of Human Society*. NC: The University of North Carolina Press.

Gutmann, D., Berger, M, & Berman, A. (2009). The division into Us-Them as a universal social structure. In Gutmann, D. (Ed.), *From Transformation to Transformation: Methods and Practice*. London: Routledge.

Hoffer, E. (1951). *The True Believer: Thoughts on the Nature of Mass Movements*. New York: Harper & Brothers.

Hopper, E. (1981). *Social Mobility: A Study of Social Control and Insatiability*. Oxford: Blackwell.

Hopper, E. (1982). Group analysis: the problem of context. *Group Analysis XV*, 2. Excerpts reprinted in Hopper, E. (2003). *The Social Unconscious: Selected Papers*. London: Jessica Kingsley.

Hopper, E. (2003a). *The Social Unconscious: Selected Papers*. London: Jessica Kingsley.

Hopper, E. (2003b). *Traumatic Experience in the Unconscious Life of Groups*. London: Jessica Kingsley.

Hopper, E. (2003c). Aspects of aggression in large groups characterised by (ba) I:A/M. In Schneider, S. & Weinberg, H. (Eds), *The Large Group Re-visited: The Herd, Primal Horde, Crowds and Masses*. London: Jessica Kingsley.

Hopper, E. (2005). Countertransference in the context of the fourth basic assumption in the unconscious life of groups. *International Journal of Psychotherapy*, 55(1): 87–114.

Hopper, E. (Ed.) (2012). *Trauma and Organizations*. London: Karnac.

Hopper, E. (2022a). "Notes" on processes of scapegoating in the context of the basic assumption of Incohesion: Aggregation/Massification or (ba) I:A/M. In S. Ashuach

& A. Berman (Eds), *Sibling Relations and the Horizontal Axis in Psychotherapy: Psychoanalysis, Group Analysis and Counselling Applications*. London: Routledge.

Hopper, E. (2022b). Group Analysis and Totalitarianism: the past and the unexpected future. Panel presentation at the 47th Autumn Workshop of the Group Analytic Society International – November.

Hopper, E. (2023a). "Notes" on the theory and concept of the fourth basic assumption in the unconscious life of groups and group-like social systems: Incohesion: Aggregation/Massification or (ba) I:A/M. In C. Penna, *From Crowd Psychology to the Dynamics of Large Groups: Historical, Theoretical and Practical Considerations*. London: Routledge.

Hopper, E. (Ed.) (2023b). *The Tripartite Matrix in the Developing Theory and Expanding Practice of Group Analysis: The Social Unconscious in Persons, Groups and Societies: Volume 4*. London: Routledge.

Leo, G. (2017). *Fundamentalism and Psychoanalysis*. Lecce, Italy: Frenis Zero Press.

Merton, R. (1957). *Social Theory and Social Structure*. Glencoe, IL: The Free Press.

Mitchell, J. (1974). *Psychoanalysis and Feminism*. New York: Pantheon Books.

Mitchell, J. (2013). The law of the mother: Sibling trauma and the brotherhood of war. *Canadian Journal of Psychoanalysis*, 21(1): 145–159.

Murray, D (2019). *The Madness of Crowds: Gender, Race and Identity*. London: Bloomsbury.

Penna, C. (2016). Reflections upon Brazilian social unconscious. In Hopper, E. & Weinberg, H. (Eds). *The Social Unconscious in Persons, Groups and Societies. Volume 2: Mainly Foundation Matrices*. London: Karnac.

Penna, C. (2023). *From Crowd Psychology to the Dynamics of Large Groups: Historical, Theoretical and Practical Considerations*. London: Routledge.

Pick, D. (2016). *Psychoanalysis in the Age of Totalitarianism*. Oxon: Routledge.

Ranulf, S. (1964). *Moral Indignation and Middle-Class Psychology: A Sociological Study*. New York: Schocken Books.

Rappoport, L. (2005). *Punchlines: The Case for Racial, Ethnic & Gender Humor*. Westport, CT: Praeger Publishers.

Robles, M. (2013). *Fanaticism in Psychoanalysis*. London: Karnac.

Sebek, M. (1996). The fate of the totalitarian object. *International Forum of Psychoanalysis*, 5(4): 289–294.

Szonyi, G. (2022). Group analysis and totalitarianism: the past and the unexpected future. Panel presentation at the 47th Autumn Workshop of the Group Analytic Society International – November.

Tajfel, H. (1981). *Human Groups and Social Categories: Studies in Social Psychology*. Cambridge: University Press.

Vogt, R. (1926). Om fundamentalisme (hyperlogisme) i religion og videnskap. *Kirke og kultur*, 33, 279–289.

Volkan, V. (2006). *Killing in the Name of Identity: A Study of Bloody Conflicts*. Charlottesville, VA: Pitchstone.

Volkan, V. (2020). *Large Group Psychology: Racism, Societal Divisions, Narcissistic Leaders and Who We Are Now*. Bicester: Phoenix Publishing House.

Yair, G. (2017). The national habitus: Steps towards reintegrating sociology and group analysis. In Hopper, E. & Weinberg, H. (Eds), *The Social Unconscious in Persons, Groups and Societies: Volume 3: The Foundation Matrix Extended and Re-Configured* (pp. 47–64). London: Karnac.

Chapter 14

On Being Tolerated as a Minority

Leyla Navaro

For long years I was raised with the concept of being 'wonderfully tolerated' as a minority in the Ottoman and then Turkish culture. I learned to feel gratitude and thankfulness toward the country where I was born and still live in. Born in Turkey as a Sephardic Jewish woman, I was accustomed not only to carry but genuinely feel this taught gratitude for many years.

When the Spanish Catholic monarch Fernando II of Aragon and Isabella I of Castile ordered the inquisition of Jews in 1492, some 500 years ago, my ancestors were expelled from Spain and Portugal. At the time, Spanish Jews were either forcefully exiled or coerced into conversion to Christianity according to the Tribunal of the Holy Office of the Inquisition (*Tribunal del Santo Oficio de la Inquisicion*). Many Jews had already converted to Catholicism (*Conversos*) in order to save their lives, yet the Inquisition also wished to nail crypto-Jews who continued their religious habits incognito. Some 40,000 to 100,000 Jews who refused to be baptized were expelled from the Iberian peninsula to those countries that would receive them (i.e. Holland, the Ottoman Empire). In 1492, the reigning Sultan Beyazid II of the Ottoman Empire allowed the emigration of Spanish Jews into his territories. He even ordered a large fleet to Spain in order to carry my ancestors into several Ottoman territories, now known as the Balkans, Greece and Turkey.

This hospitality elicited genuine gratitude among Sephardic Jews and thankfulness to the Ottoman Sultans was included in the daily prayers in synagogues. This is still practiced today towards Turkish governing presidents. Meanwhile Sephardic Jews strived to establish themselves in several regions of the Empire while importing European culture and knowhow.

Trans-generationally transmitted for 500 plus years, feelings of gratitude toward the state authorities have been the official backbone of the Jewish minority in Turkey. This was reinforced after the German Holocaust when Turkey remained neutral until the final stages of WWII, and the Turkish Sephardic Jews were mostly spared Nazi deportation in contrast to Jews of Greek, Bulgarian and Romanian origins.

Born in the northern part of Greece, Dymothicon, my father had the right insight of moving to Istanbul for commercial purposes, after which he also took

DOI: 10.4324/9781003200253-19

all his family of origin from Greece to Istanbul. Consequently, they were saved from deportation, since by decree of the German Administration (and Greek collaboration with the Nazis) all Jews of Greek citizenship were deported within two weeks. This paternal insight is one of my family's 'gratitude' stories.

In 1992, to celebrate the 500th year of their arrival in the Ottoman Empire, the Sephardic Community of Turkey created a 'gratitude foundation' (the 500th Year Foundation) and I was invited to be part of the board of directors. Up to that date, I had not questioned or reflected upon my trans-generationally transmitted feelings of gratitude. It was taken for granted that gratitude was what we, as Jewish citizens, owed to the government of Turkey who had spared our lives for having received us into their territories five hundred years ago, and moreover had not delivered us to the Nazis. Actually, upon the request of Albert Einstein to Turkey's founding leader Atatürk, tens of German Jewish university professors and academics were received by Turkey in the 1930's, thus saving their and their families' lives. They became the teaching pillars of the newly established Turkish universities. Thankfulness and gratitude were the least one could feel during that time as a Jewish citizen, or that is what we had been taught to believe.

While expressing gratitude towards the country where I lived, I started to feel a creeping uneasiness gnawing my mind. Sure I felt thankful for myself, my life, my family, my ancestors, however this gnawing feeling *of being tolerated*, its humiliation, shame, and uneasiness, together with a pinkish anger was creeping into my heart. Yes, while fleeing the Inquisition five hundred years ago, my ancestors had been hosted in this geography, yes my paternal family had been spared from deportation during WWII, yes I had the full right to exert my traditional cultural habits, yet all this was wrapped as a gift and not as an acquired citizenship right. I decided to resign from my position at the foundation.

Tolerance: A Gift or a Right?

The awareness and consciousness raised by the European Convention of Human Rights had begun to modify my perspective around tolerance. 'Being tolerated' no longer appeared a gracious gift anymore. It was a fundamental human right that I was a citizen of Turkey. I gradually realized that the experience of being tolerated had transformed me into a submissive second-class vassal distancing me from my power of assertion, open criticism, and resistance to intolerable governmental policies and actions.

In 2009, during the Gaza War in Israel, I wrote an open letter to the Prime Minister whose government was openly accusing the Turkish Jewish community of being "the killers of Gaza's children". There were several posters around the city with slogans reading: "Are you Moses' descendants? Moses himself wouldn't allow the murder of children!" The government openly targeted its Jewish community as a counter-attack on Israel and its politics.

My letter was published in a prominent Turkish newspaper where I openly questioned the government's biased attitude toward its citizens, asking whether I was perceived according to my religion and ethnicity or my citizenship? Weren't we living in a secular Republic? I was questioning the famous "500 Years of Tolerance" slogan, which had been regularly publicized as a hubristic governmental attitude. Was I considered as a natural Turkish-born citizen, or perceived according to my cultural ethnicity or my born religion? My open letter attracted a great amount of national public interest together with a multitude of reactions from both secular and religious readers. Yet the most striking part was that I got a phone call at my office directly from the then President of the State (Abdullah Gül). He mentioned that he had read my open letter with his wife, and that they were "very touched" by it. He wished to reassure me about the attitude of his government who was caring and respectful towards all minorities. Meanwhile I got several emails and phone calls from various citizens, some very supportive and others openly aggressive.

However, my feeling was that I had openly rebelled against the insidiously invasive pressure of 'being tolerated', its consequently humiliating feelings and the danger of being politically identified as a scapegoat. In my writing, I was openly claiming for my natural citizenship rights without any bias. I had finally broken the humiliating attitude of the introjected trans-generational gratitude in being tolerated as a minority.

Trans-Generational Transmission of Trauma and Gratitude

Following the sinister effects of the Spanish inquisition, being received and domiciled in the Ottoman Empire's territories had justly elicited deep feelings of gratitude in the Sephardic community. Gratitude, according to Hiles (2007), is closely linked with *trust* in good figures, therefore the wish to preserve and spare the good object predominates. The Ottoman Empire had become the 'good object' for the Sephardic community; while not wishing to lose or abandon it, feelings of gratitude were kept alive and transmitted from generation to generation. According to Hiles (2007) persistent gratification leads to more experiences of enjoyment and gratitude, and accordingly there is a wish to return pleasure. This recurrent experience makes possible gratitude at the deepest level and plays an important role in the capacity to make *reparation*.

Trans-generationally transmitted emotions may be carried on purposefully, consciously or unconsciously. Past emotions are transmitted through generations via souvenirs, memoirs, proverbs, oral history, and several identity markers such as songs, myths, language and other cultural amplifiers (Volkan, 2019). As a remembrance of transmitted deception and anger, I recall that my grandmother would repeat a couplet in Ladino while sewing a button on my jacket which said: "I'm sewing this button on the jacket of the Son of the King of Spain – May he get your troubles and may you inherit his benefits". Sewing a button on a person symbolized sewing her destiny. When asked about the meaning of the couplet, my grandmother would recall the deep deception and anger of her ancestors' rejection and past trauma. This couplet transmits the transmission of the pain and suffering that the Jewish community endured with the expulsions from Spain, and at the same time, it translates the anger and vindictiveness that such an expulsion elicited in the community. Actually, she was "depositing" the past trauma and its emotions onto me. "It is an adult in the child's life who feels compelled to add something to the child's psyche" writes Vamik Volkan (2019, p. 41). This can be compared with Anne Ancelin Schützenberger's "ancestor syndrome" where emotions experienced by ancestors are 'deposited' unto the new generations. According to Volkan (2019) "when thousands or millions of children receive the same or a similar deposited item they begin to share a 'psychological DNA'…. Depositing also includes passing along various kinds of prejudicial elements concerning the unfamiliar Other" (p. 41).

Despite changes of attitude, politics and mentality, feelings of gratitude of the Spanish-Jewish Community towards the Sultan of the Ottoman Empire were transmitted to the Turkish Government and carried on within the Sephardic Community through several generations without questioning.

Anaesthetized Minds and Silenced Emotions

The experience of gratitude and of being tolerated creates a numbing, soul silencing effect. A tacit understanding seems to function in subduing negative emotions such as discontent, resentment, anger, and rebellion. It is as if acting out on negative emotions might endanger some learned loyalty, and essentially put one's survival at stake. We may state that such an expression of gratitude is essentially a mechanism of survival. The ghost-fear of being once again targeted leads people to behave according to the obedience expectations of the dominant culture. The expected attitudes are chosen silence and submissiveness. Without being openly articulated, this tacit expectation around *minority-submissiveness* is prevalent in several cultures, be it Muslims in several European countries, Palestinians and Arabs in Israel, Rohingyas in Myanmar, Alawis and Kurds in Turkey, to enumerate a few. Consequently, any revolt or anger towards the ruling system are expected to be silenced, cowed. Yet when the mind becomes anaesthetized and natural emotions get silenced, the "*shrinking of the soul*" (Grossman, 2008) is inevitable. One becomes a candidate for subjecting one's self to the ruling power without individuality, resistance or revolt, abiding by the rules of the governing system.

Splitting

Splitting refers to the formation of two different subjective identities: the public identity behaves according to the expectations of the dominant culture, while the private identity does so according to the large group identity that one belongs to. The large group identity (Volkan, 2019) refers to a sense of belonging to a group, one that differs from other groups by reference to race, language, ethnicity, religion, affiliations or ideologies. Volkan underlines identity markers such as language, songs, mythic and historic images, religious and political beliefs, and similar cultural amplifiers (2019, p. 40).

In the case of minorities, a different way of being and a different language are used between the two public spheres: the native language (Ladino, ancient Spanish, as compared to Yiddish) is still spoken by the older generation in the Sephardic community, while the new generations speak fluent Turkish. Over five centuries, Ladino has been the private communication tool of the Sephardic community who emigrated from the Iberian Peninsula.

Splitting can be compared to Du Bois' (1903) concept of "double consciousness". In Du Bois' terms, this refers to a source of inward "twoness" as experienced by African-Americans because of their racialized oppression and chronic disvaluation in a white-dominated society. Du Bois addresses to this peculiar double-ness to the sense of always looking at one's self through the eyes of the dominant culture.

The sense of being unaccepted but only tolerated contributes to accentuating this sense of splitting: if not accepted by the dominant culture, then one's large group identity becomes necessary for survival.

Developing an Inner Identity as a Minority

I was working as facilitator and supervisor in the East and South East of Turkey with 61 women living in 23 different cities of the region with a nongovernmental organization (KAMER) for the prevention of honor killings, aggression, and harassment. The local women we worked with were from different ethnic backgrounds, Kurdish, Alawi, Yezidi, Zaza, and Sunni; nine out of 61 wore head-covers in the traditional custom. In one of my group works, lately, at the end of the day, when I asked if there were some fantasy gifts that they would like to give to each other, a young woman started to sing a song in Kurdish. She had a deep guttural voice, much like a fado singer – it was a spontaneous expression and a few women joined her singing with lower voices. To my deep surprise, tears started to roll down my cheeks, and I felt unable stop them. As I was startled by my unexpected cry, so were some of the women in the group, since I didn't understand a single word of the song in Kurdish. I'm not Kurdish, I wasn't born in the region, and I obviously didn't have similar living conditions as theirs, nor had I experienced the harsh realities of their daily lives. There was a moment of silence and other Kurdish songs followed. I was feeling an embarrassment due to my tears as the group leader. While no other woman was actually crying, despite that it was their song, their language, their emotions, their actual fate, but somehow they were mine too. Later, when I reflected upon my sudden unexpected tears, I thought that those were actually the tears of the group, of this battered region, the unexpressed, unpronounced despair of the population, the feelings of helplessness and despair of living during so many years in the heart of aggression, harassment, injustice, denial and trauma. However, those were my own tears too. Those were the tears of my social (un)conscious as a minority.

I've been reflecting on why I've been pursuing such hard work, choosing to travel to difficult and dangerous regions, choosing to share those traumatic situations that are not implicated in my daily life. My two other colleagues and I had an intimate sharing about why we were choosing to work in those conditions, loading ourselves with very harsh emotions that were not directly involved in our own daily life. One of my colleagues was traveling from Stockholm just for this work. My second colleague and myself were flying from Istanbul where our daily living conditions are definitely incomparable. My two colleagues (both Turkish and of Sunni Muslim background) spoke about a search of identity, of meeting and understanding of people of different ethnicities in Turkey, a kind of identity completion. For me, it was not a search of identity or a completion per se. Being of Jewish Sephardic origin and born in Turkey, I already know my ascendance, my ethnicity and identity. Despite my need and wish to meet and get to better know the different cultures and ethnicities in the country where I live, I felt it was a kind of 'tikkun' in Kabbalistic terms: a *repair* that has harshly torn my soul, a repair through other torn souls. On one side I'm relating to my Jewish inheritance, of the traumas that Jews went through in Europe during the last century, and also centuries ago, like my Sephardic ancestors who were expelled from Spain. It feels to me as if I'm carrying a torn soul, transmitted and experienced trans-generationally as a minority. The region I was working with is injured with deep traumas, mainly among Kurdish, Armenian, and Alawi populations. The recent history is loaded with atrocities and genocide. Many populations cannot speak their own language freely, cannot openly own their religion or ethnicity and cannot declare who they really are. Two of my group members connected with me and talked about their hidden Armenian origins. I suspect they could share this private information with me because they knew I'm a minority. The song, especially without the meaning of the words, resonated with me as the song of my minority social unconscious, echoing a deep cry of humiliation, oppression, fear, threat, losses and mourning.

This work was helping me to wake up from an anaesthetized self-mode, or sort of collective anesthesia that the on-going conflicts, threats, murders and injustices in the country have been inflicting upon our souls. To quote from David Grossman:

> I feel the heavy price that I and the people around me pay for this prolonged
> state of war. Part of this price is the shrinking of our soul's surface area –
> those parts of us that touch the violent, menacing world outside – and a
> diminished ability and willingness to empathize at all with other people in
> pain. ... The constant – and very real – fear of being hurt, the fear of death,
> of intolerable loss, or even of mere humiliation, leads each of us, the citizens

and prisoners of the conflict, to dampen our own vitality, our emotional and intellectual range, and to cloak ourselves in more and more protective layers until we suffocate.

(2008, p. 60)

Apolitical Identity

Usually an apolitical stance is tacitly and sometimes openly expected from minorities. Depoliticization may become a survival strategy: leading a personal life without getting actively involved in the country's politics. The experience of an unspoken exclusion contributes to non-involvement as a stance, not to speak of activism. This is similar to the 'good boy/good girl' syndrome where children try to be compliant and submissive in front of dominant parents. As a survival strategy, tolerated minorities mostly comply with socially expected behaviors while avoiding belligerence or revolt against the ruling power. This leads to an inactive, submissive, uninvolved citizenship stance, complying and behaving as second-class citizens. The common slogan adopted by the Jewish community "We don't meddle in governmental affairs" refelcts the 'protective' decision adopted by Sephardic elders in keeping away from politics.

This apolitical stance may create a physical comfort zone for daily survival, however the chosen silence and tacitly expected political non-activism contribute to the "shrinking of the soul". As if the survival zone provided by the governing system should feel sufficient, as if possessing the basic needs of food and shelter should feel satisfying enough. This compliant stance contributes to reinforcing the deliberately adopted status of second-class citizenship, the tacit acceptance of being tolerated. Therefore feelings of humiliation, splitting, hypocritical stance, non-assertiveness, and shame lead to the irreparable consequences so elaborately named by Grossman as the "shrinking of the soul" (Grossman, 2008, p. 60).

Identifying with the Aggressor

When modern Turkey was formed, following the Ottoman Empire, a nationalistic wave blew (1950s) and the country's official communication language became modern Turkish written in the Latin alphabet. Meanwhile the Sephardic community was extensively using the old Ladino written in Hebrew letters. As members of the new generation learning modern Turkish at school, my sister and I were transported with the nationalistic wave that demanded all its citizens to speak only in Turkish. We found ourselves exerting pressure on the older generation who spoke Ladino, demanding them to speak the country's language with the proper pronunciation. When I became a thinking and conscientious adult, I realized with some shame that my sister and I had been identifying with the aggressor. Identifying with the aggressor (Ferenczi, 1933) is a common defense mechanism stemming from powerlessness. The oppressed assume the role of the aggressor or imitate his aggressive behavior. This ends up in praising the governing system no matter what action it takes, unconsciously leading to identification with the powerful authority.

This defensive submissiveness carries a potential of being easily scapegoated. Identifying with the aggressor creates an illusion of escape from danger. Yet Frankel (2019) claims that identification with the aggressor may save the victim's life because it prevents him/her from provoking the aggressor again, which may put his/her life in danger. It may provide a temporary protection for the victim, yet it does not help to modify the status quo in the aggressor/victim dyad. On the contrary, the stifled fear and powerlessness of the victim become magnified. The loss of honor and humiliation of the fearfully identifying victim may elicit despise and anger in the aggressor. It may trigger the potential for future scapegoating. Such cases were experienced by the Kapos during Nazism, where those Jews who collaborated with the Nazis had not necessarily been spared from the fatal solution.

Scapegoat Candidature

I suggest that, particularly in times of restlessness and turmoil, being tolerated carries in its nucleus the potential of being scapegoated.

Tolerance per se requires self-awareness, self-control, education, consciousness and self-discipline, accompanied with wisdom and human generosity, those attitudes that are easier to provide in times of peace and prosperity. However in times of restlessness, war and turmoil, the scarcity of goods and facilities may hamper the necessary self-discipline in equal sharing, humanity and care for others. Being tolerated is a beneficial good-timer attitude, when social turmoil, existential danger and scarcity of goods are not in the daily agenda. Tolerance is a litmus test that changes its color when circumstances get modified. Social restlessness and existential danger trigger fear, threat and anxiety. Those forceful emotions are difficult to contain and they mostly culminate in anger and aggression. Dispatching anger and acting it out requires a specific target and it is usually the most vulnerable ones, such as children, women, needy citizens, minorities and emigrants that fall in the victimization cluster. Through projection and projective identification all 'bad' attributes are laid upon the target that gradually becomes demonized.

Scapegoating is a primitive social defense mechanism where all the bad deeds and attributes are projected unto a specific person or a group of people that are vilified. It contributes to discharge oneself from guilt, anxiety, anger, shame, and several other ambivalent feelings through endorsing the specific 'other'. Thus the illusion of being cleansed from bad deeds is adopted. Scapegoating was related in the Bible (Leviticus XVI: 21) in the form of a religious ceremony where the sins of the community were laid on to a goat that was cast out into the desert, left to die. This was a spiritual ceremony inducing that the community was cleansed from bad deeds and their sins atoned

(Schaverien, 1999, p. 74). As such many cultures use scapegoating rituals in various forms, sacrificing animals and even humans as a disposal of sins through a ritual of atonement.

Scapegoating functions through projection and projective identification: As defense mechanisms, our undesired, 'not-me' parts are projected unto others. During normal times, those defense mechanisms function rather unconsciously. But in times of restlessness and fear, the primitive need of finding specific targets to project uncontainable emotions and unacceptable 'not-me' parts may seem a survival strategy. The 'other', thus, becomes an easy target for such a disposal of vilified self-parts. Scapegoating is a collective projective identification process purposefully used by public influencers and bad-intentioned politicians.

We may state that in times of restlessness and social turmoil, the awareness and self-discipline that are the backbones of tolerance blow away. History shows that in quite rare occasions righteous people do behave according to their inherent human values (i.e. the Path of the Righteous, Yad Vashem).

Internal Racism

Migration has always been a continuous live tragedy in the world's history. Due to natural disasters, climate changes such as drought or floods, or war afflictions, people are forced to leave their native land and move out in search of survival. Expecting to be integrated is a painful process where both sides (migrating and receiving culture) feel fear, anxiety, resistance, otherness, estrangement, and alienation.

In times of social restlessness and times of war, there is regression in our defense mechanisms. The primary "stranger anxiety", as depicted by Spitz (1950) in babies, enters into function. Solan (2016) addresses to the 'biological immune system' that safeguard the familiar codes of the body and repels strange and alien invaders. With heavy migration, new arrivals trigger primitive anxieties in the receiving culture. Absorbing the 'other' is a difficult and painful process, there is a paranoid anxiety about being invaded, taken over, and modified. Especially when the "otherness" of these migrants is too directly visible (physical appearance, customs, behavior, culture) the primitive anxieties can readily be re-articulated in racial terms, especially by extremist voices mobilizing populist sentiments.

According to Davids (2017) 'internal racism' refers to a structure in the mind that mediates our relationship with members of an out-group. The relationship between the self and what Davids terms the "racial/ethnic" other is embedded in a paranoid, us vs. them duality. Davids sees this as a defensive organization that governs our relationship with 'others'. It is a phantasy system with a life of its own that generates anxiety based on paranoia (p. 1). In internal racism, the self relates to the racial other in a paranoid way and unwanted aspects of the self are projected and then lodged in the other, thus providing a measure of control over the projected content. Davids (2017) claims that what was familiar is made un-familiar through projective identification. This mode of relating dates back to the infant's earliest days when paranoid-schizoid mechanisms prevail and anxiety is managed through splitting (Davids, 2017, p. 5).

According to Davids (2017) the self-racial other relationship exists in us all. A powerful system of defenses contributes to the non-recognition of our inherent internal racism. "Without the possibility of either insight or reality testing, the danger is that the racial other remains trapped in the role of a bad object" (p. 5). Stereotypes are created according to projective identifications and they become integrated in belief systems that over-rule reality. He claims that the inner relationship with the racial other remains rooted in projective identification, with unwanted aspects of the self that are lodged in the other. Therefore these beliefs are highly resistant to change and are translated into role and behavior expectations (p. 9) that reinforce the attributed stereotypes. The "self-racial other relationship" coils as a cowed existence in our minds (p. 9). "The danger is this: the triumph of inner racist mechanisms mobilizes unconscious guilt, which is dealt with by the repetition compulsion (Freud, 1914): it is used to entrench the system further and further" (Davids, p. 11).

Again quoting Grossman (2008): "we often feel that only by some miraculous twist of fate have we been spared from becoming that detestable character ourselves, and that the possibility of being that character still exists and murmurs within us, in our genetic reservoir" (p. 38).

Acceptance vs. Tolerance

Despite that the concept of tolerance carries a positive connotation, I wish to argue that it is essentially a temporary soul-pacifier, a well lacquered conscience cleaner that helps to feel good about oneself while unnoticing the (im)perceptible haughty attitude that one is maintaining towards the tolerated. I maintain that tolerance is hubristic as well hierarchic while perspiring a (social) class difference. The tolerated are naturally in a vulnerable lower position.

Tolerance induces an imperceptible power and magnanimity to the tolerating side, feeding unrevealed narcissistic self-satisfaction. It bestows the *illusion* of self-discipline and tamed primitiveness as if one has domesticated one's internal racism and stranger anxiety. As long as living conditions remain unchanged, tolerance provides some *illusion* of human equality.

However, tolerance is transient. The narcissistic ingredients stifled in tolerant attitudes are bound to be extinguished in times of restlessness, such as war, famine, and natural disasters. Tolerance may be compared to a well-trained, domesticated pit bull dog whose inherently wild nature has been temporarily pacified and maintained under strict control. With rational and logic self-righteousness on its side, tolerance may backlash as wild intolerance at any minimal change of situation.

Tolerance has inferred conditions and implied expectancies. The tacit expectation implies that the tolerated will not complain, not create a problem, remain submissive, not try to surpass their 'secondary' rank, and remain powerless. The tolerated side is expected to feel continuously grateful, submissive and satisfied for being tolerated with no room for complaints: "what do you want more?" is the unpronounced attitude, the not displayed haughty slogan.

We may talk about tolerance for behaviors, for ideas, for adversity, yet not for people. People can be either *accepted or not*. When tolerated, a forced attitude is implicit since it carries the potential of backlashing at any time.

Acceptance has a larger scope than tolerance. Getting rid of internal fears and learned prejudices requires awareness and consciousness raising through reflection and learning. The taming of our inner fear of the 'other' demands a soulful effort. Empathy, awareness, reflection, rationalization, information and education are required efforts to tame our inner prejudices along with our 'internal racism'. Acceptance means opening the lids of our mind and soul, letting go of our primitive defenses. Acceptance is maturation, it is looking at the world from a larger angle, honor our shared humanity while embracing life with more inclusive wisdom. It requires a soul search effort and the taming of our primitive insecurities. Instead of looking for external devils, acceptance requires the struggle with our internal demons. Awareness of our primitive defenses such as projection and projective identification is an important and necessary step in the process of self-maturation.

It seems to me that teaching and learning the acceptance of the other is to a country what fitness is to a body. Just as one has always to adjust him/herself in order to remain fit and healthy, a country has to adjust itself continually to acceptance of the other in order to remain healthy. Acceptance seems to be the benchmark of a society's mental health.

References

Davids, F. M. (2017). Internal racism, Plenary Presentation, *EPF Conference: "The Familiar and the Unfamiliar"*, The Hague, Netherlands, 9 April 2017.

Du Bois, W. E. B. (1903). *The Souls of Black Folk*.

Ferenczi, S. (1933). Confusion of tongues between adults and the child. In M. Balint *Final Contributions to the Problems and Methods of Psycho-analysis*. London, Karnac Books: 156–167.

Frankel, J. (2019). Identification (With the Aggressor). In *Routledge Handbook of Psychoanalytical Political Theory*. New York: Taylor and Francis.

Grossman, D. (2008). *Writing in the Dark: Essays on Literature and Politics*. New York: Picador.

Hiles, D. (2007, November). *Envy, Jealousy, Greed: A Kleinian approach*, Paper presented to CCPE, London.

Schaverien, J. (1990). The Scapegoat and the Talisman: Transference in art therapy. In Dalley, T. et al. (Eds). *Images of Art Therapy, New Developments in Theory and Practice* (pp. 74–108). Routledge.

Solan, R. (2016). Stranger anxiety: When children face strangers. *Mental Health in Family Medicine*, 12: 223–227.

Spitz, R. (1950). Anxiety in infancy: A study of its manifestations in the first year of life. *The International Journal of Psychoanalysis*, 31: 138–143.

Volkan, D. V. (2019). *Ghosts in the Human Psyche, The Story of a Muslim-Armenian*. Phoenix Publishing House.

Chapter 15

Tolerance Amidst Racial Trauma
The South African Experience

Monica Spiro and Anne Morgan

South Africa – The Rainbow Nation?

The book 'A Companion to Ethics' uses various words to describe tolerance: forbearance, freedom from bigotry, open mindedness, magnanimity, all embracing/wide sympathies. The opening chapter of this volume proposes that tolerance is an attitude, a moral value, attained when divergent views can be contained in the service of mutual belonging with others. It is contended that tolerance is a developmental achievement negotiated through intrapsychic and relational processes.

The concept of tolerance is highly relevant for our country, South Africa, a country that received global attention in 1994 when apartheid was dismantled. At this historical time, a settlement was negotiated between the African National Congress (ANC) and the existing apartheid government that put an end to legally sanctioned racial discrimination and laws which afforded a white minority rights and privileges at the expense and diminishment of a black[1] majority; laws that endorsed gross human rights violations. South Africa and the world rejoiced in the peaceful transition to a democratic government, representative of all its citizens. The country provided a beacon of hope that violence and injustice could be set aside to allow for the harmonious co-existence of the populace. Images were captured of Black and White South Africans standing patiently in line in a spirit of hope and solidarity, waiting to cast their vote in this historic election.

Nelson Mandela was positioned as the father of this nation, a man with a history of militancy in his youth who became an icon for tolerance in his later years, embodying the dream of a unified country. His tolerance was epitomized in his capacity to embrace his captors, a strategy that saw him befriend his prison warders. The same is true for his administrative assistant, a young white Afrikaans woman who became his trusted private secretary in his role as head of state, and who remained his devoted personal aide in his retirement.

At the time, the term 'rainbow nation' was coined by social rights activist, Archbishop Desmond Tutu, to describe a vision of a society that embraces diversity. It acknowledges that multi-culturalism exists and it calls on citizens to live

DOI: 10.4324/9781003200253-20

with mutual tolerance. It presupposes a respect for differences under the unifying banner of national identity and stood in stark contrast to the divisiveness of the apartheid era. In his inauguration speech, Mandela referred to "a rainbow nation at peace with itself and the world" (cited in Manzo, 1996, p. 71).

A strongly worded constitution called on the people of South Africa to put aside the divisions of the past and adopt a path of tolerance and reconciliation. The preamble reads that "there is a need for understanding but not for vengeance, a need for reparation but not for retaliation, a need for ubuntu[2] but not for victimization" (Constitution of the Republic of South Africa Act 200 of 1993, National Unity and Reconciliation). In this spirit of tolerance, the Truth and Reconciliation Commission (TRC) was born, providing an opportunity for victims of political violence to give voice to their painful stories and for perpetrators to own their atrocities. The mandate of the commission, was to bear witness to and record the narratives of victims and offenders, grant amnesty to those who fully disclosed their involvement in politically motivated human rights violations, and offer reparation and rehabilitation to the victims. Through the mechanism of the TRC, emphasis was placed on restorative justice rather than retributive justice. Also referred to as Ubuntu justice, compassion and forgiveness were foregrounded as a way of promoting a moral culture that exemplifies tolerance.

The term "Born-Free's" was coined to refer to South African children born post-1994. As the term denotes, this generation were handed the baton of 'rainbowism' – their existence was invested with the notion that the injustices of the past had been eradicated by the democratic dispensation. It was as if they were handed a clean slate, free from the apartheid constructed socio-political identities and socio-economic inequalities. In circumstances where transformation still needed to occur, they were imbued with the notion that their "free status" would assist them in resolving these conditions.

The tolerance that was espoused in the early years of democracy was delivered with an optimism that a new system had been born that would free itself from racism and the shackles of the past. At best, a new society was envisioned using the imaginings of a post-apartheid foundation that would offer a better future for all South Africans. This emblematic vision was vested with aspirations both locally and internationally.

Now, almost 30 years on, the landscape tells a different story. Despite the transformation following the abolition of discriminatory legislation, it speaks of continued socio-economic inequalities, where a preponderance of poverty is heavily retained among the black population, a government tarnished with corruption, factions, and poor service delivery, and the failure of democratic institutions to provide the equality of opportunity that was envisioned.

It is not surprising that against this backdrop, the 'Born-Free's' coming of age resuscitated efforts to challenge the status quo in the form of the #Must Fall Movements. The call to action, which gripped the country in 2015/2016, began with high school learners challenging inherited cultural practices, norms and rules embedded in the schooling system. Their protests ignited demonstrations at tertiary campuses across the country. The burning of artwork, books and property, violent clashes, and the disruption of university life caught the attention of the nation and exerted pressure to uncover and address the perpetuation of racially biased institutionalised norms.

Through these actions, students chose to reject the metaphor of 'rainbowism' and the inherent message of tolerance that permeated the early years of democracy. They questioned the systemic racism built into our institutions and its role in maintaining a privileged elite. They interrogated the normalisation of injustices in a country that had committed itself to equality and freedom and suggested that these injustices were part of an inherited South African psyche borne out of a history of racial discrimination and colonialism. They challenged the parental generation who had brokered a peaceful settlement and accused them of negotiating a social compact that sold the black population short, predicated on a need to appease the white minority.

While the #Must Fall Movements were partially successful in their negotiations, dissention within the movement destabilised a sustained force. In particular, womxn[3] student leaders indicted the male leadership for perpetuating other forms of marginalisation, particularly gender and sexuality.

The issue of gender-based violence revisited the collective conscious with the gruesome rape and murder of a student in 2019. The incident highlighted the manifest reality of a society with one of the highest levels of sexual and gender-based violence globally (Global Peace Index, 2020). While race had been the overarching reference point to redress oppression, the recognition of other forms of marginalisation advocated for the differentiation of multiple identities and intersecting levels of oppression.

The year 2020 saw the onset of the Covid-19 pandemic in the country and worldwide,. Initial attempts at a hard lockdown further exposed the fault lines of the nation. While white people in the suburbs locked down in their walled-off homes, much of the black population, living in close quarters of informal settlements with shared ablution facilities, were not afforded the privilege of social distancing. Disparities in wealth further impacted education, with disadvantaged learners unable to access online education due to lack of computer access and internet connectivity. The socio-economic circumstances of black South Africans increased their vulnerability to the virus as they were more likely to rely on public transport, work in essential services, have pre-existing health conditions, and have less access to adequate health care. Their positioning also made them more susceptible to the economic fall-out and mass unemployment caused by the pandemic. In this way, the pandemic shone light on the schisms within our society and further widened the material gaps of inequality. Emerging international data confirmed that the pandemic was most devastating in areas of greatest deprivation, disproportionately affecting black and ethnic minority groups (Government HM, 2020; US Centers for Disease Control and Prevention, 2021).

In this climate of racial injustice and high levels of unemployment, the brutal murder of a black man, George Floyd, by a white police officer in the USA, captured public consciousness and gave momentum to the Black Lives Matter movement in the USA, igniting concomitant outrage in South Africa.

The unfolding of our recent history begs us to question the usefulness of the rainbow nation metaphor and the concept of tolerance embodied in it. Gqola, as early as 2001, identified the shortcomings of rainbowism as "an authorizing narrative of South Africa's identity that invokes a collective identity that stifles discussions of power differentials and emphasises difference while preventing the discussion that such differences evoke". Chikane more recently writes, "We are not encouraged to feel uncomfortable in the face of difference. Instead, we are encouraged to ignore difference to make it easier for us to co-exist. The rainbow nation doesn't drive us together, it forces us apart. It prioritises the acknowledgement of our differences over the understanding of them" (p. 7). This 'rainbow nation' mindset "provides a heuristic tool – a mental shortcut – to disjoin within the psyche of South Africans the old from the new" (2018, p. 26).

From this perspective, tolerance espoused in the early days may be viewed as a hindrance to a transformative process. It may serve to obscure the real healing that remains incomplete while we gloss over our inherited and ongoing hurt. While laws have the power to legally enforce desegregation, they have limitations in the arena of everyday human interaction and cannot address the importunity of social norms that have been embedded in our psyches. The past cannot simply be erased from the national psyche and exists in our fractured identities and internalised social constructions. The system of racial oppression has created casualties on both sides of the divide and the unresolved legacy serves to perpetuate a splintered society that holds racism in place.

While 'rainbowism' and the tolerance advocated by it might exist on one end of the continuum, violence and anger perhaps exists on the other end. The use of violence, not only in opposition to the status quo, but its prevalence in the fabric of civil society, indicates the way violence has been normalised and justified. South Africa is ranked as the twenty-fourth most violent country in the world, with femicide being the highest across the globe and legitimated gang violence being a feature of daily life in impoverished urban communities (Global Peace Index, 2020). The large-scale xenophobic attacks that swept across the country in 2008 and continue with flare-ups through to the present day, are a further articulation of the violence and intolerance that permeates our society. The Marikana Massacre of 2012, where police opened fire on a crowd of striking mine workers, represents a modus operandi of law enforcement where violence is sanctioned to quell conflict. Another instance of a combative response by the state was the deployment of the army into gang-ridden communities in 2019/20. The use of the military to perform policing functions again reinforces a culture of force to restore peace and security. It undermines the need to seek other alternatives and perpetuates a pre-existing code of violence.

Some would argue that our history of violent colonisation begets violence in response to it. Fanon describes colonisation as "the meeting of two forces, opposed to each other by their very nature' (1963, p. 36). Albert, a student activist, writes "Decolonisation … messes with the colonial order that maintains black bodies as subservient beings over a violent, white supremacist superstructure. Decolonisation is only violent because the introduction of colonialism was violent and the maintenance of colonialism … is through violence" (2016).

Critical Race Theory

So, how do we escape the trenches of violence and intolerance if it is not through the route of rainbowism? Is it possible? Perhaps it begins with an investigation of the complex legacies of a racialised society that persist. Critical race theory and identity politics provides some inroads into an understanding of the subjective, lived experience of our people. These very real socially constructed experiences, when they remain unexamined and often unconscious, maintain lines of privilege and racial polarisation that perpetuate inequality and trauma.

Chikane (2018) and Ntaka (2019), amongst other writers, borrow the concept of double consciousness to explicate the experience of being black in contemporary South Africa. Du Bois's (1903) concept described the experience of African Americans under the Jim Crow laws. The term referred to the conflicting reality of reconciling black identity with that of being American; "always looking at oneself through the eyes" of a racist society that negates blackness. Ntaka writes "Du Bois' theory … has helped us to understand what it means to navigate and grapple with being in between [the] 'white' and the 'black' world – and how it feels to be both 'within' and 'without' (p. 49)". Chikane writes, "My experience of racism …is linked to my experience of being made to feel inferior, not simply discriminated against. The inferiority is linked to the use of authority by someone who has been given an arbitrary superiority over me" (p. 114-115).

Fanon (1952) used the term "white gaze" when he wrote on blackness and oppression in the context of the colonial era. Current discourse confirms that his writing still speaks to the experience of blackness today where whiteness prescribes what it means to be civilized, advanced and human, and it is towards this ever moving ideal that black people must assimilate.

Steve Biko and the Black Consciousness Movement of the 1960s/70s understood the need to transform black identity to mobilize the liberation struggle. The philosophical underpinnings of the movement, to develop a positive, inclusive black identity, free from the approval of whiteness, is carried forward in the rhetoric of today's scholars.

While there has been much written about the experience of blackness within a racist society, there has been less focus until more recently on how the experience of whiteness propagates a system of structured racialised relations. The challenge in unpacking the white position has been to uncover the guise of a supposed normative position that conceals a system that continues to support white privilege. Insight into these unconscious and unacknowledged ideas and practices helps to explain the disowning of racial discrimination by white people in a society that perpetuates inequality.

Wekker (2016), has written about the white Dutch self, exploring how the denial of racism and the expression of innocence lives alongside ongoing racism and xenophobia. She argues that this expression of innocence safeguards white privilege. Diangelo (2018) further elucidates that whiteness presents as a neutral backdrop, a form of racelessness, that perpetuates white privilege.

Diangelo (2018) popularised the term 'white fragility' to describe patterns of defensiveness of white people in reaction to race discussions, particularly when they feel implicated in white supremacy. She proposes that reactions such as anger, fear, and silence serve to hold racism in place by averting the dialogue and self-reflection that could potentially result in change. She challenges the notion of racism as a conscious bias and encourages white liberals, amongst others, to engage with their less conscious, inherited socialised positioning that perpetuates racism.

Diangelo points to our investment in ideologies of individualism and objectivity as notions that serve to obscure *collective* and *subjective* experiences that prevail. She maintains that these precepts serve to ignore the unavoidable societal racialised context that shapes the core of our experience.

Group Analysis as a Meeting Ground

While much has been written to identify unconscious dynamics and positioning that perpetuates racism, much less has been written on the process of undoing these biases.

If we are understanding that racial discrimination is often deeply embedded in the unconscious and is held in place by defensive structures, the questions remain:

1. How do we see that to which we are blind?
2. How do we avoid re-enacting our assumptions and behaviour in cross-racial engagement?

It is to this end that we propose analytic groups as a possible framework in which to encounter the other, and in so doing, to confront ourselves and our unconscious racialised inheritances. Group analysis offers a space to simultaneously engage with the individual, group and society. It allows for reflection on the norms of society as expressed and contained in the group matrix. More recently there has been emphasis on an intersectional approach that appreciates positionality and the embeddedness of the individual and the group within systems of power and oppression (Aiyegbusi, 2021; Blackwell, 2020; Dalal, 2002; Kinouani, 2020; Stevenson, 2020).

With this in mind, we need to situate ourselves, the authors, as we have a subjective lens through which we are scrutinising a society in which we are also embedded. The embeddedness provides a valuable vantage point, but it also provides limitations that comes with our observational perspective. Both the writers of this chapter are white females living in South Africa. In expressing ourselves as white people, we are again centring the white voice. We are self-conscious that we run the risk of perpetuating the exact dynamic that we have documented. This is the dynamic where whiteness is given dominance and the views expressed take on a semblance of neutrality and appear to hold universal, objective truths. We considered whether we should be writing this chapter at all and concluded that we did not want to silence ourselves, but rather chose to ask a few of our South African colleagues, who might hold different vantage points, for comments on the working manuscript.

A further aspect of our context is our rootedness in Western psychological theory, and in group analysis particularly. The universality of this European import is questionable and its appropriateness in South Africa requires consideration. Our concern is that we are imposing a framework borne of the colonisers. Morgan, in a previous paper (2011), investigated the validity of group analytic concepts in South Africa. While we do not have space here to unpack the relevance of all its constructs, we will consider the foundational premise of group analysis – that the individual is constructed by the social, or at the very least, penetrated by the social. Pines (1998) suggests that group analysis "Gives rise to [an] … epistemology, one in which we can study systems, relationships and the evolution of individuals within these systems". In many ways group analysis challenges Western individualistic thinking and comes closer to the African notion of ubuntu referred to earlier. The ongoing mutual, group endeavour to communicate and to find ourselves, based on an interrelational idea about human development; the belief that through being with others in a group we can heal ourselves, corresponds with the ongoing nature of 'being-ness' contained in the concept of ubuntu.

Perhaps the greatest danger of a group analytic approach is not that it is a colonial import and that the theory may be culture bound and racialised, but that we who use it may be. Unless we have worked on these issues with others, we remain at risk of not knowing our racialised selves sufficiently well to carry out the group analytic task. We concur with Aiyegbusi (2021) that white therapists need to ready themselves to practice group analysis in a multi-racial society by working on their embeddedness in white thinking. This, to avoid colluding with defensive white reactions to confrontations and discussion about whiteness by black members of their groups. Our own experience has been to examine our defensiveness encapsulated in our position as 'white progressives' and make conscious our biases that inform our engagement. We have needed to confront our own painful feelings of racial 'othering' as well as work with such feelings as guilt, fear and shame that are evoked in cross racial exchanges. We have also had to own our white privilege and the normativity of our positioning that reinforces our unintentional but implicit bias. Our experiences in analytic groups have been useful to this end. We are aware that even if we have done a considerable amount of work, we can still face aspects of our unanalysed social legacy.

Our Experience of Using Group Analysis in South Africa

We will now offer a few vignettes that illustrate the application of group analysis in South Africa.

Case 1

One of us conducted an online median group for South African mental health professionals during the Covid lockdown. A third of the group participants were people of colour and the remaining two thirds were white. In the third session, one of the white participants recalled an incident where she had been walking with a friend on the mountainside. As she passed a black couple, she gestured a thank you to the woman who had replaced her mask on their approach. The man, who had not replaced his mask, was infuriated, and told her she should return to her home where she lives in 'white privilege' and that the mountain was available for everyone to walk freely. She spoke of feeling traumatised by the experience and indignant at the accusations levelled against her by a stranger. She felt misunderstood and the "victim of racism". The tension palpably increased in the group and a black woman responded to her by saying that she would never have any idea of the experience of racism. This woman then relayed a story where she had been driving in a car with her parents and infant daughter. When her father parked in the 'moms and tots' parking they were approached by a white person who chastised them for using the parking. She expressed the shame and rage that she felt and the sentiment that they would never have been approached if they were white. Another black woman spoke of being married to a white man, and while she felt outwardly accepted by his family, there was a level on which she always felt like the outsider and that the experience of being on the receiving end of micro-aggressions could not be understood by white people.

This reflects the racialised content that emerged in the group matrix and became the dominant focus for the five months that the group met. The opportunity for honest, cross-racial discourse saw instances of raw pain, rage, vulnerability, and shame surfacing. While the group was initiated to offer support to mental health professionals during the lockdown, the pandemic created a backdrop for issues of race to emerge. This mirrored the external world with the rise of the Black Lives Matter Movement. Complex racial trauma was witnessed and less conscious participation in a racialised system was revealed.

The conductor was challenged to empathically hold all voices, while being aware that there were a minority of black people in the group and that she, herself, was white. This raised all the possible concerns that have been illuminated in the above section. At times it felt as though the group could move towards a retraumatization through a re-enactment in the form of malignant mirroring. However, while skirting close to this possibility, the authentic engagement by all and the commitment to tolerate the discomfort, allowed for experiences to be felt, witnessed, and reflected upon.

The time-limited nature of the group was noted by some who expressed an interest in a longer process, however this sentiment was not shared by others who felt that they did not have the capacity to commit further. Resistance to working in a group with fellow colleagues and the fear of exposure was voiced alongside an appreciation of the personal insight gained to better serve our client groups.

Case 2

In a large group on a groupwork training course, the conductor was challenged about the fact that his co-conductor was a white woman. Black Members of the group were insistent that he was not the real conductor, but his white co-therapist was the one in charge. A similar issue had been raised before by black members of staff who felt their input was dismissed by participants. Maybe there was a grain of truth in that his co-conductor was older and more experienced as a group analyst. It also may have been that his co-therapist operated in a way that diminished him albeit this was not in her consciousness.

It seemed to the black therapist that he was being targeted by some of the members of the group who projected their experiences with cross racial partnerships or encounters onto and into him and then attacked him. It may also have incorporated an aspect of the history of South Africa in which mixed race marriages were legislated against during apartheid. Further in the background was the knowledge that 'Coloured' population was in fact created by mixed race relationships and for some provokes shame and guilt. It was extremely painful for him at the time to be undermined but also to be seen as a traitor.

Underlying the above there may well have been both conscious and unconscious resonance to the background mentioned. It could be difficult to believe that a black and white person would work in an equal relationship. The group went on to explore what had been said.

Case 3

One of us arranged, with a few young friends, to hold some social dreaming matrices in the centre of a small town and people from widespread backgrounds and race groups came to the meetings. One of the motivating factors of the young people for starting the meetings had been for cross-racial meeting and dialogue. When the venue closed and we moved to the black informal settlement only one white person attended. This was a serious disappointment, and the meetings were gradually discontinued.

This points to the inherited legacy of separate development that remains to some extent a physical reality, but also silently in people's minds. It seems that it was easier for cross-racial interactions to take place within the comfort zone of whiteness. White normativity is further observed in the dominant use of English as the language of communication, with most white South Africans unable to communicate in the African languages.

Conclusion

Early notions of tolerance that accompanied the neutrality of rainbowism need to be set aside for more critical and tough conversations that address the perpetuation of racism today. The current milieu requires us to interrogate the subjective reality of all South Africans and the ways in which they interact to maintain a status quo.

Our experience in South Africa cautions against the assumption that tolerance is a moral value that can simply be adopted by a diverse society in the service of mutual belonging. Tolerance practiced in societies where there are inherited differentials can serve to obscure and perpetuate inequities. The tolerance required in these circumstances is the forbearance to engage in processes where personal and collective trauma can be visited, processed, and better understood. This cannot be done in isolation, nor can it be achieved without intentional participation in cross-racial exchange that opens our vision of ourselves and others. Group analysis offers a framework for these encounters. It is a commitment to this process and tolerating the discomfort of these encounters that we believe can ultimately benefit South Africa and other societies that perpetuate psychosocial power relations in their diversity.

Notes

1 The term 'black' is used in this chapter to refer to all people of colour. While this term groups together many varied identities under one banner, it is used here to describe a social construct that creates a particular experience in contrast to whiteness within a racialised society. It does not do justice to the complexity of South Africa's racial politics inherited from an apartheid system that separated identities through distinct racial classifications.

2 Ubuntu has its roots in humanist African philosophy and is often translated as 'a person is a person through other people'. Ramose explains that ubuntu "Underlines the vital importance of mutual recognition and respect complemented by mutual care and sharing in the construction of human relations". "To be human is to affirm one's humanity by recognising the humanity of others ... and, on that basis, to establish respectful relations with them" (pp. 643, 644). Tutu writes, "[Ubuntu] ... recognizes that my humanity is bound up in yours, for we can only be human together" (2000).

3 The term 'womxn' is used by intersectional feminists as a replacement spelling in response to the sexism perceived in the standard spelling and to be inclusive of trans and nonbinary women (Dictionary.com, 2020).

References

Aiyegbusi, Anne (2021). The white mirror: Face to face with racism in group analysis. *Group Analysis* 54(3). doi:10.1177/0533316421992315

Albert, Wanelisa (2016). *How Shackville started a war*. City Press. www.news24.com/citypress/voices/how-shackville-started-a-war-20160219

Blackwell, Dick (2020). Black power – white halos. A response to Guilaine Kinouani's 'Silencing, Power and Racial Trauma in Groups'. *Group Analysis* 53(2): 255–265.

Definition of "woman". Dictionary.com. Retrieved 22 June 2020.

Diangelo, R. (2018). *White Fragility. Why it's So Hard for White People to Talk About Racism*. Beacon Press.

Du Bois, W.E.B. (1903). *The Souls of Black Folk: Essays and Sketches*. Chicago: A. C. McClurg & Co.

Chikane, Rekgotsofetse (2018). *Breaking a Rainbow, Building a Nation. The Politics behind #MustFall Movements*. Johannesburg: Picador Africa.

Constitution of the Republic of South Africa Act 200 of 1993, National Unity and Reconciliation (n.d.)

Fanon, F. (1952). *Black Skin: White Masks*. London: Pluto.

Fanon, F. (1963). *The Wretched of the Earth*, Farrington, C. (trans.). New York: Grove Press.

Gqola, P. (2001). Defining people: Analysing power, language and representation in metaphors of the new South Africa. *Transformations*, 47: 94–106.

Global Peace Index (2020).

Government Race Disparity Unit (2020, 22 October). Quarterly report on progress to address covid-19 health inequalities. www.gov.uk/government/organisations/race-disparity-unit

Kinouani, G. (2020). Difference, whiteness and the group analytic matrix: An integrated formulation. *Group Analysis*, 53(1): 60–74.

Manzo, K. A. (1996). *Creating Boundaries: The Politics of Race and Nation*. London, Lynne Reiner Publishers.

Morgan, Anne (2011). Unpublished paper presented at the Centre for Group Analytic Studies, Cape Town.

Ntaka, Noxolo (2019). Double consciousness: A comparative approach to interpreting the experiences of Black female pupils in a predominantly Black well-resourced and historically White school in South Africa? Dissertation submitted in fulfilment of the requirements for the degree: Master of Arts, Department of Political Studies University of the Witwatersrand.

Pines, M. (1998). Psychic development and the group analytic situation. In: *Circular Reflections, Selected Papers on Group Analysis and Psychoanalysis*: 59–76.

Ramose, Magobe (2002). Philosophy of Ubuntu and Ubuntu as a philosophy. In P. Coetzee and A. P. J. Roux (eds), *Philosophy in Africa*, 2nd edition. OUP.

Singer, Peter (1993). *A Companion to Ethics*. Oxford: Wiley Blackwell Publishers.

Stevenson, Stuart (2020). Psychodynamic intersectionality and the positionality of the group analyst: The tension between analytical neutrality and inter-subjectivity. *Group Analysis*, 53(4): 498–514.

Tutu, D. (2000). *No Future without Forgiveness*. Ebury Publishing.

US Centers for Disease Control and Prevention. COVID-19 cases, data, and surveillance: hospitalization and death by race/ethnicity. Accessed April 16, 2021. www.cdc. gov/coronavirus/2019-ncov/covid-data/investigations-discovery/hospitalization-death-by-race-ethnicity.html

Wekker, Gloria (2016). *White Innocence: Paradoxes of Colonialism and Race*. Durham, NC: Duke University Press.

Chapter 16

The Dyadics of Tolerance and the Tolerance of Dyadics

Shlomit Yadlin-Gadot and Uri Hadar

Introduction

The concept of "thirdness" first appeared in Charles Sanders Peirce's 1894 study of signs. Alongside the notions of "firstness" as the realm of *feeling* and "secondness" as the mode of *reacting*, "thirdness" was the mode of *thinking* (Peirce 1894/1998). Here, the subject was aware of learning, as experienced phenomena acquired a pattern and became knowable.

Psychoanalysis, from its very beginnings, has gravitated around the concept of thirdness, construing development in terms of movement from dyadic to triadic forms in both intrapsychic and intersubjective functioning. Indeed, the very concept of subjectivity often hinges on the achievement of thirdness, for the integrated modes of sensation, action-reaction and thought create the subject as a desiring center of agency and reflectivity. Whereas dyadic dynamisms necessarily involve paranoia, projection and destructive needs of control, thirdness promotes psychic tolerance and practices of mutual recognition, communication and dialogue. Consequently, psychoanalytic models of conflict resolution advocate constitution and rehabilitation of damaged modes of thirdness. This is often construed as the psychoanalytic ideal in terms of psychic development, therapeutic methodology and routes to conflict resolution (Honneth 1995).

But what happens when all acts of thirdness fail? When practices of dialogue and contract-based relations repeatedly shatter on the brick wall of suspiciousness and hostility? Here, in the context of intractable conflict, our inquiry begins. Intractable conflicts often involve multiple, inter-related issues that include incompatible values, needs for emotional security and long-standing inequalities in the distribution of resources and power (Coleman 2006). At the international level, between nations or other broadly defined groups, they are often centered around the need for discernable identity (Lederach 1995; Northrup 1989; Kriesberg 2003). When identities are experienced as threatened, defensive and offensive action is taken to protect what people see as their essence; what makes them who they are grants them distinction.

Intractable conflicts are intensified when political leaders try to resolve inner conflict by amplifying outer conflict, consciously intensifying its rhetoric and

DOI: 10.4324/9781003200253-21

practices (Burgess 2003). Burgess argues that such internal dynamics of escalation may take conflicts out of the disputants' control, pushing them towards extremes not considered desirable even in their own eyes.

In psychoanalytic terms, intractable conflicts are stubbornly entrenched in dyadic dynamisms and in the perpetual failure of practices aimed at creating thirdness in forms of dialogue, negotiation, and recognition. Here, negotiations may paradoxically exacerbate conflict. Often misconstrued as threat and insult, their stoppage intensifies the experience of danger and intransigence on both sides.

In an extensive project surveying relevant literature and documentation, Schweitzer (2009) differentiates two sets of procedures in modulating conflictual dynamics. The first focuses on analyzing conflicting interests and formulating modes of possible resolution. The second aims for deeper transformation of the conflict, effected by practices of dialogue, familiarity and recognition. Surprisingly, dialogue and reconciliation practices have been repeatedly shown to play a limited role in reducing conflict and hostility.

Our analysis of dyadic processes begins where the failure of achieving thirdness is the given point of departure. We aspire to formulate modes of tolerance derived from dyadic processes by (psycho)analyzing and teasing apart those of their elements that effect and exacerbate conflict dynamisms.

We first present some basic psychoanalytic accounts of conflict and its development in both individuals and groups, not as a comprehensive review of the relevant psychoanalytic literature, but rather for an appreciation of the existing diversity of vision. Then we examine the logic and dynamics of those *dyadic* components of intractable conflict that are given to change and manipulation, thereby forming a basis for tolerance. Finally, we examine the dialectic ties between the dyadic and the triadic consideration of tolerance. We argue that each has unique contributions, and that only through the incessant move between dyadic and triadic positions can tolerance be fully understood and promoted.

Psychoanalytic Accounts of Conflict

In the present section we present – in brief and partial manner – four nodal developmental accounts, from which the issue of tolerance may be approached. Each account articulates differential aspects of dyadic functioning and accentuates different challenges and anxieties involved in the creation of tolerance in its "slim" definition, namely, the ability of the subject to encounter otherness without extreme and violent reaction.

The Freudian Account – Castration and Exclusion

In the Freudian account, development is described in psychosexual terms and along the vicissitudes of the drive. In early stages of development, the libidinal drive manifests in oral, anal and phallic modes which determine the relations with the drive's object – the other. The oral and anal stages are characterized by an experience of omnipotence and control in relation to the object. The loved object of orality may be incorporated, "devoured" and experienced as part of the ego. In the anal stage, the loved object is a locus of control, and this is one of its prime satisfactions (Freud 1917/1963). In the phallic stage, competition emerges as an essential factor in the subject's relation with the other. It is here that the child develops Oedipal romance with the parent of the opposite sex, willing the same-sex parent to disappear and leave him as the solitary beneficiary of the beloved parent's love (Freud 1923/1961).

The traumatic aspect of the Oedipal triangle is two-fold: First, the romantic engagement of the parental couple leaves the child feeing painfully excluded. Secondly, if he dares fight this exclusion, he may be castrated by his strong adversary. Freud describes fear of castration as a frighteningly realistic possibility for the small child. The girl experiences herself as already castrated. The boy is terrified that he might share her terrible fate. Both have already experienced irrecoverable losses of experienced body-parts: the breast and the stool. In their anxiety of mutilation, castration, punishment and loss of parental love, the children withdraw romantic aspirations. Prohibition is incorporated into the psyche as its third agency, the superego: it is effectively the first form of psychoanalytic thirdness.

In Freudian analysis, the resolution of Oedipal conflicts marks the integration of libido and the unification of the psyche. The superego becomes the agent of sublimation, both incorporating and inhibiting primitive forms of the death drive in relation to the other (violence in its various expressions). The essential inhibition of the drive in the vicissitudes of sublimated Oedipal functioning allows the subject to think, mature and mentally diversify. It also accounts for both civilization and its discontents.

The Kleinian Account – Annihilation and Depletion of Resources

Kleinian thought supplies psychoanalysis with rich imagery regarding the horizon of dyadic experience, based on paranoid anxieties and fears of annihilation. In Klein's conceptualization of early experience, the infant is born into a chaotic, life-threatening world, and his psychic resources are mobilized to order it through splitting, projection and introjection. The world divides along two polarities in terms of the mother's life-giving and nurturing functions: the "good breast" satisfies, comforts, contains and feeds. It also protects the child in his phantasy from the "bad breast", which threatens with hunger, deprivation and annihilation (Klein 1940, 1957).

The infant incorporates the good breast object (primarily by introjection), projecting all discomfort and pain into the bad object which, in turn, is experienced as attacking the infant. Splitting along these lines of good and bad (respectively self and other) effectually constitutes the paranoid-schizoid position, in which the child is swamped with persecutory and annihilation anxieties. In Winnicott's elaboration of this drama, 'good-enough' mothering, with emphasis on the mother's containing function, allows the gradual integration of the good and bad objects, reducing the polarizing effects of introjection and projection and allowing growing differentiation between inner and outer realties (Winnicott 1962). When the infant realizes that the good and bad incorporate in a single object, he mourns the loss of the ultimate good, experiences concern for his object and offers reparation for his former destructive attacks upon it.

Yet, often enough, the combination of inadequate mothering and inborn aggression do not allow this optimal outcome. When frustration predominates, cycles of projection and introjection increase splitting rather than mitigate it. The basic oral hunger intensifies and colored by aggressive tendencies, develops into greed and envy. Mother's milk is then experienced as something that (s)he stole and withholds, thus triggering phantasies of both aggression and of aggressive retaliation. This evokes immense paranoid anxieties, to the extent of rendering the infant threatened with total depletion of resources, to the point of annihilation.

The Lacanian Account – Diffusion of Identity

For Lacan, subjectivity is formed in relation to the pre-existing other. Born prematurely, totally helpless and dependent on others, the infant experiences itself as fragmented, torn and exiled from the mother's body. In this terrifying realm of disintegration, the infant is offered the irresistible lure of his mirror image. This image presents a unified whole, an integrated, coordinated totality. In a jubilant moment, the infant recognizes itself in the mirror and identifies himself with this imago (Lacan 1949/2006). Clearly, Lacan notes, this recognition in the mirror-image is nothing but an absurd "misrecognition" that involves deep alienation, the inevitable consequence of the huge gulf between the unified imago and the infant's fragmentary authentic experience.

Making matters worse, the infant then enters an intense and ambivalent relation with his imago. The perfect, coherent image of himself arouses envy in the child and he seeks to own it and put himself in its place. Simultaneously, the child feels that the image is there to usurp him, to further alienate and deplete his experience of self. This pattern of what Lacan calls narcissistic 'aggressivity' then becomes the hallmark of all imaginary relations with others. Like in the Kleinian story, a basic paranoid positioning is created, dominated by the binary choice: "It's me or you".

The Name-of-the-Father saves the child from this imaginary predicament and enters psychic life when the child realizes that mother's desire is not given to her in its entirety. Some of it is painfully directed elsewhere and the child ceases to be the mother's "all". The Name-of-the-Father is not necessarily borne by the actual father, but rather represents a rule that prohibits the child's endless jouissance with the mother and that is internalized within her. On the one hand, the child experiences here a narcissistic injury yet, on the other hand, (s)he is freed from being the object of the mother's desire and is able to institute herself as a desiring subject. Of course, this is only possible within the confines of language and the law (Lacan 1953/2006). Entering this realm of lawfulness, the dyadic mother-child space is transformed into a triadic one, easing the aggressivity of imaginary relations. The urgency of experience dissipates and makes room for representational systems in the form of thought and language. This allows a measure of differentiation and safety in the face of the other.

The Relational Model – Mutual recognition

The Freudian, Kleinian and Lacanian accounts see the ability to perceive otherness as an achievement involving the gradual and successful surpassing of developmental conflicts. By distinction, leaning on contemporary infant research, Benjamin argues that the infant is born with the ability to relate to the other as subject – as an autonomous center of experience and agency. The ability to recognize the other's subjectivity is innate, but Benjamin stresses the need to cultivate it by means of maternal containment and affect regulation. When proper development fails and infant omnipotence is defensively triggered, subject-to-subject relations collapse into "escalating reactivity.... A structure of mutual accusation takes hold where neither party can truly recognize the pain or the struggles of the other.... Complementary relations are characterized by loss of agency and responsibility" (Benjamin 2006). Summoning the Hegelian logic of *Lordship and Bondage*, Benjamin construes mutual recognition as antidote to this regressive logic of complementarity, conflict, and injury. She believes that sticking creatively and tenaciously with communicative practices offers the prime route to healing (Benjamin 1995). This route is the thirdness route.

The achievement of tolerance in the Relational account leans most heavily on practices of communication and dialogue. Without them, the dyadic almost completely reduces to complementarity. Here, the absence of dialogue leaves next to nothing that can be manipulated in the service of tolerance. The other accounts, by distinction, leave more room for managing existence outside of the purview of dialogue. In Freudian theory, the fear of exclusion and castration that come with Oedipal developments may motivate the subject to seek dyadic solutions irrespective of communication. In the Kleinian account, the finality of resources plays a crucial part in presenting a world in which hunger is a threat, and the other is perceived as greedily dispossessing the subject. The Lacanian account focuses on the issue of dispossession as well, only here the dispossession is given in terms of identity; *the other threatens to be me* and thus can obliterate my existence. What is common to all accounts is an extremely fragile sense of self, one that may easily be unsettled.

Dyadic Strategies of Tolerance

In the present section, assuming the establishment of thirdness has reached a dead end, we explore cultivation of tolerance through psychoanalytic understanding of dyadic dynamisms. Trying to identify dyadic elements inherent to intractable conflict, we examine how they can be manipulated to promote tolerance. We develop our analysis by discussing several conflict-reducing strategies and showing how psychoanalytic considerations illuminate the way they effect change.

The relevant literature shows that the effort to create tolerance in intractable, violent conflicts typically involves a number of these strategies, all of which address the nodal anxieties in the psychoanalytic developmental accounts formulated above.

1. *Exclusion and inclusion effects*: Alleviation of isolation anxieties created by bestowing upon or depriving conflicted parties the privileges of belonging to a larger community. In the international arena, countries involved in violent conflict and abuse of human rights are frequently excluded from financial and security agreements and are rewarded with these memberships when violent acts and practices are ended. International pressures along the inclusion-exclusion line have proved effective, for example, in South Africa (Hook 2013).

   We argue that, in addition to concrete effects, exclusion/inclusion practices carry powerful psychological effects: They alleviate isolation anxieties by granting the conflicting parties a sense of belonging and association, as well as consolidating a stable sense of identity. These patterns cohere with Freud's Oedipal dynamics, which ties up identity with a sense of structure and continuity, positioning the child as subject in her family and transforming the mass into a group (Freud 1921/1955).

2. *Imposed limitation of resources*: Schweitzer's work on intractable conflict (2001; 2009) has shown that strategies involving manipulation of resources are effective in both reducing violent acts and in preserving ccasefires and other non-violent agreements. These strategies typically grant or withhold economic resources through direct financial and commercial aid or by imposing sanctions (e.g., on oil and arms trade), freezing assets, imposing travel restrictions and so forth.

   The effectiveness of these strategies clearly cohere with the Kleinian analysis of (dyadic) maturation inasmuch as they exacerbate or alleviate annihilation anxieties related to resources and their ownership and, with it, the sense of security in both the conflicting parties and on both personal and the group levels. In this understanding, there may also be a secondary gain that comes from re-signifying the conflict in terms of resources. The conflict that had originally been fought to *accrue* actual and imaginary resources (perceived as necessary for existence) is now experienced as *depleting* the group-subject and its resources.

3. *The sharpening of separateness*: The sense of autonomy is often a necessary precondition for tolerance. Embedded in long and brutal conflict, each conflicting party becomes irredeemably entangled with the other in establishing its identity, rather in the manner of the Lacanian mirror stage. The sense that only one identity is possible results in fear of annihilation. The developmental way out of this predicament is normally the development of thirdness through entry of the-Name-of-the-Father into the dyadic arena. However, in intractable conflict this development fails and the parties are caught in a logic where the other's identity is always at one's expense.

   In order to manage this, the subject group must disengage its identity from that of the other party. Yadlin-Gadot (2017) has called this dynamic "monadic convergence" and brought as a model the total removal of the USA from Japanese cultural commemoration of WWII destruction (as, for example, in Hiroshima and Nagasaki). In all plaques commemorating the dead there is no mention of America. The Japanese rehabilitated their sense of identity and freed themselves from hatred and threat by establishing their identity from within their own historical resources. On the international level, this process is enhanced by security arrangements, as in positioning UN forces along the borders of the conflicted parties. These arrangements often have no real effects, but they establish a clear, accentuated boundary between two identity groups.

4. *Bottom up effects*: Over time, conflict destroys cultural timelines. Hatred, fear, and memories of past atrocities are deeply entrenched and accordingly projected into the future. Creating compulsive repetitions and destroying imagined futures, the subject believes that the conflicted present is inevitable. The psychological challenge here is to rehabilitate the imagination and create an experience of possibility by means of bottom-up strategies that aim for change in the texture of life and social relations. Grassroot practices and programs, social and educational projects, economic initiatives, charitable activities and systems of reward influence both quality of life and personal experience of future possibilities (Dudouet 2006). Enhancing the wellbeing and development of the conflicted communities they create and consolidate a sense of security and create a sense of identity that is not predicated on conflict. More radically, the sense of potential, hopeful future identity transcends the despair engendered by the conflict. This kind of low-level change may create a structural-contractual transformation at some later point.

   Viewed from a psychoanalytic perspective, each of the above strategies *can be seen as rooted in a particular dynamic of maturation associated with a particular psychoanalytic perspective*. Fears of isolation and exclusion are met with offers of membership in large-scale organizations (Freudian perspective). Anxieties related to depletion of resources and annihilation are countered with economic aid, the widening of international support and the provision of security arrangements (Kleinian perspective). Finally, the unstable sense of self and identity can be facilitated bottom up, when networks of individual relations change the reality of lives, their experienced identity and imagined future (Lacanian perspective). These practices may be employed prior to the achievement of political arrangements or contractual mutual recognition (Relational perspective, see Hadar 2013).

Political Illustration of Dyadic Options

Insider's Tolerance

The manipulation of dyadic elements and their derivative anxieties can alleviate violence and paranoid anxieties *among* conflicted parties as described above. They may also trigger a dialogue between dyadic and triadic states *within* the subject (group). This dialogue may later extend from the subject to his fellow subjects within the community, a dialogue that becomes crucial when it is created between a leader and her community. Here, to fulfill the function of communication, the leader-subject needs to acknowledge both her own and her community's identifications. In terms of expression, persuasion and comprehension, a dyadic "grammar" needs to function within linguistic forms employed in the context of (intractable) conflict. An interesting example here might be the different modes of expression employed by two protagonists of the Oslo accord: Yitzhak Rabin and Shimon Peres. Their different speech modes may be described using the Wittgensteinian concept of language games (Wittgenstein 1999).

Wittgenstein contended that words acquire meaning by their use in the social practices. He drew attention to the ways in which language and action are interwoven, always already given in a social community, a way of life that effectually grants words their meanings. Different ways of life form the structure and logic of various, potentially endless, language games which, in turn, structure world views. What we have here is an inescapable inter-dependence. The structure and logic of a language game, its rules and concepts, effectually form its grammar. Different grammars produce different organizations of facts and manufacture different meanings: "Grammar is laid against reality like a ruler.... [it] is not accountable to any reality. It is grammatical rules that determine meaning (constitute it) and so they themselves are not answerable to any meaning and to that extent are arbitrary" (Wittgenstein 1974, pp. 184–185).

We use various language games in an automatic and unconscious manner, often unaware of their different underlying grammar, "for it flows along underground, as it were, without our noticing it; and not until it openly contradicts our false imagination do we suddenly become aware of it" (Wittgenstein 1980, p. 77). Often, we live entrapped within a language game, within a form of life, imagining it to be the only (valid) one to describe a world. Wittgenstein's point is that different language games construe existence differently, and that moving amongst 'games' allows the recreation of meanings. The very awareness of language games grants insight into the deep-felt sentiments and modes of living that they create, forming the workings and logic of a society.

Rabin's language game reflected the logic and structure of Israeli warfare and his 27-year career as a soldier. He served as the Palmach's[1] chief of operations during Israel's War of Independence and as the IDF's Chief of Staff during the remarkable and fateful 1967 victories. It is doubtful that the dramatic Oslo Accords could have been made by anyone with a lesser history of warfare "strength". Only a dedicated soldier could be trusted to insure the integrity of identity and the vital interests of a threatened and paranoid Israeli subject without "giving in" or "selling out". Rabin could be trusted; after all, he was the one who, as minister of defense during the first Intifada, ordered to "break the arms and legs" of Arab demonstrators.[2] Rabin's military "habitus" and soldierly bearing vouched for and validated an identity deeply ingrained in the dyadic polarities of us-them, good and evil. It allowed the reluctant Israeli center and moderate right to somehow digest his historical dramatic moves.

Equipped with a soldier's rhetoric, Rabin could remain loyal to the dyadic dynamics and grammar entrenched in his and in his group-subject's psyche. "I am a soldier in the army of peace" Rabin declared (1994), retaining the language of war. He remained for his public the strong, vigilant soldier-image that could inspire trust and security in the hearts of those experiencing mortal threat by the very idea of armed Palestinians. "Do not give them guns" was one of the leading rightist slogans, leaving unfinished the obvious continuation of the sentence: "so they won't slaughter us". This implication was obvious, no clarifications were needed. Rabin replied: "We make peace with enemies, not with friends",[3] thus not demanding that large portions of the Israeli public dis-identify with the polarities that had ordered and structured their lives for decades. Rabin realized that a psychological shift to thirdness could not, perhaps, be achieved. He did not try to promote it knowing, as he did, that dyadic time was measured by the wounded and dead.

Rabin did not expect dramatic changes in the basic anxieties of a traumatized people. He coined the slogan "a strong people make peace" addressing, yet again, the perpetual, intractable fear of annihilation. It is interesting that the two additional Israeli leaders who managed to lead Israel in territorial concessions (in Gaza strip and Lebanon) were two former IDF officers – Arik Sharon and Ehud Barak.

Insider's Idealization

To transcend dyadic hostility, the subject often resorts to ideal possibilities. Heidegger showed this logic of being when he explained his "take" on the subject as *dasein*, as an entity that *reflects* upon and questions the meaning of human existence. He described the authentic life of Dasein as rooted in the ability to project oneself into the future in terms of possibilities. This mode is the polar opposite of becoming entrapped in "facticity", namely, in the given, already signified elements of existence. This realm of possibility offers one form of thirdness, which had informed the rhetoric of Rabin's partner – Shimon Peres.

Peres had led a long political career before the times of Oslo. Despite his superior intellect and being highly esteemed abroad, Peres never inspired the public trust and respect that Rabin did in Israel. In our present line of inquiry, Peres's weak point as a political leader was no doubt related to his lack of military history, to his inability to alleviate basic anxieties of annihilation. In that sense, his was a dyadic weakness. To accentuate this weakness, Peres was also the dreamer who formulated the peace language-game, the concept and grammar of a "new middle east" (Peres 1993). Rather than inspiring hope, this concept stamped Peres as weak, naïve and out-of-touch in both Israeli and Palestinian public, equally mired in the throes of dyadic politics. Indeed, Palestinian youth called for Abas to surrender Palestinian leadership following his emotional participation in Peres's funeral.[4]

Discussion

Our illustration of the recruitment of dyadic forces to promote tolerance concentrated on political action in the Israeli-Palestinian arena and addressed anxieties related to annihilation, exclusion, and finite resources. It demonstrated how tolerance may be enhanced through the necessary manipulation of dyadic modes of experiencing and functioning.

We have tried to illustrate that in some ways, a subject firmly positioned in triadic experiencing employs a different grammar of thought and language than a subject positioned in dyadic modes of experiencing. Approaching a dyadically determined conflict in triadic terms is akin to approaching a foreigner with one's mother tongue. Even if the semantics of the triadic communication are understood, the underlying assumptions that are needed to uphold its grammar are missing, thus leaving the import of the communication necessarily distorted. Only a dyadically formulated communication can permeate and influence subjects mired in dyadic dynamics.

The move from dyadic to triadic forms is usually understood as developmental and linear. In that sense, the possibility of engaging dyadic forces for the achievement of triadic functioning is also an exploration of non-linear dynamisms, largely along lines suggested by Nonlinear Dynamic Systems Theory (NDST, see Vallacher et al. 2012). NDST construes elements of a system as interacting with each other, shaping each other, and passing information around; they are not replaceable or removable without fundamentally altering the dynamics of the whole system. By loosening our hold on the traditional ways of establishing thirdness, we may allow creativity in addressing dyadic elements in conflict, assuming that the system, the gestalt, is influenced in its entirety when any of its elements are transformed. In the context of intractable conflict, the search for comprehensive (triadic) solutions may throw parties into impasse, creating passivity and learned helplessness. Within the NDST perspective, manipulating dyadic aspects may trigger movement in static, hopeless realities.

In many intractable conflicts, the aspiration to create triadic dynamics as the sole cornerstone of tolerance may be self-defeating. Despite the moral, intellectual and aesthetic appeal of thirdness, it is of utmost importance to be able to appreciate and deploy dyadic strategies. This is especially true in regions where time spans are given and measured in terms of the wounded and dead.

In these contexts, we argue for simple and uncompromising dyadic distinctions between the violent and non-violent. Again, in dyadic terms, all violence is evil. All means to the end of uprooting it are valuable and must be pursued and cultivated. In this paper we tried to contribute towards this end.

Notes

1   The left-wing para-military group that acted in Palestine prior to the establishment of Israel.
2   Rabin's instructions as defense minister to the army in the first 1987 Intifada uprising.   https://he.wikiquote.org/wiki/%D7%99%D7%A6%D7%97%D7%A7_%D7%A8%D7%91%D7%99%D7%9F.
3   Yitzhak Rabin In a private communication to Hagai Kadmon, 1994. www.ynet.co.il/articles/0,7340,L-3971280,00.html.
4   www.ynet.co.il/articles/0,7340,L-4861900,00.html.

References

Benjamin, J. (1995). Recognition and destruction: An outline of intersubjectivity. In *Like Subjects, Love Objects*. New Haven, CT: Yale Univ. Press.
Benjamin, J. (2006). Mutual injury and mutual acknowledgement. *World in Transition Conference*, London.
Burgess, H. and Burgess G. (2003). What are intractable conflicts? In Burgess, G. and Burgess, H. (eds), *Beyond Intractability*. Conflict Information Consortium, University of Colorado, Boulder. Posted: November 2003 at www.beyondintractability.org/essay/meaning-intractability
Coleman, P. (2006). Intractable conflict. In Deutsch, M. and Coleman, P. (eds), *Handbook of Conflict Resolution*. San Francisco: Jossey-Bass.
Freud, S. (1917/1963). The development of the libido and sexual organizations. In Strachey, J. (ed.), *The Standard Edition, Volume XV*, London: The Hogarth Press, pp. 320–339.
Freud, S. (1923/1961). The ego and the id. In Strachey, J. (ed.), *The Standard Edition, Volume XIX*. London: The Hogarth Press, pp. 12–60.
Freud, S. (1921/1955). Group psychology and the analysis of the ego. In Strachey, J. (ed.), *The Standard Edition, Volume 18*. London: Hogarth Press, pp. 65–144.
Hadar, U. (2013). *Psychoanalysis and Social Involvement*. London: Palgrave.
Honneth, Axel (1995). *The Struggle for Recognition: The Moral Grammar of Social Conflicts*. Cambridge UK: Polity Press.

Hook, D. (2013). *(Post)Apartheid Conditions: Psychoanalysis and Social Formation*. London: Palgrave.

Klein, M. (1957). Envy and gratitude. In Klein, M., *Envy and Gratitude and Other Works 1946–1963*. London: The International Psycho-Analytical Library, pp. 175–236.

Klein, M. (1940). Mourning and its relation to manic-depressive states. *Int. J. Psycho-Anal.*, *21*, 125–153.

Kriesberg, L. (2003). Identity issues. In Burgess, G. and Burgess, H. (eds), *Beyond Intractability*. Conflict Information Consortium, University of Colorado, Boulder. Posted: July 2003 at www.beyondintractability.org/essay/identity-issues

Lacan, J. (1949/2006). The mirror stage as formative of the function of the I. In *Ecrits*: (trans.) Bruce Fink. New York: WW Norton, pp. 75–81.

Lacan, J. (1953/2006). The function and field of speech and language in psychoanalysis. In *Ecrits: The First Complete Edition in English*, translated by Bruce Fink. New-York: WW Norton, pp. 197–268.

Lederach, J. P. (1995). Conflict transformation in protracted internal conflicts: The case for a comprehensive framework. In Kumar, R. (ed.), *Conflict Transformation*. New York: MacMillan, pp. 201–222.

Northrup, T. A. (1989). The dynamic of identity in personal and social conflict. In Kriesberg, L., Northrup, T. A. and Thorson, S. J. (eds), *Intractable Conflicts and Their Transformation*. Syracuse: Syracuse University Press, pp. 55–82. Available at http://books.google.com/books?id=Lj2vg3xMHO8C

Peirce, Charles S. (1894/1998). What is a sign? In *The Essential Peirce, Selected Philosophical Writings, Volume 2 (1893-1913)*. Bloomington IN: Indiana University Press, pp. 4–10.

Peres, S. (1993). *The New Middle East*. New York: Holt & Co.

Rabin, Yitzhak (1994). *Address by Prime Minister Yitzhak Rabin to the United States Congress*. Washington DC.

Schweitzer, C. (2009). *Strategies of Intervention in Protracted Violent Conflicts by Civil Society Actors*. Coventry: Coventry University Press.

Schweitzer, C., Howard, D., Junge, M., Levine, C., Stieren, C. and Wallis, T. (2001). *Nonviolent Peaceforce Feasibility Study*. Available at www.nonviolentpeaceforce.org/en/feasibilitystudy

Vallacher, R. R., Coleman, P. T. and Nowak, A. (2012). Dynamical systems theory: Implications for peace and conflict. In Christie, D. J. (ed.), *The Encyclopedia of Peace Psychology*. New York: Wiley-Blackwell.

Winnicott, D.W. (1962). Ego integration in child development. In Winnicott, D.W. (1965), *The Maturational Processes and the Facilitating Environment: Studies in the Theory of Emotional Development*. New York: International Universities Press, pp. 56–64.

Wittgenstein, L. (1974). *Philosophical Grammar*. Oxford: Basil Blackwell.

Wittgenstein, L. (1980). *Remarks on the Philosophy of Psychology*. Oxford: Basil Blackwell.

Wittgenstein, L. (1999). *Philosophical Investigations*. Oxford: Basil Blackwell.

Yadlin-Gadot, S. (2017). Psychoanalytic approaches to conflict resolution: The limits of intersubjective engagement. In Ofer, G. (ed.), *A Bridge Over Troubled Water: Conflicts and Reconciliation in Groups and Society*. London: Routledge, pp. 205–212.

Chapter 17

Between Tolerance and Intolerance

Political Correctness and Populism

Haim Weinberg

Introduction

Tolerance can be defined as the acceptance of another person, viewpoint, or behavior different from our own. It is the appreciation of diversity and the ability to live and let others live. Tolerance is supposed to be the remedy to discrimination, dehumanization, repression, and violence.

The idea of tolerance as a code of conduct began in 1682, when Pierre Bayle, a French Protestant, published his book *Various Thoughts on the Occasion of a Comet*, which became a controversial bestseller. He claimed that a society would need to protect all religious beliefs if those beliefs shaped and improved people's conduct. He concluded that all people should be tolerated based on what they do, not what they say. This extraordinary early text contains the first secular justification of multicultural tolerance. Since then, tolerance became a synonym for democracy, human rights and multiculturalism. Most people in the Western world believe that tolerance and understanding the other are intertwined in the path toward human progress. No doubt – in the public discourse, tolerance is in vogue.

But how far can tolerance go? Should we tolerate cultural traditions and rituals that are perceived as repressing and against human rights? For example, should we accept women circumcision whose aim is to prevent women from enjoying sex? This female genital mutilation (also known as female circumcision: the ritual cutting or removal of some of the external female genitalia) is still practiced in some African Muslim countries, in Asia and the Middle East. Or should we tolerate "conscientious persecutors" who believe that they hold the truth, because we should respect freedom of conscience by itself?

And when do people who usually preach for tolerance and fight for diversity and for acceptance of the other become themselves intolerant? Surprisingly, some social circumstances call for more intolerance even for people who consider themselves open-minded, liberal, and welcoming differences. Usually, it happens under conditions of massive social trauma, unconsciously triggering people's emotions and affecting their behaviors.

DOI: 10.4324/9781003200253-22

In this chapter I establish a circumplex model of tolerance, based on my experience in therapy groups and draw conclusions to large social groups. In addition, I analyze the current world political/social situation, especially in the USA, to understand how polarization and intolerance governs the scene almost everywhere nowadays.

Politics and Populism

Until lately, tolerance has been in vogue, and at least in the public discourse, respect for Otherness and accepting of differences was praised and considered a virtue that enlightened and educated human beings should strive to achieve. However, it seems that in the last decade or two, and especially since 2017, political populist leaders around the world are admired by many for practicing intolerance. How did it happen?

Populism refers to a range of political stances that emphasize and prioritize the vague idea of "the people", juxtaposing and contrasting the common crowd ("the pure people") against "the corrupt elite". The term appeared in the 19th century and has been applied to various politicians, parties, and movements since that time. Populist leaders are usually charismatic or dominant figures who present themselves as the "voice of the people". They thrive and prosper in times of social unrest and distress when people are looking for a "strong" leader (whatever it means), and are easy to be influenced and convinced by emotional arguments, often, when economy falters. Populist leaders are good in abusing this need by addressing the lowest common denominator. They persuade the people who suffer from economic distress or feel socially disempowered that those "intellectual" (educated) urban folks accumulated too much economic, cultural and political power. They incite people who feel socially and economically deprived against immigrants and minorities, making them believe that those social subgroups are taking their jobs, their women, their (national) pride.

Populism is on the rise in the last two decades not only among Europe or in the US right wing, but almost everywhere: Narendra Modi in India, Donald Trump in the United States, Joko Widodo in Indonesia, Orbán in Hungary, Bibi in Israel and Bolsonaro in Brazil. How can we explain that democracy is in the midst of an unprecedented global retreat? One of the reasons for the rise of populism stems from the waves of immigrants that flooded Europe and the fear of Latin American immigrants in the USA. This global peoples' migration created a new global situation, destabilizing the secure order and evoking a feeling of unsafety. Deprived of safety, people legitimately feel alienated, distrustful, and isolated. Politically, nation after nation, this situation became a fertile ground for the rise of populistic movements, mostly right-wing, sometimes non-democratic leaders. Intertwined with increasing terror attacks, mostly by extreme Islamic people, citizens felt the earth shaking under their feet and yearned for a strong leader to save them. When these leaders rise, intolerance becomes ubiquitous, creating polarization and splitting. Populist leaders can meld the many into one, and forge people into a mob – and the mob is very intolerant. Already in the 19th century Le Bon (1895), pointed out that members in the crowd feel a lessened sense of legal culpability and that the individuals submerged in the crowd lose their self-control as the "collective mind" takes over.

The Tyranny of the Politically Correct

From the other pole of political point of view, intolerance increased as well. The politics of identities flourished in the USA since 1970, first in the academic circles and later among educated people. Its impact increased towards the end of the 20th century, and later with the spread of the Me Too and Black Live Matters movements. In general, it is an approach to politics by which people of a particular gender, religion, class, race, ethnicity, social background, etc. organize themselves politically based on the systems of oppression that they see as applying to them because of their identity. Indeed, our fundamental social identities can be a source of power or of powerlessness, a justification for inequality or for bold social reform. We should all be aware of the importance of race, class, sexual orientation or gender across a variety of important contexts, such as the workplace, family, universities, and popular culture and the implications and influences of these identities on our daily lives. Historically, the rise of democracy in the United States created troubling questions about the new power of the majority to silence minority opinion. As the will of the majority became the rule of the day, everyone outside of mainstream white American opinion, especially Indians and Blacks, were vulnerable to the wrath of the majority.

Interestingly, criticism against identity politics was voiced from both right and left political points of view. Those who criticize from the left see it as a divide and conquer strategy by the ruling classes to separate people by nationality, race, ethnicity, religion, to distract the working class from uniting for the purpose of class struggle. Some went even further to claim that when groups feel threatened, they retreat into tribalism. When groups feel mistreated and disrespected, they close ranks and become more insular, more defensive, more punitive, more us-versus-them (Berman, Berger & Gutmann, 2000). Those who criticize identity politics from the right see it inherently collectivist and prejudicial, in contradiction to the ideals of Classical liberalism. Other voices claimed that it is morally wrong to reduce identity to subjective reactions to victimhood (Berman, 2010), and to reject equal treatment under the law in favor of 'sliding scales' that are subject to infinite adjustments and flagrant manipulations.

From the point of view of intolerance, the problematic social dynamics that emerged suit the title of "the tyranny of the politically correct". Take, for example, the important idea of microaggression. There are certainly cases when people indirectly, subtly, or unintentionally discriminate against members of a marginalized group such as a racial or ethnic minority, and their verbal comments might reveal this hidden discrimination. However, since this concept is vague and subjective, it became too loose and easily used as an outcry for not enough good reason. More than that, many times instead of using it in order to draw the attention of someone who has made a mistake *unintentionally*, it is used as a way to scold, to shame and to attack those unfortunate people who transgressed. When used this way it expresses intolerance toward common human mistakes, opening a persecutive pandora box.

We can see the same process happening with the MeToo movement. Again, this movement is critically important to empower women, to change power dynamics of gender and to encourage women who are sexually harassed, attacked or raped, to loudly express in public their pain and to demand justice. Indeed, unfortunately, men used their power for centuries to sexually abuse and sexually harass women, and the MeToo movement helped women, especially young and vulnerable ones, to break their silence by visibly demonstrating how many women have survived sexual assault and harassment, especially in the workplace. However, in my opinion, it also created too many cases in which any flattering comment by a man toward a woman is considered with the same degree of severity as an abusive harassment. Those men expressing what they perceive as positive flirting comments were condemned publicly as sexists and rapists. This phenomenon is called "cancelling culture": a form of ostracism in which someone is thrust out of social or professional circles. The notion of cancel culture constitutes a form of boycotting involving an individual who is deemed to have acted or spoken in a questionable or controversial manner. The inability to distinguish between serious cases of harassment and abuse and between daily expressions of attraction and courting, and to relate to both cases as equally dangerous, created cases that seem an intolerant witch hunt against men.

The Black Live Matters (BLM) movement started showing the same polarization and extremism. It goes without saying that Black people and People of Color (BIPOC: Black, Indigenous and People of Color) have been discriminated against by the system in the US for a long time. Even though the civil rights movement in the US gained a lot of achievements, and on the surface white and BIPOC people seem to enjoy the same rights, a lot of evidence has accumulated that systemic racism is working behind the scenes, from the highly unreasonable proportion of incarcerated black people to the low, unexplainable proportion of black people in leadership roles in any organization. Protest against incidents of police brutality and all racially motivated violence against black people is crucial in order to change the unconscious social injustice and the unequal power that white people (especially white males) have in American society, but as pointed out above regarding the other social movements, it carries the danger of the tyranny of the politically correct as well.

Take, for example, Robin DiAngelo's (2018) important concept of white fragility. In her book she describes the disbelieving defensiveness that white people exhibit when their ideas about race and racism are challenged, and particularly when they feel implicated in white supremacy. Since white people respond automatically with defensiveness and avoid dealing with systemic racism in the USA, DiAngelo believes that it shows their fragility. There is no doubt that this phenomenon exists and contributes a lot to the continuation of systemic racism in the US. However, in public discussions and in the public discourse, "white fragility" became a slogan that is easily pulled out whenever a white person disagrees with any argument that BIPOC people or their avid supporters bring. In a way it acquired the same problematic use that the concept of resistance acquired in the psychoanalytic field: Whenever you disagree with your psychoanalyst, you are resisting; whenever you disagree with BIPOC people and their supporters, you show your white fragility. In some circles it seems as if white people are required to repeat some ritual and say certain sentences in order to appease the angry attacks on white people. In short, strong, almost rigid intolerance is dramatically shown among people who are fighting for tolerance, human rights, equality and diversity.

How can we understand this strange phenomenon? A simple explanation is the mechanism of identification with the aggressor. Following decades and sometimes centuries of oppression, minority groups internalize the outside oppression and abuse by the majority. It can be expressed as an internal oppression, such as accepting themselves as inferior, diminishing self-worth and acquiring learned helplessness, but when they gain power and they protest, they might unconsciously use the same oppressive mechanisms that were directed at them. In a way it a scapegoating process by those who were previously scapegoated.

Another explanation is based on Hopper's (2019) fourth basic assumption of Incohesion: Aggregation vs. Massification. Hopper argued that under conditions of massive social trauma, social large groups regress and manifest behaviors that stem from that basic assumption: shifting between extreme aggregation (becoming isolated, fortressing rigid individual boundaries and selfishly taking care only of one's needs) and massification (loosing individual boundaries, merging into a crowd, and becoming undifferentiated and non-reflective mob). The massification pole can trigger thoughtful sensitive adults to lose their acceptance of differences and to become very intolerant.

In conclusion, under some conditions liberal and human right movements can create "the dictatorship of the political correctness", pushing people to react by throwing the baby with bath water, renouncing tolerance.

The Impact of Social Media

We cannot ignore the social media revolution of the 21st century and its deep impact on our culture, some of it is still hidden from awareness. A culture of immediate gratification has emerged, racing for "likes" as a sign for being socially popular, easily creating massification by a viral spread of messages, and enhancing cyberbullying. Cyberbullying is the use of an electronic device to bully, threaten, or intimidate another person. It exists since the creation of social media. In a culture of rising incivility, combined with many that are both sensitive and passionate about their beliefs, people are using bullying or harassing behavior and labeling it as activism. Traumatic social conditions that were mentioned before, such as the viral spread of the video of George Floyd's killing by a police officer in Minneapolis, accelerate the development of intolerance on social media and the digital world and poison the public discourse. Online political discussions are experienced as angrier and less civil than those outside social media. Networks of partisans co-create worldviews that become more extreme. Disinformation campaigns flourish.

The relative ease of sending, publishing or forwarding nasty shaming messages, attacking someone online in the name of justice, makes social media a dangerous arena, reducing tolerance to zero. Reflection and self-control are not encouraged online. Connecting through the Internet lacks the body-to-body interaction that creates empathy (Weinberg, 2014; Weinberg and Rolnick, 2020), and it gives people a license to become hurtful. The philosopher Emmanuel Levinas (Cohen, 1996) claimed that responsibility begins in seeing the face of another human being. In one of his interviews, he said: "The face says to me: you shall not kill." Not seeing the face of the person that is attacked, is compared to the act of the pilot who releases the bomb on an enemy village, without seeing the pain of those who were attacked. Social media can also become suggestive and viral. Haidt and Rose-Stockwell (2019) wrote about "the dark psychology of social networks". They claimed that human beings evolved to gossip, preen, manipulate and ostracize. We are easily lured into this new gladiatorial circus of social networks even when we know that it makes us intolerant, cruel and shallow. Facebook and twitter are not for deep thinkers and for thoughtful reflections.

The Relational Model

Relational approaches (Mitchel & Aron, 1999) shifted from a "one-person" psychology to a "two-person" psychology, explaining people's behaviors as co-created through the interaction. Pathology and problematic behavioral expressions are no longer considered a result of inner unconscious dynamics only, but as stemming from interactions or relationships of which people are unaware. This radical view of human problematic relational manifestations, focusing on intersubjective processes since the 1990s, was actually expressed much earlier by Foulkes (1964) the father of group analysis, who considered the "location" of pathology outside the individual – in society. The location of the disturbance is not in the individual but *between* individuals. Following Foulkes, Robi Friedman (2013) discussed what he called "relational disorders" – dysfunctional relationships that are co-created when powerful emotions are not contained by the group. His description can easily be expanded to include social dynamics and subgroups. In the Deficiency Relation Disorder there is a split between the powerful and the weak, with lack of reciprocity around give and take. Roles are fixed and no change is possible. This relational social disturbance created years of white supremacy and gender inequality. Rejection Relation Disorder creates unconscious scapegoating dynamics which are socially demonstrated in projecting "badness" onto minorities such as Jews or Blacks, resulting in racism and fantasies of getting rid of the scapegoated social minority. In Relation Disorders of the Self people give up their needs looking for a hero (a charismatic leader) and a victim (immigrants, minorities). In the last social disorder, Exclusion Relation Disorder, there is an inability to contain differences, and (sometimes unconscious) manifestations of envy and rivalry. The need to be in the center creates a dynamic of exclusion and a chronic normalization of powerful social hierarchies. No social movement is allowed, and minorities are marginalized and under-function socially. The important factor of this model is that it is co-created by all social subgroups who participate in these dynamics. Intolerance exists in each of these social disturbances, but no one is to be blamed specifically.

The group analytic concept of the social unconscious (Hopper, 2003; Hopper and Weinberg, 2011, 2015, 2017) completes the relational paradigm by exploring social deviation as co-created by people who belong to the same social grouping, originating from their social unconscious.

The spread of populist leaders and rise of right-wing governments around the world in the last decade, is highly connected to the tyranny of politically correct, all described above. The more rigid and intolerant the politically correct advocates became, the more it threatened some people who emphasize "law-and-order" and pushed them to hold more extreme anti-human rights position, and vice versa: The more extreme and intolerant some social subgroups became towards immigrants and minorities, the more intolerant human right people became since they felt threatened as well and had to hold their lines more fortressed. In short, polarization and divisiveness replaced tolerance and acceptance of the other in both sides. Some of the social dynamics described above are a backlash against the tyranny of the "politically correct" atmosphere disconnecting the highly educated folks who accrued significant economic, cultural and political power from blue collar working class (and vice versa). Thus, polarization and splitting became ubiquitous. There is no way of separating between the two poles and blaming only one side, and it does not matter "who started". Extremists from both sides feed one another and are co-created.

The relational model praises a dialogue in which each party listens to the other party's point of view, trying to understand their point of view. It's an intersubjective model in which the subjectivity of each participant is valued and encouraged. Such a dialogue is crucial in creating acceptance and tolerance among opponents. Unfortunately, in the current social and political circumstances, and especially last year during the global traumatic conditions of the Corona pandemic, dialogue is rarely encouraged or achieved. The public discourse focuses on who is right and who is wrong, and not on understanding the other and their point of view.

A Clinical Vignette

In an online forum of an American mental health professional organization dealing with group therapy that includes some professionals from outside the USA, a discussion started about BLM (Black Lives Matter) following the protests against police brutality and discrimination towards BIPOC. The posts were very emotional and angry, focusing on systemic racism in the US and how black people are threatened every day or do not get the appropriate health care, bringing many examples from last year. One of the members from outside the States asked why the group is focusing only on black lives and suggested adding intersectionality to the discussion. He brought examples from his country about police brutality against LGBTQ people. He argued that a comprehensive anti-systemic oppression work on racism cannot be hijacked and diminished as related only to color, as deep understanding regarding changing a system from the inside demands multicultural, intersectional and international perspectives analysis where color, sex, gender, ethnic origin, class, intergenerational traumas are some of the categories that influence our social unconscious.

His message was responded to with very angry posts. People attacked him for using the words "colored people" instead "people of color" (ignoring the fact that he might not be aware of the politically correct terms in the USA since he lives in another country). He was called a racist, accused of demonstrating white fragility, and was sent "to do the work" and read DiAngelo's book and other articles about white supremacy and fragility. He was perceived as holding extreme right-wing ideas (alt right) and was accused that his deliberate intention was to weaken the fight for BLM and reduce the importance of protecting Blacks. To the author of this chapter, it felt as if an angry vocal subgroup on that forum tries to silence and scapegoat one member for bringing a different point of view, so in response, the author of this chapter wrote:

> We are experts in group processes and group dynamics, so why don't we use this expertise and try to understand the dynamics of this forum? I want to suggest my understanding and analysis. I am sure that there are other ways to analyze the processes and I invite you to share your understanding and observations.

I continued to suggest that the forum is not involved in a dialogue in which each member tries to listen and to understand the other person's point of view, but in a divisive fight in which there is "right" (my side) and "wrong" (the other side). I pointed out to the possibility of scapegoating dynamics on the forum, since the person from abroad who brought a different point of view was silenced and marginalized (in a parallel process to what happens to minorities and of course to BIPOC in society). As a response to my post, I was called a racist as well and I was attacked as an old white male who is not ready to give up his privileges!

This example shows how educated, rational, adult professionals who passionately fight for human rights and for tolerance for the other, can become very intolerant in traumatic times (both the pandemic times and the social traumatic situation during Trump's regime) and lose their professional ability to reflect on psychological and group processes involved in a discussion, when strong emotional issues trigger them. An interesting extreme example of losing the ability to think clearly and mentalize the other in this discussion was the demand not to ask black people for their experience since people should "do the work" themselves and read about the experience of BIPOC and not put the burden on them to describe their experience. While I can understand the logic of this this idea and agree that a single BIPOC in a group might become a representative of their social group and be burdened by this role, the extreme demand not to ask BIPOC for their experiences in order to learn from them negates everything we teach about groups where people usually learn from one another, since interpersonal input is one of Yalom's (2020) therapeutic factors. The intolerant dynamics described above underline the common goal of all the discussants in that forum: fighting social injustice and supporting human rights. Instead of uniting and fighting together against the real danger of racism and discrimination, people who have those same values fight against one another. The conversation is ending by reenacting the same social dynamics between majority and minority: by the silencing of repressive voices.

A Circumplex Model of Tolerance

The dilemma regarding tolerance is: when is it necessary for building a healthy society and when what looks like "over-tolerance" (which is actually pseudo-tolerance) leads to a strong negative backlash? Sometimes too much tolerance to behaviors that are extremely out of the range of common accepted social behavior increases social deviation and encourages pathological behaviors. If we take an extreme stance of tolerance, we might end up allowing, and even encouraging, problematic social behaviors such as pedophilia. Indeed, some writers argued that pedophilia should be accepted as an unchangeable sexual orientation, and should not be condemned, just as we accept LGBTQ people for their sexual preferences. They try to separate between this sexual innate tendency, and between practicing it as it leads to harming children.

In the case of pedophilia, it is easier to negate this unhealthy abuse of tolerance, since pedophilia is condemned and socially unaccepted nowadays all over the world, but what about attitudes that are considered normal in one society and unhealthy in others? Even if we disregard the extreme ritual of female circumcision, mentioned at the beginning of this chapter, there are more moderate traditional rituals that are controversial. For example, wearing a burqa (traditional face covering) by women in the Moslem world reflects the values of a conservative society in which men's power and privileges are the norm. However, such a discriminative attitude (as perceived through Western eyes) towards women is unacceptable in the West. Should liberal citizens in Western countries agree and accept the existence of the burqa in their countries in the name of tolerance and liberalism? It sounds contradictory that tolerance, which is supposed to encourage and support human rights, will be used for justification of taking basic human rights from women.

This is not a theoretical discussion: In 2010 the France parliament banned the wearing of face-covering headgear. France became the first European country to impose a ban on full-face veils in public area. This act was followed by heated public debates over nationalism, secularism, immigration, security and gender. The main argument was that forcing women to cover their faces is sexist and Moslems living in France should assimilate into traditional French norms.

Taking the above into consideration, I want to suggest a circumplex model of tolerance: Moderate amounts of tolerance are healthy and contribute to the development of a democratic, inclusive and pro-human-rights society, while high levels of both tolerance and intolerance are unhealthy and can create more polarization and division. In fact, each pole of the tolerance-intolerance dimension can easily push for a backlash in which (as explained by the relational model mentioned above) the more some social subgroups are intolerant, the more it pushes other social subgroups to be overly tolerant, and the more some parties are overly tolerant, the more other parties are pushed toward more extreme intolerance. In short, the model I suggest is not contrasting tolerance with intolerance but contrasting intolerance (which I suggest calling under-tolerance) with pseudo over-tolerance.

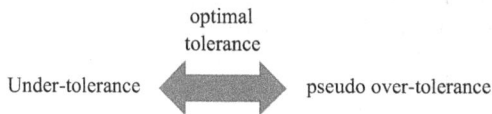

This circumplex model is helpful in determining when tolerance contributes to diversity and negate discrimination, dehumanization, repression, and violence, and when (given in overdose) it paradoxically encourages more violence, discrimination and divisiveness. It can help policy makers establish some constraints against over-tolerance and under-tolerance and contribute to the difficult public discourse around this topic.

Concluding Thoughts

While writing this chapter I became aware of how cautious I am in choosing my words and how much I feel the need to express support for liberal social movements (such as MeToo and BLM) before expressing any criticism about unjustified exaggerated attacks from supporters of these movements on people who belong to the majority. I certainly feel the danger of encountering intolerant reactions to what I have written and being labeled a racist, as I described in that professional forum. This inner process might show how much the topic in discussion is not theoretical and distance for our own experience but is personally relevant to each of us.

Although the circumplex model might help resolving some of the difficulties around being over or under tolerant, it is a theoretical model, and the question still remains how to practically determine the boundaries of optimal tolerance. It might be easier to agree that should be no tolerance for people who publicly encourage violent acts against other people (whether it's encouraging violence against minorities or encouraging terrorist actions against innocent citizens). However, what about people who deny the holocaust in public? Should it be considered an antisemitic attitude that might lead to discrimination and aggression against Jews?), or take an even more controversial issue: Should critiques of the Israeli government actions against the Palestinians tolerated by Israelis or should they be considered as anti-Semites as well? We can quickly see that the range of optimal tolerance is subjective and in fact it is determined by our personal resilience and ability to expand our range of acceptance for others.

References

Berman, A. (2010). Post-Traumatic Victimhood. In I. Ulric, A. Berman and M. Berger (eds), *Victimhood, Vengefulness and the Culture of Forgiveness*. New York: Nova Science Publishers Inc.

Berman, A., Berger, M., & Gutmann, D. (2000). The division into us and them as a universal social structure. *Mind and Human Interaction*, 11(1): 53–73.

Cohen, R.A. (1996). *Face to Face with Levinas: Dialogue with Emmanuel Levinas*. New York: State University of New York Press.

DiAngelo, R. (2018). *White Fragility: Why It's So Hard for White People to Talk About Racism*. Boston. MA: Beacon Press.

Foulkes, S.H. (1964). *Therapeutic Group Analysis*. London: George Allen and Unwin.

Friedman, R. (2013). Individual or group therapy? Indications for optimal therapy. *Group Analysis*, 46(2): 164–170.

Haidt, J. and Rose-Stockwell, T. (2019). The Dark Psychology of Social Networks: Why it feels like everything is going haywire. *The Atlantic*, Dec 2019 issue. www.theatlantic.com/magazine/archive/2019/12/social-media-democracy/600763/

Hopper, E. (2003). *The Social Unconscious: Selected Papers*. London: Jessica Kingsley Publishers Ltd.

Hopper, E. (2019). The Tripartite Matrix, the Basic Assumption of Incohesion, Fundamentalism, and Scapegoating in Foulkesian Group Analysis: Clinical and empirical illustrations including terrorism and terrorists. *Group*, 43(1).

Hopper, E. & Weinberg, H. (eds) (2011). *The Social Unconscious in Persons, Groups, and Societies—Volume I: Mainly Theory*. London: Karnac.

Hopper, E. & Weinberg, H. (eds) (2015). *The Social Unconscious in Persons, Groups and Societies: Volume 2: Mainly Foundation Matrices*. London: Karnac.

Hopper, E. & Weinberg, H. (eds.) (2017). *The Social Unconscious in Persons, Groups and Societies: Volume 3: The Foundation Matrix Extended and Reconfigured*. London: Karnac.

Le Bon, G. (1895, English translation 1896). *The Crowd: A Study of the Popular Mind*.

Mitchell, S. A. & Aron, L. (1999). *Relational Psychoanalysis, Volume 1. The Emergence of a Tradition*. New York: Routledge.

Weinberg, H. (2014). *The Paradox of Internet Groups: Alone in the Presence of Virtual Others*. London: Karnac.

Weinberg, H. & Rolnick, A. (eds) (2020). *Theory and Practice of Online Therapy: Internet-delivered Interventions for Individuals, Families, Groups, and Organizations*. New York: Routledge.

Yalom, I. D., & Leszcz, M. (2020). *The theory and practice of group psychotherapy*. Hachette, UK.

Part 5

Tolerance and Intolerance in Organizations and Institutes

Chapter 18

Beyond Tolerance in Psychoanalytic Communities

Reflective Skepticism and Critical Pluralism

Lewis Aron

Recent developments in the philosophy of science suggest that scientific knowledge grows not by accumulating supporting evidence but by subjecting our beliefs to the staunchest criticism we can gather. This paper argues for approaching contemporary psychoanalytic multiplicity with an attitude of "reflexive skepticism" and "critical pluralism." We can gain the most from the diversity of psycho- analytic theories by moving beyond mutual respect and tolerance toward a genuine appreciation of others, for the critical perspective that they can offer to us and that we can offer to them. The other, the other school, viewpoint, or orientation, can provide a function that we cannot do for ourselves nor they for themselves. In this view, the criticism of the other can become a unique gift, mutually exchanged among schools.

The only good then is for a person to seek out honest friends who will enlighten his eyes to what he is blind and will rebuke him out of love, thus rescuing him from all evil. For what a man cannot see due to his inability to see fault with himself, they will see and understand and warn him, and he will be protected. On this scripture says: "in abundance of counselors there is salvation" (Mishlei 24, p. 6).

Psychoanalysis is widely known for its long history of splits and schisms among schools of thought. It has for this reason often been compared to religion where schisms frequently involve mutual accusations of heresy. In the United States, for many decades, psychoanalysis was largely under the hegemony of American Ego Psychology, which dominated the psychoanalytic mainstream. The fall of this largely monistic psychoanalytic consensus coincided with the decades of the decline of the prestige of psychoanalysis as a male medical specialty, with the increasing feminization of the field; challenges from psychopharmacology; the health care industry; managed care; alternative therapies; the demand for empirically supported and evidence-based medicine; the Freud Wars and the new Freud Studies; a growing self-help movement; the critiques from feminists; gay, lesbian, and queer studies; and the loss of the status and institutional bases of psycho- analysis in psychiatry and clinical psychology (this history is reviewed in Aron & Starr, 2015).

DOI: 10.4324/9781003200253-24

With this loss of status and prestige has come a newly found and hard-won plurality of perspectives. Psychoanalysis is no longer psychoanalysis but rather many psychoanalyses. Multiplicity and pluralism is the state of the discipline today around the world. Many psychoanalytic institutes now teach multiple points of view and have various diverse tracks and orientations; each school tends to support its own journals, assign different core texts, maintain separate canons of literature, speak its own idiom; and each school has its founding heroes or patron saints as well as its denigrated enemies.

For some observers and commentators, our present state of multiplicity is a sign of the demise of psychoanalysis. Stepansky (2009) told the story of a once-cohesive discipline that has splintered into rivalrous "part-fields" and now struggles to survive under siege. He viewed our multiplicity as a fragmentation, the result of the inevitable marginalization of any profession that resists integration into the scientific mainstream of its time and place. Other scholars, notably Wallerstein (1992), called for reestablishing common ground rooted in our shared clinical experience in consulting rooms where therapists relate comparably to the immediacy of the transference and countertransference interplay with their patients. Many other psychoanalytic leaders applaud and celebrate our multiplicity, not as a sign of disintegration and demise but to the contrary as the mark of creativity, intellectual excitement, and generativity. Mitchell (1993), for example, described pluralism in psychoanalytic thought as essential and nourishing of growth. Cooper (2008), although welcoming this "pluralism," made the point that it is unfortunately a multiplicity of authoritarian orthodoxies, multiple monistic views, each derived from a thinker and tradition. Cooper holds out the hope that empirical research might solve the problem. Some analysts, such as Govrin (2016), have even called for a future of psychoanalysis in which dogma and pluralism can coexist in what he refers to as "fascinated" and "disenchanted" communities.

In this article I argue that our multiplicity is not inherently good or bad, but what will determine its value is what we do with that diversity, how we view each other and make use of the range and variety of approaches now available. Until the 1970s there was hardly any discussion of "comparative psychoanalysis," a term associated with Schafer, who first used it in 1979 (Schafer, 1979). How could there have been a discipline of comparative psychoanalysis when analysts were convinced that any disagreement with the dominant view was heresy? In our own era, there have been passionate calls for a comparative and integrative approach (Willock, 2011). I argue here that we need to move beyond "comparative psychoanalysis," and even beyond theoretical integration. In my view, informed by recent developments in the philosophy of science, the multiplicity and diversity of psychoanalysis, the many diverging psychoanalyses, may be best utilized when we focus in a balanced way on both common ground and difference, not for comparison and contrast alone, or to achieve integration, but to learn from each other's opposing views. We can gain the most, I believe, by moving beyond mutual respect and tolerance toward a genuine appreciation of the other, for what they can offer to us and what we can offer to them. The other, the other school, viewpoint, or orientation, can provide a function that we cannot do for ourselves nor they for themselves. In this view, the criticism of the other can become a unique gift, mutually exchanged among schools.

Critical Pluralism

The ideas that I develop in what follows are derived from the work of the Israeli historian and philosopher of science, Menachem Fisch.[1] Trained in physics, philosophy, and the history and philosophy of science, Fisch has argued for a contemporary philosophy of science that steers a course between the Scylla of uncritical dogmatism and the Charybdis of radical relativism. His approach is influenced by Karl Popper's "critical rationalism," the contention that scientific knowledge grows not by accumulating supporting evidence but by subjecting our beliefs to the staunchest criticism we can gather. Although Popper himself dismissed psychoanalysis as a "pseudoscience" because he believed its propositions could not be "falsified," that is empirically tested and challenged, I argue that, ironically, the post-Popperian approach articulated and applied by Fisch befits the current challenges of psychoanalysis. Although it is beyond the scope of this essay to present in any detail, it is of interest that Fisch utilizes his philosophy of science not just to understand developments in the world of natural science but to facilitate interreligious dialogue and critique. That his approach lends itself to the study of religion as well as science may point to its relevance and suitability to psychoanalysis, which has affinities with both realms of discourse.

As a philosopher and historian of science, Fisch studies how one scientist gets another scientist to change his or her mind about a theory. It seems to me that this question should be of much interest to psychotherapists who are always trying to get patients (as well as colleagues) to change their ways of thinking.

Fisch's "reflexive skepticism" suggests that self-doubt and self-criticism is our best attitude toward our own convictions because to assume that we are imperfect, limited, or just plain wrong is the attitude that will most likely lead us to ongoing problem solving and improvement. If we allow ourselves to expose our vulnerabilities and our shortcomings and remain open to criticism, then we are in the best position to continually problem solve and improve. This is not a call for self-effacement or masochism, as Popper's theory was among the most optimistic and constructive of scientific philosophies; it is rather an appeal to the value of ongoing improvement and refinement that is gained by continuing dialogue and unending critique.

In today's psychoanalysis, we have improved our attitudes toward one another's communities greatly. In some societies and institutes there is respectful dialogue across perspectives and the various schools of thought have more often found ways to coexist. Our reading lists now refer to theories beyond our own schools and journals. But getting along and mutual respect, peaceful coexistence, is not sufficient. Fisch's reading of the history and philosophy of science calls on us to go beyond liberal tolerance. Tolerance is essentially the granting of the right for the other to be mistaken, but not in any way a recognition of their viewpoint being of value. In Fisch's model, the other is not seen as a threat but comes to be regarded as an asset, providing an essential benefit. Others challenge our assumptions, raise questions that we might not think to ask, upset our complacency.

The underlying assumption is that self-critique is always somewhat limited, or perhaps another way of stating it is that we are not as good at self-observation and self-criticism as we often like to imagine. Our beliefs, assumptions, and convictions are often egocentric, and we are so invested in these norms and suppositions that we take them for granted. As fish, we may not notice the water we swim in. It is only when our breathing is disturbed that we pay attention to the air. By focusing on our weaknesses and limitations, and by exposing these to analysis by those who have somewhat different beliefs, we gain a unique opportunity to improve.

Recent developments in psychoanalysis have, I believe, been overly influenced by an overly simplistic utilization of the excesses of postmodernism and associated trends in philosophy of science. Ludwig Fleck (1981) articulation of the idea of "Thought Communities," Thomas Kuhn's (1970) model of "Paradigm Shifts," and perhaps especially Rorty's (1979) "pragmatism" have been used to argue for the "incommensurability" of theories. Whether an intrinsic problem of Kuhn's or a result of a faulty misapplication, this has led to a form of radical relativism where it is argued that scientific developments do not proceed rationally but are more like changes in taste or aesthetics. The problem, as I understand it, is this: If we believe with full conviction that our own views are correct or the most highly developed, the best, or absolutely true, then why would we bother talking to those with other, more "primitive" views? But if we cannot systematically compare our theories and argue rationally for the advantages of one or the other, then why should we bother talking to each other? We might agree to live together, respectfully, with liberal tolerance, but if our theories are incommensurable, if we cannot agree on any shared norms, then on what basis could I expect that you could ever convince me of the rightness or wrongness of your views? Whether monists or relativists, absolutists or pragmatists, there is no need to talk with or learn from those others who have different beliefs. We might liberally tolerate them, but we have no need for them in their very otherness. For reflexive skeptics, the other is not merely tolerated but is regarded as essential in and for their very otherness.

The Framework Problem

Now we must ask, How could the other ever convince us that we are wrong? If they persuade us that we are incorrect on one level, isn't it because they have appealed to our norms, to our framework of understanding, on a higher level? If they persuade me that my theory of mind does not capture the complexity that another theory reveals, it is because they can appeal to my wider frame of belief regarding the psychical. If not, then on what basis could I conclude that I had been mistaken? But then how can they convince me that these background assumptions are themselves limited? Only by appealing to a yet higher level of assumptions. But this model would lead to an infinite regress in which there would always be a need for yet some higher level of norms and assumptions that would serve as the basis for challenging one's beliefs and convictions. In philosophy of science this is called "the framework problem."

Fisch and his colleagues have proposed a solution to the framework problem along the following lines. Essentially Fisch argued that although we cannot be convinced by others, because of the framework problem, we can be "ambivalated" by critics. By ambivalated he means that our convictions may become destabilized, some hesitation or unease is introduced, and then we can promulgate these doubts within our own communities. To become so ambivalated, however, we must have sufficient "trust" in these outside critics.

Often this comes in the trading zones of ideas outside our immediate scientific communities, in teaching to nonspecialized audiences or at conferences where we meet people in related disciplines or associated schools of thought. In the process of this trading and conversing outside of our immediate like-thinking colleagues we may be open enough to destabilizing and ambivalating forces of external criticism.

Why do we need criticism from the other? Why isn't self-criticism sufficient? We are simply too close to our own ideas, and even if we can challenge our own ideas, it is even harder to challenge the norms and values upon which these ideas rest. And even if we can challenge those values, it is even harder yet to challenge the underlying norms upon which those values themselves rest, and on and on. The respectful challenges, criticisms, questions of the other are essential in our efforts to improve.

The Chimera and Like-Enough Subjects

It is here that I think psychoanalysis itself may make a small contribution to Fisch's thought. I would suggest that Bach's (2016) symbol of the chimera is a useful metaphor for understanding Fisch's solution to the framework problem. Here is how I understand it. We are all egocentric, especially about newly acquired ideas and theories, but also about all our beliefs and convictions. Decentering is always a challenge. In Bach's terms, we tend toward a narcissistic state of consciousness, a state of being, heavily leaning toward subjective self-awareness. In this state of being, the other is perceived as a threat to our very existence. Why would we risk trusting our own mind to that of a stranger? Our narcissistic defenses are designed to deal with the other's strangeness and to gradually allow the other to be recognized, affirmed, and slowly metabolized. The immune system classifies a foreign body as distinct from the self, and therefore as dangerous, but this must change to take in a foreign body. The other must become the self, or like enough to the self to pass. It is this process that Bach calls chimerization.

This process is also reminiscent of the affect regulation literature when developmentalists like Gergeley and Watson (1996) showed how mothers teach infants to define and evaluate their feelings by "marked" matching responses. Human caregivers provide "marked" affective mirroring signals, expressions that are altered displays of the responses that the caregiver would normally use to express affect states. In other words, the parental mirroring is not like a real mirror, but rather it mirrors with a difference. It is close to the child's affective experience but not the same, and it is precisely in its commonality and yet difference that it is taken in as a marked response.

I translate the preceding to mean that to take in the other, we must generally make them "like-enough subjects," to paraphrase and condense Winnicott (1965) and Benjamin (1995), or transform them into chimeras, with mixed or shared DNA, such that we take them in as parts of ourselves. Their criticisms of our theories, of our assumptions, norms, and values, must share enough commonality so that we are fooled into thinking that they are us. We can then take in their criticism as if it were our own without our antibodies attacking their criticism. In short, we identify with their criticism, which is what allows their ideas to penetrate our defensive narcissistic barriers and destabilize us, "ambivalate" us from the inside-out. Relational theory adds to Fisch's model that mutuality facilitates change. We would be much more likely to open ourselves up to becoming "ambivalated," if we saw that our other was influenced by our criticisms of them. Benjamin (2018) suggests that if we embrace the centrality of learning from rupture and repair, of acknowledging our vulnerability and imperfection, then the other's protest can be turned into an asset and advantage. This approach to protest and criticism strengthen Fisch's model and is valuable in inter-school psychoanalytic dialogue and debate.

The question for psychoanalytic communities is the following: Do we want only to sustain, protect, and perpetuate our schools, our approaches? Or do we want to continually test them, challenge, and improve them? Is preservation alone a recipe for stagnation? Are we best off maintaining that our own school of thought (Contemporary Freudian, Kleinian, Kohutian, Relational, Lacanian, or whatever) is the most advanced, deepest, most sophisticated, most comprehensive, answering all the problems with which we deal? Or are we better off assuming our theories and approaches are limited, problematic, incomplete, and in need of constant improvement to be brought about only by being challenged and criticized? Reflexive skepticism is the neo-Popperian attitude that respects the other precisely for the challenge that they provide, stimulating our own questioning and self-examination.

Freud as Reflexive-Skeptic

In this regard, I want to argue for a view of Freud's achievement somewhat different from the way he is often imagined and presented. Especially with the rise of the New Freud Studies, Freud's embattlement, and his excommunication of dissenters, has been highlighted. It is thought that Freud had little use for anyone who disagreed with the shibboleths that he enumerated (the unique importance of sex, Oedipus, dreams, and the unconscious). But I want to suggest that although Freud politically may have exiled his dissenters, nevertheless he took their criticism seriously and often in fact made their criticisms his own—even while he disavowed such influence. An example of this is his paper "On Narcissism" (Freud, 1914). The paper is unfortunately read as part of teaching Freud's work, without reading the works of Adler and Jung that had led up to it. It is essential in my view that one reads these works, and especially Jung (1972), who also criticized Adler for his overemphasis on the psychology of the self, and criticized Freud for not having a self-psychology. When one reads "On Narcissism" in this context, not only does one understand Freud's paper differently, that is, as a response to, and attempt to integrate, the criticisms of Adler and Jung, but one sees that Freud spent years struggling with his critic's arguments. It is not simply that Freud was trying to persuade his followers that his views were superior to Adler's and Jung's – that is not the only or superordinate concern. Freud may have denigrated their theories and contributions, he may have split them off politically and socially from the psychoanalytic profession, but he took their criticism seriously and spent years struggling with their perspectives, even if he often took their arguments and ideas and made them his own. I am not suggesting that this is proper personal conduct or good ethics but rather that Freud did use others' criticism to bolster his own theory. In his *Interpretation of Dreams*, he had written that "My emotional life has always insisted that I should have an intimate friend and a hated enemy" (Freud, 1900, p. 483), and Freud made excellent use of these many enemies to criticize, challenge, and improve his own theories.

One can readily see that despite his polemic writing style, that often made him seem so certain about his contributions, that there is another Freud, perhaps an altered and dissociated self-state, a second state of consciousness, a Freud who was very much a reflexive skeptic! To add one illustration, consider how Freud made use of the challenges of critics to reconsider his wish fulfillment theory of dreaming when confronted with traumatic dreams. Even concerning such a favored and hypervalued contribution as his own theory of dreams, Freud in fact maintained a reflexive skepticism that allowed him to revise his theories. I understand that this may be considered a very generous reading of Freud, and I acknowledge that it is not the only Freud we are familiar with, but it is one of his multiple selves.

Freud seems to have used the criticism of others (external criticism) to facilitate his self-criticism (internal criticism). Self-criticism and self-examination are essential, but when used alone they are weak tools. Whereas Mitchell (1993) described self-reflection as the distinguishing characteristic of the analytic function, it should not be forgotten that this analytic self-reflection takes place in the relationship with another, that is, with the patient, who as Bion (1980) described is the analyst's "best colleague." Try as hard as we may, as sincerely as we might, we are egocentric beings who take many of our assumptions for granted, and it is hard for the eye to see itself (Stern, 2004). Stern argued that the eye can see itself, that we can begin to self-observe using our multiplicity. But that multiplicity is itself discovered through enactments with others who hold and embody other versions of ourselves. I would suggest that what Stern called "snags" and "chafing" (p. 208), which he described as some tension, a sense of something wrong, contradictory, or uncomfortable, is quite like what Fisch described as becoming "ambivalated." Self-criticism and self-examination need to be supplemented and amplified by criticism from significant and like-enough others so that we can take in their criticism in the form of chimeras, we can identify with their criticisms and make them our own.

The Relational Tradition: Internal and External Criticism

Relational Psychoanalysis was arguably the first American school of psycho-analysis to emerge following the decline of the dominance of Ego Psychology and the resulting proliferation of multiple schools of psychoanalytic thought (Aron, 1996). Its initial formulation was the result of a comparative psycho-analytic project (Greenberg & Mitchell, 1983). Mitchell once spoke to me of relational psychoanalysis as a form of "critical eclecticism."[2] Certainly, it became a big tent, an overarching perspective, which is why Mitchell and I (1999) referred to our first collection of relational articles as "the emergence of a tradition" rather than a school. It was also, undoubtedly, offered as a correc-tive to what were perceived to be excesses in what had previously been viewed as the "mainstream." Important as well, its rise coincided with the development of the Division of Psychoanalysis (39) of the American Psychological Association and therefore offered a new perspective to a national audience of psychologist-psychoanalysts, many of whom had been excluded for decades from the main-stream. It was a broad and unifying theoretical framework that was fresh, contemporary, post-women's movement, postclassical, post-gay rights, and per-haps most important uniquely its own and not that of the heretofore medical association.[3] This is not to reduce important theoretical developments to poli-tics and professional factors alone, but rather to emphasize that there was a sociopolitical context within which the relational tradition could burgeon.

That efflorescence of the relational tradition occurred in the 1980s and it has now been almost 30 years since its institutionalization. It went from being an intimate and local movement in New York City to quickly become a national movement and eventually an international force in psychoanalysis.

It is typical among psychoanalytic schools to argue for the advantages of one school over another, for leaders to point to the deficiencies of other schools and to champion their own. This can be part of a healthy development. The competitiveness of the schools for students and adherents can be constructive and may stir a sharpening of conceptualization and formulation. As I have argued throughout this paper, external critique, when respectful and based on sufficient common ground and shared values, can be useful and even essential to growth. It is required for generativity that each school be receptive to learning from these critiques and not just defending against them. Why do we not have a tradition for schools of psychoanalysis to openly and publicly engage in self-critique (critique by insiders)? In retrospect, this is surprising. After all, doesn't every doctoral dissertation and published research always include a section on the study's limitations and inadequacies? Why wouldn't we expect that psychoanalytic texts would also be willing to expose their limits, restrictions, and biases? As I argued earlier in the paper, this is not a call for masochistic submission to the other, nor does it require us to be overly hesitant or modest in our formulations. We can and should argue for and persuade others of our convictions as much as any school of thought. We can speak and write strongly, and yet remain open, vulnerable, responsive to criticism and to corrective feedback. This is a strength and not a weakness.

Relational psychoanalysis was based on conceptualizing the nature of transference and countertransference not as distortion, displacement, and false connection but as a personal idiosyncratic but plausible construction. This shift in our understanding of transference phenomena led the relational clinician to respond to so-called negative transference as based on plausible perceptions of the analyst's participation with the patient, rather than dismissing the observations as distortions and displacements from past objects.

Why would relational writers reject theoretical criticism as based on misunderstanding, misreadings, distortions of relational theory, when these same analysts listen to criticism from patients and strive to understand the plausibility of the criticism? We no more believe that our patient is always "right" than we assume that our critics are always right. What we do believe is that when external criticism seems to be accompanied by good will and an effort to understand and respect our point of view, it may offer us valuable insight that we would and could not achieve as readily on our own. Internal and external criticism dialectically inform each other. Criticism that may have been rejected when it came from outsiders may have nevertheless been sufficiently internalized such that it led to some "destabilization," and this slight shaking up of perspective may then spread among insiders.

When we acknowledge the contributions of others, this in turn may make them more likely to accept our own reciprocal feedback about their approach. Psychoanalysts have increasingly been promoting an ethos of "mutual vulnerability" (Aron, 2016). Such an attitude among the "schools" might prove valuable as well. As in any transitional phenomena (Winnicott, 1953), it may become impossible to say whether the criticism came from inside or outside. This is the chimera (Bach, 2016), with its mixed DNA, a selfobject that allows us to internalize otherness, without fearing for our lives because we have metabolized the other's feedback, and the other has become us. This chimera may then save our lives.

For our approaches to grow, thrive, remain alive and vibrant, we need the dialectic of internal and external criticism and we need to allow ourselves ongoing ambivalating. To facilitate its occurrence, psychoanalytic educators need to make space for students and practitioners to "practice ambivalating," that is, to practice being responsive to the snags and chafing that inform us of limits and contradictions and allows us to awake from our dissociations.

The seemingly dualistic opposition of "internal" and "external" critique fails to capture the richness of the critical process, and instead I suggest that we view internal and external critique as a dialectic rather than a binary (see Aron & Starr, 2015). The point is that the very distinction between internal and external critique is simplistic precisely because of the arguments made in this chapter.

Internal critique would be weak indeed without the benefit of a viewpoint outside of one's own perspective. We need more than one vertex to decenter. Luckily, we each have multiple self-states, and we have identifications in multiple directions that allow us to feel some snags and chafing such that the eye can come to see itself (Stern, 2004). Internal and external create, sustain, and define each other dialectically.

Perhaps you will disagree with these arguments. You may point out the limitations of my thesis and contradictions in my propositions. As a reflexive skeptic, I hope to have argued strongly and stated my proposal with conviction. I do, after all, wish to persuade and convince and promote my own ideas as much as monists and relativists do. If you have reasoned objections and can prove me wrong, well then – that would certainly make my point, wouldn't it?

Notes

1 Menachem Fisch is a prolific author, and a good select bibliography of his work may be found in Tirosh-Samuelson and Hughes (2016), which also includes several representative articles, an editorial overview, and an intellectual overview. I am not a historian or philosopher of science and have no expert competence in evaluating Fisch's professional contributions. I have been influenced by his work, but the responsibility for any misuse or misunderstanding of his theory is mine alone. Other books of his that I have studied are included in the reference section: (Fisch, 1997; Fisch & Benbaji, 2011). Special thanks to Daniel Marom for introducing me to the philosophical writings of M. Fisch. Marom is responsible for curricular and pedagogical development at the Mandel School for Educational Leadership in Jerusalem, where we have been collaborating in an ongoing study of psychoanalytic education.

2 Unfortunately, I have not been able to find a published reference to his using this phrase to describe his own form of theorizing, but there are several times when he did speak against "uncritical eclecticism" or "muddled eclecticism," and this usage does support my memory that he considered his own approach a form of "critical eclecticism.".

3 It is significant that Greenberg and Mitchell's (1983) book coincided with the first annual meetings of Division 39, and that the establishment of the Relational Orientation at NYU's Postdoctoral Program in Psychotherapy and Psychoanalysis

in 1988, and the establishment of *Psychoanalytic Dialogues* in 1990, immediately followed the lawsuit against the American and International Psychoanalytic Associations, which was settled in November 1988 with the institutes promising not to discriminate against psychologists or other "nonmedical candidates" (see Wallerstein, 2013).

References

Aron, L. (1996). *A Meeting of Minds*. Hillsdale, NJ: The Analytic Press.

Aron, L. (2016). Mutual vulnerability: An ethic of clinical practice. In D. M. Goodman & E. R. Severson (Eds), *The Ethical Turn*. London, UK: Routledge.

Aron, L., & Starr, K. (2015). *A Psychotherapy for the People*. London, UK: Routledge.

Bach, S. (2016). *Chimeras and other Writings*. Astoria, NY: International Psychoanalytic Books.

Benjamin, J. (1995). Sameness and difference: Toward an "Overinclusive" model of gender development. *Psychoanalytic Inquiry, 15*(1), 125–142. doi:10.1080/07351699 509534021

Benjamin, J. (2018). *Beyond Doer and Done To*. London, UK & New York, NY: Routledge.

Bion, M. (1980). *Bion in New York and São Paulo*. Perthshire, Scotland: Clunie Press.

Cooper, A. M. (2008). American psychoanalysis today: A plurality of orthodoxies. *The Journal of the American Academy of Psychoanalysis and Dynamic Psychiatry, 36*, 235–253. doi:10.1521/jaap.2008.36.2.235

Fisch, M. (1997). *Rational Rabbis: Science and Talmudic Culture*. Bloomington: Indiana University Press.

Fisch, M., & Benbaji, Y. (2011). *The View from Within: Normativity and the Limits of Self-Criticism*. Notre Dame, IN: University of Notre Dame Press.

Fleck, L. (1981). *The Genesis and Development of a Scientific Fact* (T. J. Trenn & R. K. Merton, Eds). Chicago, IL: University of Chicago Press.

Freud, S. (1900). The interpretation of dreams. *Standard Edition, 4*, (ix–627). London, UK: Hogarth Press.

Freud, S. (1914). On narcissism. *Standard Edition, 14*, 67–102. London, UK: Hogarth Press.

Gergeley, G., & Watson, J. S. (1996). The social biofeedback theory of parental affect-mirroring: The development of emotional self-awareness and self-control in infancy. *International Journal of Psycho-Analysis, 77*, 1181–1212.

Govrin, A. (2016). *Conservative and Radical Perspectives on Psychoanalytic Knowledge*. London, UK: Routledge.

Greenberg, J., & Mitchell, S. A. (1983). *Object Relations in Psychoanalytic Theory*. Cambridge, MA: Harvard.

Jung, C. G. (1972). *C. G. Jung's Two Essays on Analytical Psychology* (Collected Works of C.G. Jung, Book 7). Princeton, NJ: Princeton University Press.

Kuhn, T. S. (1970). *The Structure of Scientific Revolutions* (2nd ed.). Chicago, IL: University of Chicago Press.

Mitchell, S. A. (1993). Reply to Bachant and Richards. *Psychoanalytic Dialogues, 3*(3), 461–480. doi:10.1080/10481889309538987

Mitchell, S., & Aron, L. (1999). *Relational Psychoanalysis: The Emergence of a Tradition*. Hillsdale, NJ: The Analytic Press.

Rorty, R. (1979). *Philosophy and the Mirror of Nature*. Princeton, NJ: Princeton University Press.

Schafer, R. (1979). On becoming a psychoanalyst of one persuasion or another. *Contemporary Psychoanalysis*, *15*, 345–360. doi:10.1080/00107530.1979.10745584

Stepansky, P. E. (2009). *Psychoanalysis at the Margins*. New York, NY: Other Press.

Stern, D. B. (2004). The eye sees itself. *Contemporary Psychoanalysis*, *40*(2), 197–237. doi:10.1080/00107530.2004.10745828

Tirosh-Samuelson, H., & Hughes, A. W. (2016). *Menachem Fisch: The Rationality of Religious Dispute*. Boston, MA: Brill.

Wallerstein, R. S. (1992). *The Common Ground of Psychoanalysis*. New York, NY: Aronson.

Wallerstein, R. S. (2013). *Lay Analysis: Life Inside the Controversy*. London, UK: Routledge.

Willock, B. (2011). *Comparative-integrative Psychoanalysis: A Relational Perspective for the Discipline's Second Century*. London, UK: Routledge.

Winnicott, D. W. (1953). Transitional objects and transitional phenomena: A study of the first not-me possession. *International Journal of Psycho-Analysis*, *34*, 89–97.

Winnicott, D. W. (1965). The maturational processes and the facilitating environment. *International Psycho-Analytic Library*, *64*, 1–276. London: Hogarth Press and the Institute of Psycho-Analysis.

Chapter 19

The Challenge of Tolerance between Psychoanalytic Institutes

Psychoanalytic Insights into Establishing New Psychoanalytic institutes

Avi Berman and Gila Ofer

In this chapter, we describe the establishment of two psychoanalytic institutes and the slow and painful process of transitioning from resistance, rejection and intolerance towards the creation of constructive competition and inspiration for beneficial changes for all involved.

Introduction

This chapter is written from the perspective of two psychoanalysts and group-analysts who have initiated and took part in the founding of two new institutes: the Tel Aviv Institute for Contemporary Psychoanalysis (TAICP) and the Israeli Institute of Group Analysis (IIGA). We experienced first-hand both the emergence of the motivation for establishing a new institute as well as the reactions this initiative elicited. We encountered the resistance and heard the critiques and the reservations directed at us. We looked for dialogue, in hopes of presenting ourselves and achieving recognition. We were hurt by rejection. We felt the fear of letting others down and the threat of potential failure. We approached well-known teachers and were heartened by their positive responses. With their help, we created training programs that measured up to high and conventional standards, avoiding the most orthodox rigidity. We made sure that the qualification of each of our alumni is conducted by senior and established psychoanalysts and group-analysts, who had not been part of the training process. We were significantly supported by established psychoanalysts and group-analysts – some of whom were affiliated with the very same institutes that opposed our endeavor.

Now, some 20 years after the foundation of these two institutes, we look back at this long process and explore it from the perspective of tolerance and intolerance. We assume that many of the processes that took place at the time are *universal processes* involved in the establishment of any new psychoanalytic institute and that some of these are even common to relations between competing organizations in any field.

DOI: 10.4324/9781003200253-25

The challenge of tolerance towards the establishment of a new psychoanalytic institute includes, first and foremost, the recognition of its right to be born and exist as a new sibling in the community. It also refers to motivations stemming from oedipal strivings and ambitions (killing a father) and 'binding-of-Isaac' power struggles (killing a son).

Tolerance

Tolerance is grounded in the acceptance of the disapproval between different views and people and their inclusion as nevertheless belonging to a shared field or territory. The most significant manifestation of tolerance is coexistence, in which the people with whom I disagree live alongside me in the same environment and their rights are fully recognized. Tolerance requires the containment of difference and the relinquishment of the total 'rightness' or privilege of any one side. Such tolerance welcomes pluralism.

Tolerance between psychoanalytic institutes may exist under these same conditions: mutual acceptance in spite of differences and areas of disagreement as well as mutual acceptance of the other's right to belong to the field of psychoanalysis. Aron (2017) addresses the issue of difference and tolerance between psychoanalytic institutes, suggesting that difference can be tolerable and even fruitful, when similarity and difference are at an equilibrium. In one's personal experience, a lack of similarity turns the other into a foreign body that is either potentially threatening or irrelevant to the self. The same holds true for the "other institute". Its foundation may be perceived as a threat by the existing institute, or it may be considered excessively different and therefore 'non-psychoanalytic'. This means it will not be considered as part of the field of psychoanalysis and will become excluded, out of bounds.

Thus, a new institute that wishes to be included in the field must be perceived by existing institutes as 'like-enough' to them. For such tolerance to succeed, both sides must be committed to it: the new institute must offer sufficient similarity to existing ones and the latter, on their part, must strive to see the former's similarity and 'make it' a like-enough subject. Aron argues that coexistence-facilitating tolerance between psychoanalytic institutes is not merely an ethical position. It is a position that allows mutual enrichment to the benefit of all sides: "we can gain the most, I believe, by moving beyond mutual respect and tolerance toward a genuine appreciation of the other, for what they can offer to us and what we can offer to them" (2017, p. 273).

We, the authors of this chapter, are among those who believe in the benefits of pluralism and the striving for tolerance inherent in it. Tolerance between organizations presupposes that there is room for two (or more). Passion for psychoanalysis and the effort put into psychoanalytic training are not the exclusive property of any single organization. Furthermore, from the vantage point of the twenty years that have passed, we have indeed come to realize that, in both cases we present, it is the emerging coexistence that led to the thriving of psychoanalysis and group analysis in the same environment and, along with it – the thriving of all the organizations involved. Everyone profited.

However, despite the conceptual clarity presented here, in reality there is no external third party who decides whether an institute is 'like-enough' or has the right to belong to psychoanalysis. In inter-institutional relations, subjectivity and inter-subjectivity have the final say. A psychoanalytic institute could be attributed with an "ego-ideal" and a "super-ego". The institute's identity is defined by these terms and by the training, certification and affiliation regulations derived from them. Institutional socialization entails resistance to and avoidance of any divergence from these regulations. Therefore, it is possible that a new institute that aspires to be considered psychoanalytic, may, from the very outset, be suspect of falling short of being 'like-enough' to be accepted into the field. It may be rejected beyond the bounds of the tolerance of coexistence.

Both the desire to establish a new institute and the resistance thereto are expressed through an explicit and well-reasoned discourse. But, as the psychoanalytic perspective argues, this discourse is underpinned by a host of hidden, known-but-unspoken motivations, as well as unconscious motivations and turbulent feelings of apprehension, insult, anger, envy and ambition. In this chapter, we address all of these. Even though we are among the new founders, we hope to offer an unbiased perspective. We believe that such a perspective requires recognition of the subjectivity of each party and the espousal of their respective points of view. We therefore wish to begin with the conscious, explicit and well-reasoned aspect of the conflict surrounding the foundation of the new institutes as well as recognition of the importance of these core arguments.

Many of those affiliated with the existing organization fully believe that they are upholding the tenets of psychoanalysis and of the proper training of new candidates. They believe that they are devoting considerable effort and energy to this goal. They thus suspect the founders of the new institute as favoring the easy road or cutting corners. They believe that those affiliated with the new institute might end up harming the profession and lowering its standards, or encouraging new psychoanalytic approaches that might end up being heresy disguised as innovation. To those affiliated with existing institutes, the founders of new institutes might be biased by personal ambitions that have not been fully analyzed. From this perspective, pluralism is associated with the potential risk of harming the essence of the profession, misleading clients and even keeping them from getting suitable help.

The new founders experience their initiative as sincere and professional. Their desire is to facilitate innovation in psychoanalysis and an openness to dialogue about it. Some would like to establish another institute in order to break the monopoly established and maintained by the existing institute. They experience the resistance to this as a barrier to growth.

Differences in terms of professional values and theoretical approaches are not the only source of crisis and controversy. The foundation of a new institute within the same environment also leads to competition over resources, such as the recruitment of candidates and faculty. Organizations working in the same environment might end up competing on an economic level and in terms of prestige. The economic setbacks such emerging competition might bring, could be especially painful to those who have spent their lives working hard to uphold their professional principles. Such realistic fears are common knowledge but are seldom spoken about in public settings, constituting an 'unspoken-known'.

The position of the new founders also entails an 'unspoken-known' element: some of them feel angry and offended by having been rejected by those affiliated with existing institutes and respond to it with a kind of rebellion. Even this wish for independence and for getting out from under the wing of established analysts may be an unspoken-known.

Sharing Our Own Experience

In what follows, we wish to share, in a manner that is as balanced as possible, our memories and experiences of the process of founding two new institutes. Thus, we are looking at the material from the perspective of participants-observers, making use of our subjective experience while aspiring to objectivity. However, in the time that has passed since, we have been in dialogue with some of the members of the existing institutes who had taken part in these events and include their views.

Between 1999 and 2001, two new psychoanalytic institutes were established in Israel: the Tel-Aviv Institute for Contemporary Psychoanalysis (TAICP) and the Israeli Institute for Group Analysis (IIGA). In the field of psychoanalysis, the growing acquaintance with the relational approach was a significant contribution to this. This approach voiced its reservations about the orthodox understanding of patient-therapist relations and doubted the therapist's ability to remain neutral, objective and uninvolved in what was taking place in the therapy as well as the therapeutic benefits of absolute commitment to such orthodox views.

We believe that some of the inspiration for the initiative of founding new psychoanalytic institutes came from a general social-cultural context of pluralism and a social-political climate that entailed hope for the future. The two initiatives began with much hope and enthusiasm and in the context of the backdrop of the national sense of elation that followed the Oslo B Agreement and the hope for peace between Israelis and Palestinians. The vision of creating new institutes in Israel was born in this optimistic atmosphere (Ofer and Hadar, 1998; Hadar and Ofer, 2001).

Prior to 1999, there was only one psychoanalytic institute in Israel: The Israeli Psychoanalytic Institute (IPS). Toward the end of that year, three senior clinical psychologists (Michael Shoshani, Batya Shoshani and Gila Ofer) started the process of establishing a new psychoanalytic institute: the Tel Aviv Institute for Contemporary Psychoanalysis (TAICP). They invited other psychoanalysts and senior clinicians interested in becoming psychoanalysts to join them. They contacted the late Stephen Mitchell (2004), who helped the group to form the first training criteria, advisory board, and international qualifying committee for its first cohort of candidates: those founding members who were not yet analysts. The founders made it their first priority to achieve and maintain a high level of training, which, beyond its strictness, also assured that members developed their freedom of thought.

Several months after that, Mitchell came to Israel to participate in a conference and declared that the most exciting experience he had on his visit was his meeting with the founders of the new institute. At the time, the professional community in Israel was in turmoil regarding this new enterprise: until then, the Israeli Institute of Psychoanalysis (IPS) had a monopoly on training psychoanalysts and only accepted about twelve candidates every two years. There were many more talented psychotherapists for whom there was simply no room. A few people within the IPS thought it was important to have a second institute, were tolerant to the idea of inter-institutional competition and offered us their help. Nevertheless, the majority of IPS members opposed the idea of a second institute. The reasons they gave for their opposition were presented as professional criticism, which stemmed from a sense of responsibility for maintaining a high level of psychoanalytic practice and training.

They argued that members of the new group were underqualified professionally and intended to shorten the training process; that they wanted the status of being psychoanalysts without having to put in the effort required; and that they did not appreciate the essence of psychoanalysis. The chairperson of the existing institute called them "a bunch of rejects", referring to those who, in the past, had not been accepted as candidates to the IPS. Interpretations had also been offered about members of the new group still suffering from unelaborated oedipal transference to their analysts.

The faculty of the Psychotherapy Program at Tel-Aviv University also voiced their strong opposition to the foundation of the new institute. One of the founders of the TAICP, who served on the curriculum committee of that program, was presented with an either-or ultimatum: either she resigns or she must refrain from any further involvement in the process of establishing the TAICP. This demand was presented solely to her and not to other colleagues, who were members of the IPS curriculum committee. With much pain and anger, she chose to resign. This step was justified by the fear that the establishment of the new institute will mean the damage the program; anger and suspicion were ubiquitous.

On the other hand, psychoanalysts from abroad supported us in our effort. Throughout the first two years of studies, they came to Israel, advised us throughout the establishment process and lectured on different psychoanalytic themes as part of the training of the new candidates.

On October of 1999, the official establishment of TAICP was announced with eleven members, four of whom were certified analysts. In March 2004, the institute already had fifty members and more than thirty-five applicants for training each year. Today, the TAICP has some 200 members.

We would now like to describe the establishment of the Israeli Institute of Group Analysis (IIGA). The institute was established following the sudden and traumatic discontinuation of a training-diploma course in group analysis led by group analysts from the London IGA.

The latter institute saw itself as the flag-bearer of the group-analytic tradition and as its professional leader. It was even perceived as such in Europe at that time and this status also had historical roots. Foulkes, the conceptual father of group analysis, was a German Jew who immigrated to England after the Nazis came to power – thus saving his own life. The London institute was established through the inspiration he offered and the help of a small group of group analysis enthusiasts. A tradition was developed by which the London IGA was the core institute that trains and certifies group analysts. In the early stages of group-analysis in Israel, both the Israeli community and the London institute eagerly accepted the idea that the former should be sponsored by the latter. With the help of a local organizing committee, a course was set up for senior Israeli group-therapists, who began the London institute's training process with willing excitement.

Thus, in 1995, the London IGA started its first group analytic training course in Israel. Candidates had to be experienced and certified individual and group therapists and had to undergo four years of training by a senior group analyst from the London IGA. Such overseas training courses were conducted as "block trainings", with candidates gathering six times a year for a five-day intensive, which included theory, supervision groups and group analysis sessions (like individual psychoanalytic training, candidates had to experience group analysis as patients themselves). The detailed program of the training course was given to the candidates in advance and was strictly adhered to. A local committee was charged with administrative communication between staff members and candidates.

Towards the end of the first year, candidates sensed growing tension between staff members. The staff consisted of four group analysts: two women and two men. One of the two women had initiated the Israeli course and served as its coordinator. It was eventually discovered that the coordinator and one of men on the staff had disagreed about the requirements and the fees for the candidates. As a result, the first 'block' of the second year opened with an announcement by the coordinator that the course requirements are changed, the fees are being raised and new participants are joining.

Course participants understood that some financial mistake had been made and that the changes were intended to ensure its continuation. But during the year this event was repeated and the atmosphere among the team members became murkier. The additional change this time aroused resentment and concern.

The majority of course attendees sent a letter to the IGA board, protesting these sudden changes of the setting and the requirements and what they experienced as the "unstable holding" of the course. This letter was sent in hopes of initiating a dialogue between course attendees and the body representing the training program. For the Israeli trainees, this letter represented a desire to discuss and impact the decisions affecting the training and, therefore, the very fate of group analysis in Israel.

In response to the letter, a IGA delegation came to meet with the trainees. While the trainees expected empathy, a problem-solving approach and the re-stabilization of the unsettled program, they were shocked to find out that the London training committee had decided to stop the course altogether. Candidates were sent away mid-training and the conductors returned to London. This decision by the overseas training committee to stop the course was abrupt as it was final.

The sudden discontinuation of the course happened in the middle of the trainees' deep involvement in therapy and learning, with no apparent concern or consideration for the emotional and practical impact this would have on the candidates or for the violation of professional codes of conduct. This took place at the same year when prime minister Itzhak Rabin was murdered; elation and hope for peace turned into sadness and worry. The Israeli ex-trainees were dispersed and felt deserted, disappointed, depressed and angry.

Then, new initiatives were born. In 1999, Avi Berman, as a member of the Israeli Association of Group Psychotherapy board, initiated the founding of a new Israeli Institute of Group Analysis, through which those who attended the interrupted ("broken") course would be able to conclude their training process. The intention was to create an institute that would not be dependent on the London IGA, to adopt the rules established by the European Group Analytic Training Institutions Network (EGATIN) and to invite qualified, internationally-recognized group analysts to serve as the course's teachers, supervisors and therapists. In early January 2001, the training course was reopened, this time as an independent Israeli project, relying on staff from abroad. Thirty-three trainees from the original interrupted course, signed up for this first course; most of them are graduates today. In 2003, another course was opened, training forty additional candidates.

The Israeli Institute of Group Analysis was thus founded as an act of leaving the sponsorship and the auspices of the London institute. Through this step, the Israeli institute was born on equal terms and was no longer the 'protégé' of another central institute. The unilateral nature of the interruption of the original course was eventually answered with the establishment of an independent institute.

A Psychoanalytic Perspective on Inter-Institutional Intolerance

Manifestations of intolerance may be disguised as professional statements. At the same time, the existence of competition diminishes both the capacity and the willingness to engage in organizational self-reflection. In this situation, mutual projections might remain undeciphered.

The history of psychoanalysis has seen disputes which occasionally entailed the exclusion and marginalization of both people and ideas. It seems that some of these disputes involve an element of intolerance towards the prospect of coexisting with differences of opinion and new ideas. On the political-organizational level, the fierce debates between Freud and his opponents are well-known in the psychoanalytic world. Jung, Adler and Ferenczi were all rejected and marginalized when they sought to put forth ideas that differed from those of Freud. Later it was Klein and Anna Freud or Klein and the British independent school. In France, splitting between colleagues or between analysts and their analysands fueled the establishment of more and more psychoanalytic institutes.

Hopper's (1996; 2003) definition of the social unconscious suggests that all facts and social forces are unconsciously reactivated on the individual, group and organizational levels. We suggest that the founding of new institutes in the same territory in which existing ones operate may stir unconscious oedipal anxiety and aggression from both sides. This perspective, which is based on the analysis of Oedipal wishes, argues that the existing institute is experienced as a father-figure for the new one, and their unconscious relationship is informed by an Oedipal transference. Such transference suggests a clear hierarchy between the two institutes, with the existing institute having the higher – and potentially domineering tatus. As for the new institute, it becomes a kind of son, who might be submissive and placating or, quite the contrary, rebellious and prone to patricidal wishes (Freud, 1921).

Senior members of the existing organization may experience the initiative of the new founders as an aggressive oedipal attack on the latter's metaphoric fathers. Reaction-formation mechanisms might transform Oedipal vulnerabilities and anxieties on both sides into anger and vengefulness, leading to provocative acts and militant conflicts. The potential for dialogue and coexistence might be lost in the enactment of these unconscious mutual Oedipal dramas.

However, the Oedipal conflict can also be viewed from another angle: Loewald (1979) elaborates on this idea and explores the importance of "killing" the Oedipal parents and claiming their authority as a metaphoric experience which leads to the transformational internalization of the child's experience of their parents: an experience which is the very foundation of the emergence of a self that is responsible for itself and towards itself. In the same vein, Loewald argues that every generation of analysts is tasked with using, destroying and re-inventing the creations of the preceding generation. This is the tension between influence and originality when one generation replaces another. In this manner, a new psychoanalytic institute both murders and internalizes, both uses and creates at the same time.

There is yet another way of exploring the relations between an existing and a newly founded institute from a psychoanalytic perspective: Juliet Mitchell's (2006) discussion of sibling relations. According to Mitchell, in the older sibling's experience, the birth of a new sibling is an existential threat: the newcomer robs them of their mother, of their exclusive relationship with her and of their identity as her child. One potential reaction to such a threat is murderous rage (to the extent of actually harming the newborn sibling).

While we have no intention of undermining the validity of the various rational arguments against the foundation of a new institute in terms of otherness, we propose taking seriously those regressive motivations that equate the foundation of a new institute with the birth of a new sibling. The new institute may pose an actual threat to the status of the existing one (which had been hard won over many years), forcing the latter to compete over the same pool of therapists and patients.

Indeed, the failure to achieve tolerance towards newly established psychoanalytic institutes means, among other things, emotions such as envy, jealousy, revenge and fear. According to Klein (1957), envy is "the angry feeling that another person possesses and enjoys something desirable – the envious impulse being to take it away or to spoil it" (p. 181). Jealousy is based on the fear of losing an advantage one has to another person (ibid., p. 182). We suggest that any situation in which one's advantage might be lost to some new contender, may arouse jealousy. Thus, a newborn institution may arouse both envy and jealousy. We suggest that there is an *envious* component in the emotional attitude of the new founders and a *jealous* component in the emotional attitude of the veterans.

What might be envied by the new founders in their relation to existing organizations? We assume that some of the new founders experience envy as a result of feeling excluded by such a prestigious organization. Others may envy the safe and privileged position of these established, senior figures. They may envy the pioneering experience of new beginnings that the existing organization must have had. In their fantasy, founding a new institute transforms fear and pain into a victorious and heroic new creation.

We suggest that, on the part of the existing institute and its affiliates, jealousy is aroused by the foundation of new institutes. Losing its monopoly, priority, prestige, clients and money to a new competitor undermines the old institute's hard-won advantage. When intentions of founding a 'rival' institute become widely known, they are likely to evoke anger and condemnation. There may be a devaluation of the new founders and their initiative; predictions of the new organization's future failure (potentially revealing unconscious wishes for such failure) may be publicly voiced; and the new organization may be publicly referred to as a potential danger to the high standards of the profession. Finally, the founders of new organizations might be punished by being excluded from their present professional positions.

A Note on a Benign Resolution of Envy and Jealousy

Frankel and Sherik (1977), who observed envious behavior in infants, found that, at the age of 18–24 months, children seemed to envy of the better fortune of other children. They appeared very hurt and angry and reacted vengefully and aggressively to another child's advantage. At this early age, children's behavior seems to closely match Kleinian theory. Yet, according to Frankel and Sherik's observations, envy-based interpersonal motivations and behaviors undergo a crucial transformation at about three years of age: the motivation to rob or destroy one's 'better-off' counterpart is transformed into the wish for equality. This is a transformation from "I want this", to "I want something like this" or "I want this too". This is the age at which children learn to present demands and negotiate. They learn to approach a third party for help in closing the gap that was created between them and their peer. Through such transformations, envy and jealousy become much less destructive, making way for more benign competition and cooperation between competitors.

We suggest that processes of envy and jealousy may be resolved in a similar way in adults as well: through parallel growth and coexistence, rather than mutual destruction. These processes may be transformed into benign competition and mutual success. Self-actualization may be motivated by envy, while also keeping it in check, creating benign competition and resulting in the coexistence of competing institutes and a certain degree of cooperation. While envying the share of the existing institute, the new founders may choose to compete by founding an institute of their own. They can transform their envy into a striving for an equal share through self-fulfillment. The jealousy of existing institutes may be also contained and resolved in a similar way. In the best-case scenario, both envy and jealousy can be resolved while creating mutual inspiration and revival.

Back to Tolerance between Psychoanalytic Institutes

We suggest that the successful resolution of conflicts stemming from the foundation of new institutes depends on the conscious and thorough elaboration of these issues, which culminates in tolerance towards the other.

Tolerance between psychoanalysis institutes is the result of a long process. Perseverance, patience and the efforts to establish and maintain dialogue are all vital parts of this striving. We have found that most of the efforts to belong to the shared territory of psychoanalysis must be made by the newly established institute. To the extent that the newly-established institute wants to preserve and refine its innovativeness, towards belonging to the field of psychoanalysis, it would do well to make an effort to be a 'like-enough institute'.

At this point we would like to note the importance of relationships with established psychoanalysts who support the foundation of the new institute. The positions of such figures are taken into account by both sides, helping create a climate of tolerance towards the potential for shared belonging to the field of psychoanalysis. Such a third party helps those affiliated with the existing institute take the new institute seriously. At the same time, it helps those affiliated with the new institute be more attuned to those conditions in which their institute can be shaped as 'like enough'. This third party helps create a shared potential space, in which the process of foundation and belonging is, to some extent, elaborated in a shared manner.

As founders hoping to establish such belonging, we chose to act as if the onus of proving that we were a like-enough institute was on us. We made a point of creating a strict training program, in the spirit of well-established psychoanalytic institutes. We reached out to recognized teachers. We also made a point of approaching teachers from the existing institute to serve as faculty on both newly established institutes, even though only some of these teachers responded to our invitation. Those who supported us were people who knew us personally, who knew our commitment to the highest standards and who believed in our professional vision. Some of them recognized the importance of new approaches and supported their inclusion – even within the framework of another institute. Other supporters wanted to prevent the field from being monopolized by any one institute and were fundamentally in favor of the foundation of an additional institute.

Epilogue

Today, in 2021, the Tel Aviv Institute of Contemporary Psychoanalysis agenda includes pluralism, social engagement and interdisciplinary studies. It has considerable influence on the professional community in Israel and abroad and its members regularly publish papers in leading psychoanalytic journals and play prominent roles in the psychotherapeutic and psychoanalytic communities in Israel and abroad.

Today, the Israeli Institute of Group Analysis consists of 110 members, members and candidates. Institute members are involved in all international professional group analytic activities. Programs of group analytic training are being assimilated into analytic psychotherapy programs of some of the leading universities.

Some two decades after the foundation of these two institutes, it seems that they both exist in the field of psychoanalysis with a desired degree of tolerance. Many relationships between existing and new institutes and those affiliated with them have formed: their respective representatives speak side by side at professional conferences and their papers are published in the same journals. It seems that the foundation of the TAICP – with its openness to a plurality of approaches and its emphasis on the relational approach as one of its central tenets – has even led to changes in the existing institute (the IPS), which has been moving towards a similar pluralism of different approaches. In contrast, many TAICP members are asking to join the well-established international association (IPA). The mutual influence between institutions is evident and appears quite fruitful. Not only has their coexistence in the same environment, as well as the certain degree of competition between them, not decreased the number of candidacy applications, it has considerably increased it, as well as the general interest in the field of psychoanalysis. In the field of group analysis, the new institute (IIGA) has been fully accepted as an equal among equals in the international community, with which it has a relationship that entails both cooperation and mutual appreciation.

Acknowledgement

Three tragic deaths occurred during the training phase of both new institutes. Robin Cooper was killed in a climbing accident in the Alps during a summer vacation. Bryan Boswood passed away. Steve Mitchell died of a heart attack. We still mourn these losses.

References

Aron, L. (2017). Beyond tolerance in psychoanalytic communities: Reflexive skepticism and critical pluralism. *Psychoanal. Persp.*, 14(3): 271–282.

Frankel, S. and I. Sherik (1977). Observation on the development of normal envy. *Psychoanalytic Study of the Child*, 32: 257–281.

Freud, S. (1921). Group psychology and the analysis of the ego. *S.E.* 18, pp. 65–144.

Hadar, B. and Ofer, G. (2001). The social unconscious reflected in politics, organizations and groups. *Group Analysis*, 34(3): 375–385.

Hopper, E. (1996). The social unconscious in clinical work. *Group Analysis*, 20(1): 7–42.

Hopper, E. (2003). *Traumatic Experiences in the Unconscious Life of Groups*. Jessica Kingsley Publishers: London.

Klein, K. (1957[1975]). Envy and gratitude. In *The Writings of Melanie Klein* (pp. 176–235). London: Hogarth.

Loewald, H. W. (1979). The waning of the Oedipus complex. *J. Amer. Psychoanal. Assn.*, 27: 751–775.

Mitchell, S. A. (2004). *Relationality: From Attachment to Intersubjectivity*. Routledge.

Mitchell, J. (2006). Sibling trauma: a theoretical consideration. In P. Cole, *Sibling Relationships* (pp. 155–174). London, Karnac.

Ofer, G. and Hadar, B. (1998). The social unconscious in politics, organizations, and groups: A case of overseas training course. *Mikbatz*, 3. (Hebrew).

Chapter 20

The Paradox of Tolerance

On the Therapeutic and Social Value of Not Tolerating the Intolerable

Uri Levin

Introduction

One Friday afternoon in 1965, in the heart of the city of Jerusalem, two Israeli Poets met for the first time (a meeting initiated by a mutual friend). One of the poets was Zelda Schneurson Mishkovsky – known to her readers simply as Zelda – 51 years old at that time. She was the daughter of a prominent Hasidic rabbi from the Chabad dynasty. The other poet was Yona Wollach, 30 years younger than Zelda, a promising yet undiscovered young and provocative poet. At the time of their meeting, Zelda was almost unknown to Israeli poetry-lovers, even though she had been writing poems since her early adolescence, and a few of them had been published for some years.

Wallach asked to read a few of Zelda's poems and was enormously impressed by what she read. She decisively urged and encouraged Zelda to publish her poems. She lent Zelda her typewriter, on which Zelda then typed her first book of poetry – *Pnay* (Leisure). The book enjoyed great success, making Zelda both respected and recognized as a poet. That meeting started a meaningful relationship between the mature, religious, subtle Zelda and the young, anar-chist, and impulsive Yona Wollach. After a second meeting, Zelda published "Two Elements" (1982) – a poem outlining the vast gap and contrariness underpinning their relationship. Despite this contraposition, the two orphaned poets went on to enjoy each other's company for some years.

However, everything changed in the spring of 1982 when Yona Wallach's poem "Tefillin" (Phylacteries) was published, arousing an enormous storm. The poem's graphic depiction of a Sado-Masochistic sex performance using phylacteries crossed the line for many people. In addition to numerous threat-ening letters and phone calls to the journal's editorial offices, there was also a letter from Zelda. "When I saw Yona's poem," wrote Zelda to the editor of the journal who published the poem, "I thought that I wished I was dead, because I could no longer bear to hold in my hands a magazine that had published such a thing" (Tzvi, 1984). This letter sealed the end of the friendship between Wallach and Zelda, who thereafter refused to have any contact with neither Wollach nor the journal that had published the poem. It seems that Zelda had

DOI: 10.4324/9781003200253-26

felt that "poets can either revive, or put to death, the other's poetry, and in Yona (Wallach) these two possibilities exist" (Tzvi, 1984).

I believe, that this historic event, can easily resonate in all of us our own life stories – true friendships that ended with a broken heart; close family members who no longer utter a word to each other; a former loved spouse who turned into a loathed enemy. Aren't we all acquainted with the feeling that our boundaries are so crossed, that like Zelda, we just cannot go on with something, or someone, unless we would be willing to deplete ourselves completely? Tolerance is a key factor in the beneficent development of individuals, groups, organizations, and societies. However, perhaps sometimes, especially amongst psychotherapists, is it being overrated? Moreover, when discussing relations, should we not, perhaps, consider *intolerance* as a key factor of no less importance than *tolerance*?

In this chapter, I will explore a few aspects of the complex dialectical relations between tolerance and intolerance in our clinical work, as well as in our role as citizens of our societies and cultures. Theoretical consideration will be presented, demonstrated by two clinical vignettes.

Tolerance in Psychoanalytic and Group-Analytic Theory

In most, if not in all psychoanalytic theories, some aspects of tolerance are a *sine qua non* for the development of a healthy personality. In Freud's drive-theory, one aspect of the need for tolerance is reflected in the movement towards the dominance of the 'reality principle' over the 'pleasure principle' (1911). In Melanie Klein's object-relations formulation, tolerating ambivalence towards the object is embedded in the notion of developing the depressive position and of the infant's weaning from the massive use of splitting (1946). In Winnicott's model of 'good-enough' mothering, it is the infant's tolerance of its mother's (hopefully minor) failure to completely adapt herself to its entire needs, which enables the transition from a state of complete dependency towards 'object-use' of the social world (1969).

For Bion, who formulated a theory of thinking and the advancement of a 'Homo Cogitans', it is the infant's *capacity for toleration of frustration* that will determine its developmental course (1967). According to Bion, the frustration is derived, predominantly, because of the inevitable gap between the infant's 'preconceptions' (its inner predisposed expectations of the breast) and the 'realizations' (the breast itself). Mating preconceptions and realizations will always end with a 'no-breast' experience, or in other words, with a frustrating 'absence'. Bion postulated that

> if the capacity for toleration of (that) frustration is sufficient, the "no-breast" inside becomes a thought, and the apparatus for "thinking" it develops … thus enabling the psyche to develop thought as a means by which the frustration that is tolerated, is itself made more tolerable.
>
> (p. 112)

In other words, tolerating frustrations consolidates a positive vicious circle; one in which tolerance of frustration generates the ability to 'think' this frustration, which in turn generates more tolerance, and so forth. But, on the other hand,

> if the capacity for toleration of frustration is inadequate, the bad internal "no-breast" ... confronts the psyche ... (and) tips the scale in the direction of evasion of frustration (in a way that) what should be a thought ... becomes a bad object ... fit only for evacuation.
>
> (p. 112)

This evacuation, mainly through projective identification, results in a disturbance of the development of 'an apparatus for thinking', overtaken by a hypertrophic development of an apparatus of ridding the psyche of bad internal objects. 'To think or not to think' is Bion's fundamental pondering, which echoes throughout our entire life: "the crux lies in the decision between modification or evasion of frustration" (p. 112).

The Value of Intolerance in Clinical Work

Intolerance is valuable, both in our day-to-day life and in our practices. We cannot accept everything. We should not allow everything. We must not tolerate everything. In biology, accepting, allowing, and tolerating everything results in the end of the cell, of the organ, of the organism. However, when it comes to psychotherapy, *tolerance* is the *bon-ton*. For example, Ogden (2005a) reminds therapists that they should contain the patient's intolerable characteristics, since from the outset these characteristics goaded the patient to come to the analyst for help. In his illuminating phrasing of how he conceives the analytic process, he writes:

> A person consults a psychoanalyst because he is in emotional pain, which, unbeknownst to him, he is either unable to dream (i.e. unable to do unconscious psychological work) or is so disturbed by what he is dreaming that his dreaming is disrupted. To the extent that he is unable to dream his emotional experience, the individual is unable to change, or to grow, or to become anything other than who he has been.
>
> (p. 1)

Ogden (2005b) goes on interpreting the analyst task vis-a-vis the patient intolerable psychic organization and its defensive manifestations, namely to tolerate, contain and (from time to time) interpret the unconscious communication of the patient:

> (the analyst) recognize that a patient's inhumane behavior (often directed against himself) is usually a reflection of the psychological illness for which

he came to the analyst for help. The analyst neither condones the patient's inhumane behavior (for example, the patient's relentless self-debasing thoughts and actions or his burning himself with cigarettes), nor does he respond to the patient with an expression of revulsion. Rather, he treats the behavior as an urgent plea for the analyst's aid. Up to a point, the analyst responds by engaging in conscious and unconscious psychological work in which the patient's inhumane behavior is treated as an unconscious communication.

(p. 9)

However, Ogden reminds us that therapists might confront circumstances that require an act of intolerance, as the therapist reaches a point:

when the way in which the patient is communicating his pain is so cruel (to himself, to the analyst, or to others) that it would be unconscionable for the analyst to proceed with 'analysis as usual'.

(Ogden, 2005b, p. 9)

It is crucial for the sake of the therapy, and of the therapeutic relations, that alongside his flexibility and tolerance, the therapist will also serve as the "gate-keeper" of the therapy:

I believe that there is no such entity as psychoanalysis under conditions in which the analyst allows extreme inhumanity on the part of the patient to take place, such as leaving very young children unattended for long periods or torturing animals to death.... When a patient's inhumane behavior reaches an unacceptable level, the analyst must treat the situation as an emergency requiring decisive action. By behaving in this way, the analyst shows the patient, in an un-self-righteous way, who the analyst is, what matters most to him (and, by implication what is important to the values inherent in psychoanalysis).

(Ogden, 2005b, p. 9)

So here, Ogden advises us to bear in mind that by showing intolerance towards the intolerable (which is, at least to some extent, subjective and reflecting the therapist's values and morality), we offer our patients an important model of differentiating right from wrong. Psychoanalysis, group analysis, or any other psychotherapy, is not just about tolerating everything in our patients, but also about setting limits. By tolerating much, but not everything, psychotherapists help their patient to live their lives in a more humane manner than they might do. The following vignette demonstrates this idea, with its complexities and dualities.

A senior colleague of mine shared with me an intervention he had with one of his patients. My colleague's patient, a male in his forties, had not paid for his therapy for a long period. All of my colleague's efforts to work the issue through were eventually unproductive, and the patient withheld his payment. The patient used to mock the therapist for trying to make him understand why he didn't want to pay, and continually promised to pay at their next meeting, which he never did. After many months of frustration, and after countless consultations and supervisions, my colleague told the patient that they would have to stop the therapy if he didn't pay his debt. The next meeting, the patient entered the room holding a huge plastic container, overflowing with small coins of NIS 1 (about 20 cents). He sat down in his armchair, and with a triumphant demeanor emptied the container on the floor of my colleague's clinic. Thereafter, with a sadistic tone, he told my colleague that he was going to enjoy the image of him bowing down to collect the scattered coins and that in their next meetings that image was going to give him pleasure. My colleague commented by saying that the patient was both right and wrong – right to assume that the therapist would be crouching down collecting the coins, but wrong in assuming that there would be a future session. He declared an end to the therapy and advised the patient to consider seeing another therapist.

Over the years, I have shared this vignette with many colleagues of mine, and I was impressed by the wide spectrum of reactions I received. As you might expect, many condemned the therapist for his non-empathic countertransferential reaction towards the patient. Others expressed understanding of his behavior, nevertheless considered the therapy at large a complete failure. A few evaluated positively the therapist's way of conducting the therapy and its final session. Only some considered the last intervention an empathic one, reflecting to the patient that there is a limit to cruelty that even an empathic therapist would tolerate. I have found myself oscillating between these therapeutic attitudes, hoping I will not, one day, have to face such a dilemma. Was my colleague's reaction only an unconscious enactment, or was it also a legitimate and response of intolerance, to the intolerable destructive behavior of the patient? I rather leave it an open question, as a reminder of the difficulties psychotherapists might face vis-à-vis some patients' behaviors.

In a second vignette, taken from a group I conducted many years ago, I shall describe the interplay of tolerance and intolerance. I view this interplay as fundamental to understanding the process of projective identification, as an intersubjective communicative process. For Klein (1946) projective identification was mostly an intra-psychic process, involving a phantasy of evacuating a part of oneself into another person. Bion (1959, 1962) offered a radical revision of Klein's intra-psychic model, conceiving projective identification as an interpersonal process, (i.e., between the infant and the mother, or between the analysand and the analyst). In Bion's model, the 'projector' exerts (mostly unconsciously) pressure on the 'recipient' to experience himself and behave in a way congruent with the unconscious projective fantasy. For projective identification to "work", namely become a transformative process, the recipient (partially) experiences himself 'in somebody else's phantasy', so in a way, he is being tolerant to that which is being projected on him. Nevertheless, if the recipient is "too" tolerant, i.e., totally identifies with the unconscious phantasy of the projector, he becomes *the* projector, failing to return to the projector anything other than what has been projected on him. Think of a crying infant and its anxious mother, who is identifying with her infant's anxiety, to the point where she becomes as helpless and desperate as her infant, and can no longer relax the infant. It is critical that at the same time the recipient identifies (tolerates) the projected phantasy, he will be able to use his own subjectivity, and "to shake himself out of the numbing feeling of reality that is a concomitant of this state ... (and) if he can do so, he is in a position to give ... the correct interpretation" (Bion, 1959, pp. 149–150). In other words, the mother must also show intolerance to the (or at least to some of the) projected phantasy, if she is to be of any help to the infant. Here is the vignette:

> In Israel, upon turning eighteen, all young people, with minor exceptions are required to serve in the army; men for a minimum of three years and women for at least two. Thereafter, they have to do periodic reserve duty until the age of about forty. In Hebrew, we call this duty *"milu'im"* (army reserve service). In my *milu'im* service, I was stationed with a Casualty Notification Officers (CNO's) unit. My duty was to help the CNOs by providing both mental and emotional support; in counseling cases where young children were involved; or debriefing them after their return from their most difficult duty. Young CNOs undergo a very professional qualification training process, and then usually serve for many years without a refresher or new learning courses. I initiated a course for senior CNOs, and after a long year of preparation, I opened the first senior CNO course for the IDF (Israel Defense Forces). The group consisted of twelve officers in well-pressed uniforms, all in their late 30s or early 40s (I was 26 at the time). They sat before me, looked at me semi-suspiciously, and seemed almost disinterested in the workshop. I opened my presentation by introducing myself and letting them know we would be working together in the coming days in a workshop titled 'The Role Perception of the Senior CNO'.
>
> After presenting the primary task to the group, I suggested we open by each person introducing himself, and sharing with all of us his expectations of the workshop. The first officer to speak was a young, good-looking officer, who presented himself with a smile, adding he was most pleased with the idea of the course being opened. Hesitantly, he added that he was a bit surprised they would have to spend two days with a psychologist and that he was thinking they might enjoy "different stuff", but, still, he hoped it would go well. The second officer to speak, on the right of the first, was less smiling and less hesitant in his criticism, letting me know that he believed it was a waste of time to spend two days with a psychologist, rather than meet with high-ranking and more experienced officers to learn from them. The third officer to speak was angry at the situation. "How can you possibly help us? Have you ever experienced what we do in the course of our duty? We do not

need academic theories. We need some *real learning*" he finished with a mixture of rage and contempt.

As you might imagine, at this point I was already a bit uneasy in my chair. Nevertheless, I tried to keep my feelings hidden and let the group members understand that it was OK to keep sharing any feelings or thoughts they might have. Therefore, that was exactly what they did – they kept sharing their resentful attitude, their objection to the plan, and to the fact that I assumed they might need and enjoy a workshop of this nature. The process turned into a "rolling snowball" of criticism and disappointment. I felt bombarded, became more and more irritated and began experiencing feelings of panic. Although I did not explicitly show my feelings, I had to cope with them, and with the three pressing thoughts I was contemplating. The first was that all the CNOs in the room suddenly looked ugly, disgusting, and monstrous. The second feeling was immense anger with these ungrateful men, for not appreciating my initiative and contribution. The third and final idea was that, at the end of the first session, I would suggest to the officer in charge, that we change the plan and ask him to hastily find some other officers to work with them, on whatever they would be interested in. In other words, I was thinking of abandoning my assignment.

Finally, the session approached the time for a break. I resented the group, and I was afraid they resented me even more. The catastrophe was looming closer and closer, but then, five minutes before the break, I felt relaxed, when I suddenly understood what had taken place in the room for the past hour.

The last CNO ended his speech. The room was tense and quiet. The group looked at me – anxiously and with anticipation. I took a deep breath, and told the group that I had carefully listened to all they said, and that I would like to thank them for opening my eyes, as to what being a CNO really meant. They looked a bit surprised, as I kept telling them I now knew, with more awareness and comprehension than I had before, that a CNO is someone who has to keep performing his job, in the last place on earth that he is wanted and welcomed. Everywhere he goes, the CNO is unwanted; everybody wants him out of their house and of their lives – yet he has to stay grounded and professional, and contain all that is projected on him. I also told them, that I felt they had had to work hard to make sure I would get this point, which was crucial for them in order to make sure we could work together. The group was silent, but this time the silence was less tense and more comforting. We took a break, and on our return from it, we got back to work and kept on working for two more days, fruitfully and productively.

On Stiffness and Toughness of the Therapist

In his most practical paper 'On beginning the treatment', Freud (1913) offers psychoanalysts a few 'recommendations' about the opening stage of the treatment. He refrains from formulating strict rules, preferring not "to claim any unconditional acceptance for them" (p. 123). However, when he comes to discussing the rule of payment for the therapy, he takes a hard line and with a stringent tone, he states that he:

> adhere strictly to the principle of leasing a definite hour. Each patient is allotted a particular hour of my available working day; it belongs to him and he is liable for it, even if he does not make use of it... *no other way is practicable* (Italics mine). Under a less stringent régime, the 'occasional' non-attendances increase so greatly that the doctor finds his material existence threatened; whereas when the arrangement is adhered to, it turns out that accidental hindrances do not occur at all.
>
> (pp. 126–127)

When a therapist follows the technical psychoanalytic rules, e.g. strictly keeps the time-boundaries of a session, or charges a patient for a missed session, he or she might be uncomplimentary diagnosed by their patients, colleagues, or supervisors, as "rigid", "stiff" or "inflexible" therapist. Therapists who, in contrast, are not that firm regarding keeping the technical rules are usually flatteringly considered "flexible" or "elastic". This terminology tends to overlap the contemporary split between "classical" psychoanalysts and "relational psychoanalysts" – the former are described many times as inflexible and rigid, whereas the latter as flexible and tuned-in to the patient's needs.

Kallner (2009, p. 138) hypothesizes that Freud's resolute stance about payment arrangements regarding missed sessions (namely, that the patient has to pay if he doesn't show up for his meeting) derived from Freud's (justified) prediction, that this rule would be greatly objected, resisted, and confronted. Indeed, many therapists find this rule too difficult to implement, up to the point it is entirely abandoned. Many therapists have adopted compromising arrangements, even when they identify with the professional commitment to keep the therapy's setting in terms of time and money. Kallner, who strongly advocates Freud's instructions, differentiates between "stiffness" and "toughness" when it comes to evaluating clinical interventions, especially ones that relate to issues of the therapeutic setting. She suggests (p. 199) that 'stiffness' (rigidity) indicates an object – be it a person, a matter, or a law – that on occasion, was supposed to present changeability and flexibility, but due to a certain flaw is unable to present the expected changes. The Challenger exploded in 1984 because a rubber O-ring seal, which was never tested in extreme cold, became stiff (less flexible than it should have been), and failed to seal the joint it was supposed to seal. In contrast, 'toughness' means something which, or someone who, from the outset, was supposed to remain resistant and unchangeable in the event of pressures. A building may collapse if the construction is not tough enough. In psychoanalytic or psychodynamic psychotherapy, stiffness is never desirable, since it implies a lack of required adapting abilities. However, meeting pressures to change the therapeutic setting (in a flexible way) is an acquired ability, one that the therapist may set as a professional objective.

Tolerance and Intolerance in Societies

Tolerance has also become a crucial element of the liberal political order, especially after Locke. When individuals in society "are sufficiently tolerant, political disagreements can be dealt with amicably; there is little risk of shifting into a Hobbesian state of anticipation because of conflicting political values" (Muldoon, Borgida & Cuffaro, 2011, p. 322). In the Lockean tradition, free and equal moral persons are motivated to tolerate one another in lieu of an obligation to assist others. Intolerance is often devaluated because the most salient examples of intolerance are usually of bad behavior with a negative connotation. This is unfortunate, since:

> while tolerance is often necessary for us to all get along and better understand each other, no one who defends tolerance could consistently hold that it can be unlimited. Some things are truly intolerable: murder, rape, child abuse. The problem is where to draw the line when we move beyond such evidently intolerable things. Disagreements about which acts are intolerable give rise to some of our deepest moral and political conflicts.
>
> (Pianalto, 2010)

To illustrate this point, have a look at this photo, which is presented at the "Topographie des Terrors" (Topography of terror) museum in Berlin:

In the photo, you see spectators and workers of the Blohm & Voss shipyards during the singing of the national anthem following the "Führer's address" given by Adolf Hitler in Hamburg, June 13, 1936. While all those present raise their right arms in the obligatory "German salute", one man refuses to do so and crosses his arms. He is probably August Landmesser, who had run afoul of the Nazi Party over his unlawful relationship with Irma Eckler, a Jewish woman. He was later imprisoned and eventually drafted into penal military service, where he was killed in action.

Landmesser, known as "Be This Guy" man, took a kind of action against the intolerable. We might call this kind of action a 'non-violent interference'. In his book *The Open Society and its Enemies* (1945, Vol 1) Karl Popper, the great Austrian-British philosopher of science, coined the phrase "The paradox of tolerance". Popper states that if a society is tolerant without any limit, its ability to be tolerant will eventually be destroyed, or seized, by the intolerant. His paradoxical conclusion is that "to maintain a tolerant society, the society must be intolerant to intolerance". We can consider Popper's assumption regarding societies also relevant to individuals, groups, and organizations. We might postulate that each organism is at risk, should it not develop proper mechanisms for defense against intolerance that is addressed against the organism itself.

Morris Nitsun's concept of the 'Anti-Group' (1996) is another reminder of the negative power groups might present (by "groups" Nitsun means different levels of groups: therapeutic groups, families, organizational, cultural, and political systems, or societies.). The anti-group describes the destructive aspects of the group towards the group itself. If not recognized, contained, and (sometimes) restricted, the consequences of such an anti-group process might be impasses, severe conflicts, and even the disintegration of the group. In such circumstances, more active intervention might be needed, e.g. keeping the boundaries, stopping violence, or even the removal of that part of the group, that threatens its survivability.

Concluding Comments

The Covid-19 epidemic, which was quickly followed by the development of a successful vaccine, has caused society to reconsider their tolerance for challenging sub-groups such as 'Vaccine hesitancy' or 'Anti-vaxxers.' Civilian-rights clashes are on the rise, posing a threat to the fragile social order. How far should society and governments go in mandating vaccination or frequent PCR testing on the public? Is it ethical for a teacher to decline immunization and still keep his job? Is the government, on the other hand, allowed to dismiss him? Furthermore, what will the trade unions' stance be in such a conflict?

Personally, I believe that the current scenario is a good example of Popper's "paradox of tolerance". Democracy, at its core, aims to integrate as many perspectives and views as possible. However, there comes a time when society must be intolerant of the intolerance of certain of its subgroups in order to sustain a tolerant society.

References

Bion, W. R. (1959). *Experiences in Groups and Other Papers*. New York: Basic Books.

Bion, W. R. (1962). A theory of thinking. In *Second Thoughts*, pp. 110–119. New York: Jason Aronson, 1977.

Freud, S. (1911). Formulations on the two principles of mental functioning. *The Standard Edition of the Complete Psychological Works of Sigmund Freud, Volume XII (1911-1913)*: The Case of Schreber, Papers on Technique and Other Works, pp. 213–226.

Freud, S. (1913). On beginning the treatment. (Further recommendations on the technique of psycho-analysis I). *The Standard Edition of the Complete Psychological Works of Sigmund Freud, Volume XII (1911-1913)*: The Case of Schreber, Papers on Technique and Other Works, pp. 121–144.

Kallner, N. (2009). *The Camel's Hump: On the Technique of Dynamic Psychotherapy*. Modan Publishing House Ltd (Hebrew).

Klein, M. (1946). Notes on some schizoid mechanisms. *Int. J. Psycho-Anal.*, 27: 99–110.

Muldoon, R., Borgida, M. & Cuffaro, M. (2011). The conditions of tolerance. *Politics, Philosophy & Economics*, 11(3): 322–344.

Nitsun, M. (1996). *The Anti-Group: Destructive Forces in the Group and their Creative Potential*. Routledge.

Ogden, T. H. (2005a). *This Art of Psychoanalysis*. Routledge.

Ogden, T. H. (2005b). What I would not part with. *Fort Da*, 11(2): 8–17.

Pianalto, M. (2010). In Defense of Intolerance. *Philosophy Now*, 79, https://philosophynow.org/issues/79/In_Defense_of_Intolerance

Popper, K. (1945). *The Open Society and Its Enemies*: Volume 1: *The Spell of Plato*. Routledge Classics, 2003.

Winnicott, D. W. (1969). The use of an object. *Int. J. Psycho-Anal.*, 50: 711–716.

Tzvi, A. (1984). The yearning for friendship. *Hadarim*, *4*: 16–31 (Hebrew).

Zelda (1982). "Two Elements". In *Zelda's Poems* (1985). Hakibbutz Ha'Meuchad (Hebrew).

Index

Pages followed by "n" refer to notes.